A TRIBU

Best Wishes
Happy reading

Tony Ltt

4/2010

ALL IN
MY CORNER
A TRIBUTE TO SOME FORGOTTEN
WELSH BOXING HEROES

Tony Lee

Edited by Elizabeth Lee

Published by
TL Associates

Copyright © 2009 Tony Lee

Published in 2009 by
TL Associates
128 High Street, Ammanford
Carmarthenshire, SA18 2ND
Telephone: (01269) 597599

A CIP catalogue record for this book is
available from the British Library.

ISBN 978-0-9564456-1-2 (hardback)
978-0-9564456-0-5 (paperback)

Printed and bound in Wales by
Dinefwr Press Ltd.
Rawlings Road, Llandybie
Carmarthenshire, SA18 3YD

Front cover photo:
*Standing, left to right: Danny Evans (Welterweight Champion of Wales),
Randy Jones (Cruiserweight Champion of Wales).
Seated, left to right: Ginger Jones (Featherweight Champion of Wales),
Johnny Vaughan (Mentor/Manager),
Billy Quinlen (Lightweight Champion of Wales).*

Back cover photo:
The author with signed gloves.

Contents

I wish to dedicate this book to my wife Elizabeth,
for the editing and for her patience with me,
and to all my family for their support.

Acknowledgements

A life-long interest in boxing, particularly Welsh boxing, has given me some fascinating experiences and made me many friends. Sadly, the boxers I knew and admired have passed away; some of them very recently—like Cliff Curvis from Swansea. They all gave me so much help and encouragement. I already knew the Ammanford boxers: Danny Evans, the Peregrines and the Quinlen family, and I was introduced to boxers like Glen Moody, Len Beynon and Big Jim Wilde, through the Swansea ex-boxer's Association.

When Mrs Maud Vaughan entrusted to me her late husband's diaries I felt very honoured but wondered what to do with them.

Eventually, based on the Johnny Vaughan diaries, I wrote a series of short articles on local boxers for the *South Wales Guardian*, the local weekly based in Ammanford. It was a way of telling a younger generation about the achievements and the courage of young men from the past who had lived and fought in the same small town and its surrounding area. It also turned out to be a nostalgic trip down memory lane for some of the *Guardian's* older readers and their interest was an unexpected pleasure. They began to tell me about relatives who had been boxers and to give me newspaper cuttings and photographs to add to my collection. Some of them thought there was a book to be written about the local old-timers whose poverty was the reason they took up boxing. It's taken me too long to get round to writing the book, but I hope it's better late than never.

My grateful thanks are due to:

Miles Templeton, Bob Lonkhurst and Harold Alderman MBE, for their generous help, advice and encouragement.

The late Mrs Maud Vaughan, and the late Edgar Vaughan, for Johnny Vaughan's diaries.

Terry Norman, for help with local historical context.

Dave Owens, Merthyr.

Morwen Davies, Swansea, for information on Dai Chips.

Vivien Burgess, freelance newspaper researcher, Colindale.

Ken Fifield, Swansea.

Bryan Reading, Wendover, for the cartoons.

Jim Jenkinson, Liverpool.

Geraint Richards, Aberystwyth.

Mrs Jayne Jones, Ginger's daughter.

The many not mentioned by name, who have encouraged me or expressed an interest in, this project over the years.

My dear late friends in the boxing fraternity, especially Bryn Ginger Jones, Danny Evans and Tommy Davies, Bryn Edwards and Don Chiswell—this is for you, boys.

Tony Lee

Foreword

Johnny Vaughan was a man steeped in the sport of professional boxing. He had been a decent fighter himself in the days before and during the First World War and had fought against some of the best men in Wales, including the great Frank Moody. After his retirement he started to manage and train boxers in his home town of Ammanford and by the 1930s he had established himself as a Welsh boxing sensation. In the 1930s Ammanford was a small town with a population of around seven thousand. Situated between the Welsh Valleys, a boxing hotbed, and mid-Wales, a boxing hinterland, it was remarkable for the quality of boxers that it produced and this was down to Johnny Vaughan. I have in my collection a photograph of Johnny alongside four of his boxers, each of which held the Welsh title *at the same time*. For Johnny to have made such an impact on the sport, from such a small place, was an outstanding achievement.

Tony Lee is a man who has long been interested in all aspects of the sport in Wales. I know from the many conversations I have had with him just how passionately he feels about the subject. He likes to get 'inside' the characters and personalities of the game and to understand what made them, and the sport itself, tick. He is lucky enough to have possession of Johnny Vaughan's original diaries and it is upon these that he has based his story. His tales of the events and the boxers of the 1930s and 1940s would have been in danger of being lost forever, but for this book.

As someone who had spent most of my life researching boxing and boxers from this period I am acutely aware that there are very few of them left alive today to hand down their memories. Tony was fortunate in that he knew most of the boxers he writes about and many of the anecdotes were passed on to him first hand. He writes with genuine affection for his subject and tells a story which is well worth the telling.

Miles Templeton (Boxing Historian)
www.prewarboxing.co.uk

Chapter 1

A Golden Day

I suppose in common with most people I never thought there was anything particularly interesting about the place where I grew up. Penybanc, or hill top in English, is a mile outside the small mining town of Ammanford in Carmarthenshire. From Penybanc 'square'—a rather elevated name for the junction bordered on one side of the road by the Golden Lion public house and on the other side by what was a butcher's next to a chip shop—you can see Ammanford stretched out in the valley below you. The butcher's and the chip shop are now long gone, I'm sorry to say, along with the post office and a small general store. Even the pub has recently closed, though the rugby club is still a thriving part of village life.

Into this lively little community I was brought at the age of five, and grew up there happily surrounded by friends, taking those around me for granted as a child does.

It was years later that I 'discovered' that some of our neighbours were very well-known in the world of boxing, as well as rugby. One 'son of Penybanc' was Johnny Vaughan, boxer, trainer, manager and promoter —a man of many talents.

One Monday evening when I was 12 years old my Dad and I settled down at home in front of the radio to listen to a boxing match. It was a British title fight to decide the heavyweight championship, vacant because of the retirement of Don Cockell, and the winner would receive the Lonsdale belt. What made it more exciting was that the contenders were both Welshmen: Johnny Williams then of Rugby, and Joe Erskine of Cardiff, whose trainer was our local hero, Archie Rule.

Johnny Williams.

It was 27th August 1956, nine days after my twelfth birthday and during the school holidays, and thus I was allowed to stay up and listen to the broadcast. The venue was the Maindy Stadium in Cardiff, an open air arena which unfortunately resulted in the spectators getting soaked in a 'torrential downpour'.

Although Erskine scored more points than his opponent from the start, Williams inflicted more damage and Erskine was cut over his left eye in the fourth round. Continuing to outpoint Williams and nearly flooring him with a left hook, Erskine then lost a little ground because Williams engaged him in some in-fighting and holding at which he was superior, and Erskine emerged from the ninth with a split right eyebrow. Williams, however, was unable to capitalise on this after some patching-up in Erskine's corner, and Erskine, displaying the ring skills for which he became famous, remained stronger throughout.

2

I remember I jumped up and cheered when the commentator described Erskine's hand being raised by Johnny Williams himself, before Erskine was even declared the winner. Such sportsmanship! Erskine put on the solid gold Lonsdale Belt and his Tiger Bay fans went wild.

As I got ready for bed I decided that when Dad had finished with the next day's newspaper I would cut out the account of the fight and the pictures and paste them in my scrapbook.

The next day I was out all afternoon; maybe doing a bit of sparring with my friends who would, no doubt, have argued about which one of us was playing Joe Erskine's role. We were always pretending to be somebody or other. The Lone Ranger and Tonto, American gangsters we'd seen at Saturday morning pictures; anyone we thought was a hero, or a villain. One by one we made our way home. My stomach told me it was way past tea-time. The skies had turned ominously grey and it wasn't long before the rain came down. I was just about to pass the Golden Lion when instead, I decided to shelter just inside the pub's open doorway.

Ducking in from the rain two men appeared. I saw the familiar smiling face of none other than Archie Rule. *'Beth wyt ti'n neud fan'yn? Ti'n dan oedran!'* ('What are you doing here? You're under age!') he was laughing. Archie asked me if I knew who the other man was. I looked at him. He was big, he had a long black coat and sunglasses and he was carrying a black case. Immediately images of gangster films I'd seen at the pictures came to my mind. Sunglasses in the rain? And what was in the case? In films I'd seen similar ones which contained machine guns.

I swallowed hard and said I didn't know him. Had it not been for Archie I would have considered braving the rain and running home. He beckoned to me still smiling.

'Dere mewn i fi gael dangos i ti beth sy' da'r dyn hyn.' ('Come here and see what this man has got.')

I followed them into the bar, whereupon the case was put on a table and opened. Inside was a truly beautiful shining object which took my breath away.

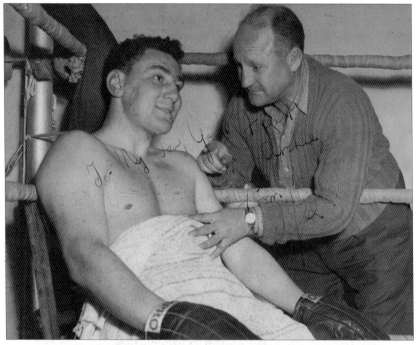

Joe Erskine and Archie Rule.

'This man, my boy,' said Archie with a flourish, 'is the heavyweight champion of Great Britain, and this is his Lonsdale Belt. Meet Joe Erskine!'

The men in the bar were all crowding round now, wanting to try the belt on. There was handshaking and backslapping all round and many an offer of a pint for the champ and his trainer. Totally awestruck, I stood with eyes and mouth wide open, and the big man smiled at me slowly and painfully.

Joe Erskine took off his sunglasses and I saw the price he'd had to pay for that belt.

Within minutes I was home, breathless and desperate to tell my father all about it.

Dad, stopping only to get his jacket on, lost no time in calling round for our neighbour before setting off to the 'Golden' for a pint.

I was always interested afterwards to follow the fortunes of that particular Lonsdale Belt—the last solid gold Lonsdale Belt in heavyweight circulation, it was originally awarded to another great Welshman, Tommy Farr, when he beat Ben Foord of South Africa to win the British and British Empire titles in 1937.

Joe Erskine's first defence of the British title against Henry Cooper in September 1957 was successful. He outpointed Cooper in a lacklustre fight, which was close throughout.

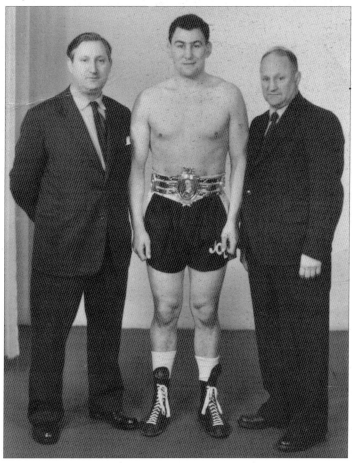

Benny Jacobs, Joe Erskine and Archie Rule.

Then in June 1958 Erskine met Brian London and lost title and belt. *British Boxing Yearbook,* 1985, describes the fight:

> Brian London won the title once held by his father (Jack London) when he knocked out the crestfallen Erskine. When the Welshman's eye went, London was transformed into a fighting fury, smashing his opponent twice to the canvas where he was counted out on one knee.

Such are the vagaries of boxing that when London met Cooper in his first title defence, in January 1959, he was beaten 'by the length of Blackpool pier', according to the *British Boxing Yearbook*. Both men suffered eye injuries, but though London took severe punishment, there were no knockdowns and Henry Cooper won on points.

In November 1959, Erskine tried to regain the title in 'one of the best heavyweight fights for years'. But Cooper retained the title with 'a first-class demolition job on the Welshman. Floored four times in the twelfth, Erskine was counted out lying backwards over the bottom rope.'

But plucky Joe must have wanted that belt back really badly and on 21st March 1961 he was up for another try. This time both boxers had 'boxed extremely well' until the fifth when Erskine retired, a victim to Henry's famous left hook. Thus Henry Cooper, having successfully defended the British title twice, won that beautiful belt outright.

Thirty years later I met Joe Erskine for the second time. The occasion was the fiftieth birthday banquet of the Welsh Area, British Boxing Board of Control, and this time I had the presence of mind to ask the great man for his autograph. I told him about our first meeting all those years ago and he chuckled, but didn't recall the incident.

Five years after that on 7th September 1984, I attended the 75th anniversary dinner of *Boxing News*. I had a pair of boxing gloves given to me by Howard Winstone, and I asked the champions who were there to sign them. Among these signatures is that of a man I was delighted to meet that night. He brought back memories of my boyhood and my father telling me of the great boxers of his youth: he was the 1930 Junior World Welterweight Champion, Jack Kid Berg.

Chapter 2

Jack Kid Berg

Jack Kid Berg was my father's hero really. They were born two months and maybe eight miles apart—the Kid in Whitechapel in the East End of London; my Dad just round the corner from White Hart Lane in Tottenham.

My Dad, George William Lee, was born in April 1909 and grew up, along with his two sisters, in Tottenham. His father, Thomas Henry Lee, was a tram driver though he had learnt the trade of a saddler and harness maker. His mother, Ethel, had long periods of illness during his childhood and died when he was 18 years old.

In due course, his schooling finished, Dad was apprenticed to a Jewish dental practice as what was then called a 'dental mechanic', where he learned how to make dentures. It was during this period in the 1920s that he developed his lifelong interest in boxing, accompanying his work colleagues to the lively shows at such venues as Premierland. Among the colourful vibrant Jewish community in East London were multifarious characters involved in professional boxing but one of their favourites at this time was the up-and-coming Jack Kid Berg of whom great things were expected. It was hoped that he would emulate some of the successful pre-war Jewish boxers like Americans Abe Attell and Battling Levinsky, and another 'Kid'—Ted Kid Lewis—who had come from the same background in the East End of London, and who had won the World welterweight title in 1915.

It was not a cosy life into which 'Jack' Bergman was born in June 1909 and named Judah, after his father.

His parents fled from Poland or Russia in the early years of the last century. His father had wanted to emigrate to the United States but somehow the family never made it and they ended up in the burgeoning Jewish immigrant area in Whitechapel, where Judah senior learned tailoring. Jack was the third child of Judah and Mildred, and the first to be born in Britain. At least one grandparent must have crossed the Atlantic though, because Jack remembered his grandmother visiting from Canada. Family legend had it that at the end of her visit she travelled back on the *Titanic*.

Jack grew up rough—by the age of thirteen he was only at home twice or three times a week—and famously tough, invariably coming out best in gang fights and earning a reputation by walloping any Gentile who picked on smaller Jewish boys. As 'Yiddle' (Jack's street nickname meaning 'little Polish Jew') was always looking out for ways to make some pocket money, it was pretty natural for him to graduate towards boxing at a young age.

Jack's hero was Ted Kid Lewis, who had returned to Britain in 1919 after spending five years conquering America, where he had won the World welterweight title. He had lost the title to his arch rival Jack Britton six months before his homecoming, but that did not diminish his stature in the East End one jot and he went on to fight thirty-seven times between 1920 and 1924, including British, European and World title fights.

Jack Kid Berg was fourteen years old by then and, in spite of his father's appeals to him to stay out of the ring, he had his first professional fight at Premierland on 8th June 1924, against Young Johnny Gorden, whom he stopped in eight rounds. He went on to have a further fifty contests at Premierland—with an occasional foray to the Royal Albert Hall or Blackfriars—losing only two of them.

By the time he was sixteen and four months he was a little over featherweight, and actually failed to make the weight when he met Johnny Curley, British featherweight champion, and beat him. Had it been a title fight he would have been the youngest-ever British champion. As it was, by the time a proposed re-match, this time for the title, could be arranged, Berg would never have made featherweight. Interestingly, four years later Johnny Curley was beaten at Premierland by feather-weight Ginger Jones of Ammanford, one of Johnny Vaughan's boxers.

Jack turned lightweight and began to study the technique of a fellow East End Jew, then current British lightweight champion, Harry Mason. Although he admired his boxing, Jack said the violin-playing Mason was bigheaded and not 'my cup of tea at all'.

Some commentators, including the famous Bombardier Billy Wells, thought Berg would not be a worthy contender for Mason's title at this time. Nevertheless, various attempts were made to match them, but the two men never met in the ring, mainly because Mason had by then moved up a weight.

However, Ammanford's Danny Evans, also managed by Johnny Vaughan, fought Mason in April 1934 at Swansea in an eliminator for the British welterweight title. He had previously held Harry Mason to a draw in Cardiff so thought he was in with a good chance for a crack at the title. Sadly, Danny lost on points over fifteen rounds. Many years later he told me that Harry Mason was the best boxer he ever fought.

Then, while he was still only eighteen years old, Jack followed in the footsteps of both Mason and Ted Kid Lewis, and took advantage of an offer to try his luck in the United States of America.

He sailed on the SS *Berengaria* in March 1928, courtesy of his new American manager, Sol Gold, who cabled that he had fights lined up for him. His training and sparring on board were watched with growing interest by sizeable crowds of his fellow passengers. (Eighteen months after this my Uncle Will made the same journey on his way to New Mexico to work in a coal mine.)

By 1930, the name of Jack Kid Berg had become well-known in the States as a seemingly tireless 'value for money' boxer with some con-vincing wins under his belt. During this period he was given another nickname to add to 'Yiddle' and 'Kid'. Onlookers, bemused by his flail-ing arms style which he could keep going for a full three minutes in every round, dubbed him 'The Whitechapel Windmill'.

But it was back at the Royal Albert Hall that what was arguably Jack's finest hour occurred. American fight promoter Jeff Dickson (scourge of the fledgling British Boxing Board of Control who had refused him a licence), arranged the match between Berg and American Mushy Callahan to decide the Junior Welterweight Champion of the World, on 18th February 1930.

There was a big build-up to this contest in the press, with the *Sporting Life* announcing to the fans on 7th February, that 'contrary to expectations' Jack Kid Berg had not begun to train hard yet:

> Instead Berg went riding in Windsor Great Park. Like his former mentor, Harry Mason, Berg has a fancy for horsemanship, and his manager is permitting him to go riding again today. After that he must settle down in earnest, and on Monday begin his boxing practice with a number of sparring partners who are going down from London.

On 12th February, they reported that Mushy Callahan had had difficulty finding sparring partners although his manager offered £1 per round to boxers willing to spar.

By this time, some confusion about the status of the contest had arisen because of news from New York of a decision to strip Callahan of his title; this was quickly rescinded but left fans bewildered about whether or not this was to be a World title fight.

However, for the crowd gathered in the Albert Hall on 18th February, there was more drama to come.

As the MC announced the contest, Lord Lonsdale himself stood up and said: 'This fight is not for the championship of the World!'

Unlike Sol Gold in Jack's corner, who yelled at the noble lord that he was a 'Limey son-of-a-bitch!', Jack was apparently completely unfazed by the uproar and went on to score a decisive victory when Callahan's corner threw in the towel just before the eleventh round. Callahan wept in his corner as Berg danced around the ring. Clearly the title was real enough to both of them, as indeed it was to countless fans on both sides of the Atlantic.

Later, in an interview with *Boxing* magazine Lord Lonsdale qualified his outburst:

Jack Kid Berg Poster. 8th July 1933, Vetch Field, Swansea.

The point is that there is no such thing as a 'junior' championship. It is against all the rules of the game in this country. In America they used to have such titles but I believe they have forbidden them there now . . .

How can there be a junior championship at any weight? You might just as well add a few more categories to each class of boxing and have, say, a sub-junior championship. There would be no limit to the titles claimed.

A pedantic view? Perhaps, but what would Lonsdale have thought of the fragmentation, and many would say, devaluation, of world titles today?

About the American rules at the time Lord Lonsdale was only partly right. Although New York authorities no longer recognised junior titles, the NBA did, and Jack's NBA belt remained one of his most prized possessions throughout his life. The *Sporting Life* acknowledged that junior championships had 'not been abolished entirely in America' and *Boxing* commented that they were surprised that the British authorities appeared 'slavishly prepared to kow-tow to American nervousness at the prospect of losing a precious world title.'

Altogether Jack Kid Berg had some sixty-three fights in American rings and was a very popular figure among US fans. His opponents included all-time favourites Tony Canzoneri and Kid Chocolate.

Back on British soil in 1934, Jack was now after the British title and his opponent was Harry Mizler. It was no problem for Jack:

> The contest developed into a grim, dour struggle and Mizler developed damage to both hands early on. The fury of Berg's attacks increased and the champion was punished steadfastly with only his fighting instinct saving him from being destroyed. At the end of the tenth round Mizler was retired by his corner when the situation became irreversible.
>
> —*Boxing Yearbook.*

Two months before Jack took the British lightweight title from Harry Mizler, on 4th August, yet another of Johnny Vaughan's boxers had met his opponent first! Billy Quinlen fought Mizler at the Vetch Field in

Jack Kid Berg.

Swansea. It was Mizler's first defence of the title and it went the distance, with Billy losing in a close contest.

While Jack Kid Berg pursued his career through 1934, winning his British title in October, my Dad had other things on his mind. It was in March of that year that he married Iris Jones, who had nursed him through a bout of rheumatic fever in Oldchurch Hospital, Romford.

It may be romantic to marry your nurse, but there can be complications. In this case, Iris was suffering from a severe attack of *hiraeth*—she was homesick for Wales. Well, George was a qualified dental mechanic and looking to set up business on his own and Iris completed her training in Oldchurch Hospital (and had her appendix removed there), so why not move to Wales?

By the end of the year, George found himself surrounded by numerous in-laws, in Iris's home town of Ammanford, near Swansea. He set up business making and repairing dentures, and the business was known as Jones's Dental Laboratory.

He soon began to realise that he had moved to an area which was a veritable hotbed of boxing—Ammanford's starring role in the Welsh boxing scene was to last for another few years before gradually declining.

As it was he was an avid listener to bouts which were broadcast on the radio and he remained so until we eventually had a television set. George and Iris listened on their crystal set, sitting up at three o'clock in the morning along with thousands of others, to hear Tommy Farr put up the fight of his life against Joe Louis in the Yankee Stadium, New York, on 30th August 1937. I believe it was the first live broadcast of a World title fight to be cabled from America. Although, as history records, Joe Louis won, Tommy Farr returned to a hero's welcome in Wales, including an official reception hosted by the Lord Mayor of Cardiff. His name remains among the greatest in British and Welsh boxing annals.

Tommy Farr was a well-known figure in our parts. During the early 1930s, just a few years before he made history in America, he was often to be seen at the boxing booth belonging to Joe Gess. In the late twenties and the thirties Gess's booth was a regular attraction in Ammanford, and also travelled between Garnant, Pontardulais, Ystradgynlais, Clydach and Pontardawe. Tommy was the star attraction in the couple of years before he took the British title. At the end of the evening, he would set off, always whistling, to walk five miles down the railway line to his digs in Pontardulais.

He was almost as proud of his musical talents as he was of his boxing achievements. As well as his ability to whistle tunefully he had a good singing voice and made a number of records, crooning in the style of the day, and even co-writing some songs.

Farr certainly did not win all his early fights. On one occasion at Ystradgynlais, he was stopped in five rounds by Myrddin Ellis Davies, known then as Young Ellis, from Ystradgynlais. Later he was also called Tiger Ellis or the Mad Mullah; he became Welsh welterweight champion in March 1932.

In 1939, the Second World War intervened in everyone's life. My Dad, exempted from compulsory call-up because of his trade, joined the Home Guard. Towards the end of the war in August 1944, Iris, my mother, produced me.

Chapter 3

Down the Mountain
and off to the Fair

The history of boxing in Wales is as complex as it is in the rest of Britain. In the beginning there were no rules at all. It is hard to say when prizefighting began in Wales, but in the early days there were men known as mountain fighters whose devastatingly violent fights were held in secretive rocky arenas where the militia would not find them. They were of course bare-knuckle fights, often going on for hours or as long as both men were still standing. It is easy to imagine the terrible damage inflicted by bare fists, especially to the boxers' eyes. The bloodthirsty promoters and spectators at these events would bet huge amounts of money on their man so that the winner—occasionally literally the survivor—was highly prized indeed. However, much of the payment for the fighters consisted of the nobbins or nobbings, that is the money thrown into the ring or in a hat passed round to show appreciation for a 'good' fight!

Similarly the exact beginning of fairground booth fighting is impossible to pin down, but it had until its gradual demise, certainly been around for two hundred years. In the early days it would have been a bloody, little-controlled and unedifying spectacle, because that was what the spectators paid their money to see, and many of the early booth boxers, as well as the challengers, were from the same stock as the mountain fighters.

In the middle of the nineteenth century prizefighting, discredited through sharp practice, had seen a great decline in public interest, and

Bassets' boxing booth.

prizefighters, unable to make a living elsewhere, ended up giving displays in the booths that accompanied travelling fairs.

Fairs in those days were a bit different from the dodgems, rides and candyfloss variety we have today. They became annual events in certain towns for specific trading purposes: 'St Faith's fair outside Norwich, for instance, where drovers from all over the country assembled their beasts on Bullock's Hill and for a fortnight the place looked like a prairie round-up,' or Sturbridge where: 'in long streets of booths . . . English merchants rubbed shoulders with merchants from Venice and Genoa . . .' Later there were hiring fairs, known as 'mops', where men and girls looking for work would attend with little symbols of their trade to show the kind of work they were able to do: '. . . cowherds with a strand of cow hair in their buttonholes; shepherds with crooks and servant girls with mops and other such emblems . . .' At the end of the day a lighthearted atmosphere prevailed. These folks who shared trades and acquaintance, liked to linger, frequent the inns and look for entertainment.

> One by one the naphtha-flares were lighted, whose rustle somehow penetrated even the din of a thousand laughing voices. Pennies might buy less time on roundabout or swing but that time was the more hilarious. Rifle shots cracked through the music; screaming girls were swung so high it seemed that the creaking boats must fling them out at last, and somewhere a bell sounded as a village lad, testing his muscles with a wooden mallet, won the admiration of glancing eyes. Hoop-la, cokernut shies, Aunt Sallies, a coloured boxer ready to take on all comers, a shooting range, a peep show—such were the titillations . . .
>
> *Fairs, Circuses and Music Halls*—M. Willson Disher.

As far as the boxing was concerned, it has been suggested that there may have been an element of 'stage-managing' some of the fights with previously worked-out blows and exaggerated groans as part of the entertainment. In the early days, purses amounted to a few shillings and side-stakes were counted out in coppers, so perhaps it is not surprising that they weren't always prepared to shed blood.

It is also the case that the booth owners were basically showmen who made their living out of entertaining the public. Jack Scarrott, boxing booth owner, remembered a six-round draw he had witnessed at rival Joe Gess's booth between Jim Driscoll and Fred Welsh: '. . . to tell you the truth I don't think it was a genuine fight. They were just making a show for the money.' Probably the audience were prepared to pay just to see these two men in the ring together as they were among the greatest Welsh boxers of all time.

Most of the fighting that went on in fairground booths was certainly real and bloody enough but, over the decades, proprietors were very seldom bothered by the constabulary. They would advertise the shows as 'assaults-at-arms' or 'exhibitions' and the prizefighters would take on members of the public at 'sparring' over three rounds. Providing they held their fairground licences, booth owners were generally left alone.

The name John Scarrott, or 'Jack' as he was known, crops up over and over again in the story of boxing in South Wales; he was a key figure in the shaping of the careers of Jim Driscoll, Tom Thomas, Jimmy Wilde, Percy Jones and many others who came to fight for him in his booth.

In 1936, at the age of sixty-nine, when he had 'been in the game' for fifty years, Jack Scarrott gave a series of remarkable interviews to William Hughes for the *South Wales Echo and Express*. In them he portrays a world which was sometimes extremely violent; where pubs and even whole villages were no-go areas after dark because of the fighting. He describes 'the very first fight I ever saw' at Black Pill, Mumbles, when he was a small boy between a gypsy called Jack Hearn and a Martin Fury; a bare-knuckle fight:

> . . . Hearn was a very fine man, about 15 stone in weight, about 5ft.10in. in height, and all strength and ruggedness from head to foot, while Fury was only about 11 stone 6lbs. None of the gypsies could believe that Hearn could get beaten for he had licked all the gypsy fighters that came his way, and those gypsies in those days didn't fight for money, for there was nobody about to offer them purses, but just for the love of fighting.
>
> But this Fury turned out to be a very fast fighter and clever. He kept on ducking and dodging in and out, and playing on Hearn's face, until it was dreadfully swollen and battered. They must have fought for an hour and a half, but how many rounds I don't know, for a round lasted until a man went down, but Fury beat him up in the face so bad that he blinded him in both eyes.
>
> The gypsy women were now shouting to go for the police and the fight was stopped, but a gypsy shouted: 'We will lance his eyes and get him to see, and he can fight again.' They did it and the fight went on, but Hearn was blinded again, and the man could fight no more. Five minutes after the fight, the police came and an old gypsy woman said to them: 'My dear men, you're too late.'

Born in Newport, Jack Scarrott was twenty-one years old when he started his own boxing booth, having already spent some years scrapping for other booth owners. He had spent his formative years among such giants in their world as Shoni Engineer (John Jones) of Treorchy, and fellow showman William Samuels, the self-styled Champion of Wales.

He could neither read nor write but, over the next half a century Scarrott 'handled big deals, paid substantial purses to hundreds of boxers and raised many thousands of pounds for charities'. He was a friend to: '. . . practically every boxer of note that South Wales produced during what may be described as the golden age of boxing,' many of whom boxed in his booth. Among the well-known names was Llew Edwards, and it may have been through him that Jack Scarrott knew Johnny Vaughan and George Rule, of Penybanc, Ammanford. Scarrott would sometimes visit George, father of Archie and Crad Rule, and Johnny Vaughan almost certainly fought many of his early unrecorded bouts for Scarrott's booth.

He was a wonderful storyteller and a larger-than-life character. A consummate showman, he was interested in all kinds of entertainment involving feats of strength, apart from boxing. Once Scarrott engaged an Italian strong man, called Montano, whose act involved weight-lifting and wrestling with members of the public who would be offered £1 per minute in the ring with him.

> But his greatest and final feat was to have a cannon fitted to his shoulders and fired. I had never seen him doing this performance and I let him get on with it. He loaded the cannon with powder, some men lifted it on to his shoulders, and it was fired off. Mister, it fairly shook the town. All the paraffin lamps in my booth went out and there we were in darkness. People came running from all directions to see what was the matter. We men on the booth didn't know exactly where we stood. Men and women from the houses close by said the explosion had jarred their houses from top to bottom.
>
> An inspector of police came up and asked me what I was doing. I explained to him that I had engaged this Italian as a turn, but that as I had never seen him rehearse his act I didn't know what he was going to do. Had I known that the explosion of this cannon would be so terrific I would not have allowed him to do it.

But there was no doubt about it, this Italian's weightlifting and wrestling performances were very good.

Early in the twentieth century it is fair to say that the showmen who owned the boxing booths had started to clean up their act considerably. Jack Scarrott observed: 'Education and the churches and chapels did that.' Fairs were after all, attended by families.

'Boxing' was now thought of more as the 'art of self-defence', following the example of the National Sporting Club, Lord Lonsdale and the rules that stipulated among other things, that gloves must be worn.

The general idea was that the travelling fair would bring with them a large tent or booth in which paying spectators would watch the proprietor's boxers take on all comers from the audience. Many of the challengers had had a bellyful of beer and were full of bravado. They made easy pickings for the boxer who had to be careful though to avoid uncontrolled flailing fists. He must also beware of the odd hustler, an experienced boxer maybe fallen on hard times and eager for the prizemoney. However, sometimes a youngster with talent would show up and be spotted by the proprietor/trainer who might then take him under his wing.

As well as employing boxers to take on challengers up-front, the owner of a booth would put on advertised boxing shows between professional boxers.

A reporter for the *Daily Express* described a visit to one of these shows. This was written in 1937 but, apart from the prices and the currently-popular tune, nothing of the atmosphere of the pre-First World War booth had changed in the period between the two wars:

> There were three bouts, a ten-rounder and two six-rounders. A crowd of 400 men and boys filled the booth to watch them. I went along with them. Prices were: adults 1s, unemployed 9d, boys 6d.
>
> There were no seats; we all stood on sloping boards, first row men and boys leaned against the ring. Some of the boys' heads came just above the sawdusted floor of the ring. From outside came the shriek of

Brian Reading.

women and children on the swings; a mechanical organ blaring out 'September in the Rain'.

All the six-rounders on the bill were paid 10s. each. The ten-rounders received £2.10s.

Six-rounders are never paid more than 12s.6d, but a ten-rounder can get as much as £4 for a fight if he is good.

Among those who learned their trade in the fairground booths in Wales from 1900 and through the 1930s were Jimmy Wilde, Jim Driscoll, Frank Moody, Ginger Jones and his brother Harold, Billy Quinlen and Tommy Farr.

The best-known boxing booths, or pavilions, in the Neath and Swansea valleys through many decades were Scarrott's, Taylor's and Basset's; Carmarthenshire (including the Amman Valley) and Pembrokeshire were served by Joe Gess's booth. Throughout the 1920s-30s Joe Gess had weekly boxing shows, moving from Ammanford to Brynamman and Ystalyfera, as well as travelling with the fairs. Many of the booths (including Gess's) were also frequently to be found in the towns of the Rhondda Valley where there were probably more hungry fighters per square mile than anywhere else in Wales.

Most of these boxing booths had disappeared by the nineteen-sixties but Ronnie Taylor kept a branch of Taylor's booth going in the North of England and was consequently able to boast a personal appearance by none other than Muhammad Ali in 1977, in South Shields. According to Ronnie, Ali was so taken with the booth that he asked if Ronnie could take it over to the States, saying: 'Our fairs have nothing like this at all.' Later, Ronnie and his wife received an invitation to Ali's wedding.

In the nineteenth and early part of the twentieth century, before the National Sporting Club rules, there were obviously no official champ-ions, nor any properly recognised weight divisions other than the attempts of promoters or booth proprietors to match boxers in order to produce a fair fight. This led to all sorts of claims, and counter claims, by boxers who, having usually beaten many opponents, called them-selves champions. These claimants would then wait for challengers to their 'title' whom they may, or may not, agree to fight. One such Champion of Wales was William Samuels, a boxing booth proprietor himself, who travelled in South Wales from Cardiff through to Carmar-thenshire and Pembrokeshire in the latter part of the nineteenth century. He weighed between twelve and thirteen stone which I guess made him a heavyweight champion and certainly his fighting ability was renowned and prodigious. It was also, at least when he was young, bare-knuckle, brutal and over as many rounds as both boxers were able to carry on.

According to Jack Scarrott, Samuels once boxed against the great John. L. Sullivan at the old Philharmonia Music Hall in Cardiff. He also fought the 'West of England champion', Tom Vincent of Plymouth, when he was reputedly sixty-five years old!

Not all the Welsh boxers of those early days were of the same rough-hewn type as William Samuels. In the true sense of the word, and in spite of having also spent much of their early lives in the boxing booths, men like little Jimmy Wilde and Jim Driscoll were gentlemen.

Jimmy Wilde, who was memorably known as 'The Ghost with a Hammer', came from Tylorstown—his other nickname was the 'Tylorstown Terror'. It has been said of him that, pound for pound, he was the greatest boxer of all time. Although he weighed a tiny 108 lbs. in his prime, he possessed that elusive and most-valued asset: a knockout punch.

Jack Scarrott was accused of 'brutality' by the crowd when he first featured sixteen-year-old Jimmy Wilde on his booth. 'They got quite angry about it,' remembered Scarrott, 'and told me to take him away before somebody hurt him. I said to them, "Now, don't you get excited at all, gentlemen. There's no need for you to worry about this lad getting hurt. You wait until the boxing starts and you'll see who's doing the hurting."' According to Jack Scarrott, that night little Jimmy knocked out a mountain fighter weighing about 12 stone, with a right to the chin in the second round, and it took them ten minutes to bring him round. The following night, a challenger protested at the suggestion he should be matched with Wilde, saying he'd come to fight grown men, not boys. He lasted fifteen seconds.

The precise number of knockouts that Wilde had during a career of perhaps one hundred and forty recorded fights, is disputed. According to some records it was over seventy.

The number of knockouts he achieved in perhaps hundreds of fights during his early career in the booths is completely unknown.

Wilde's favourite story about Scarrott's booth was one he often told: Meeting Scarrott by chance one day in 1916, after he had finished boxing for him and had already won a Lonsdale Belt, he accepted Scarrott's offer to box in the booth for over four hours for a purse of £40. He claimed that he knocked out nineteen opponents in three and a half hours that day in the booth, before complaining to his old friend that he was in need of refreshment!

'Of course!' said Jack, 'come into the caravan, have a cup of tea and a bun, and you'll be all right after.' They sat down for half an hour before Scarrott, who clearly wanted more than his money's-worth, opened up the booth again, charging a second admission fee, and Jimmy boxed on, beating another four opponents in the remaining half-hour.

In December of that year, Wilde beat American Zulu Kid for the World Flyweight title, which he held until June 1923 when he lost it to Pancho Villa.

When he was boxing for Scarrott, a few years before the First World War, Jimmy Wilde had three encounters with another boxer from his home town, Dai 'Chips' Davies. Wilde claimed there was a feud between the two families, but this was denied by the Davies family. The interesting thing is that at the time, well before he became famous, Wilde briefly met his match in Dai 'Chips'. Jimmy Wilde had a devastating right and Dai had a mighty left. They first met at Tylorstown and the referee, a Mr Llewelyn of Pontypridd, had no hesitation in awarding the verdict to Davies. A return match was fought at Tonypandy over four rounds and the result was a draw.

A 'decider' was arranged by Wilde's manager, Mr Teddy Lewis—this was a twelve-round contest to be held at Tonypandy. A newspaper recollection of the fight, written in 1934, claims that 'Chips' was definitely ahead in the sixth round, when the referee stepped forward to separate them. Immediately afterwards Wilde caught 'Chips' off his guard and closed the latter's eye. In the eleventh, Davies landed a solar plexus punch but there were cries of 'foul!' and the referee gave Wilde a rest, so it was claimed. Wilde recovered and the fight went the distance, with Wilde declared the winner . . . 'But there are lots of sound judges in the Rhondda Valley who will tell you that he was extremely lucky.'

Dai 'Chips' Davies claimed he was never stopped in 150 contests. Two years after his third fight with Wilde he joined the Army and was sent off to war. Half the muscle of his leg was shot away in France. He died when he was about forty years old.

Jimmy Wilde died in Cardiff at the age of 76, in 1969. They said he was never the same after he was beaten up by a gang of muggers on Cardiff Station. He had been one of the world's greatest boxers; they saw only a tiny vulnerable old man: easy pickings, for a gang of them.

A real gentleman was Percy Jones, a firm favourite with Jim Driscoll, who was his mentor, and with Jack Scarrott, who 'thought very highly' of him and remembered the young Percy fighting for the booth when-

*Jim Driscoll with his protégé, Percy Jones, who became
flyweight champion of Europe and the World.*

ever it was in Porth, which was Percy's home town. It caused Jack some
consternation for, happy as he was to have the talented youngster in his
booth, he had to keep the fact of Percy's boxing from his mother who
was vehemently against it, though his father was proud of his son's
success.

Percy Jones was the first Welshman to win the World flyweight title,
three years before Jimmy Wilde got it, but he was not recognised as
World champion in America until 1982 when Gilbert Odd of *Boxing
News* got Percy's name added to the *Ring Record Book*. Gilbert Odd
described the circumstances in which Percy gained three titles in one
'sensational' fight:

> By the beginning of 1914 Jones was recognised by the National Sport-
> ing Club as a challenger for the British Flyweight title and Lonsdale
> Belt which Bill Ladbury had taken from Sid Smith, together with his
> claims to being World and European Champion.

They met on January 26 and at the weigh-in, to the consternation of the Welsh party, Percy was 6ozs. over weight. This was a red light if ever there was one, but the usually astute Welshman decided to ignore it.

The champion magnanimously offered Percy until 9 p.m. to make the necessary reduction, but Driscoll knew that to leave it as late as that would leave his protégé as weak as a rat. He took the Porth lad for a trot round the houses, well wrapped up, then gave him some intense skipping and other vigorous exercising, so that an hour later he made the weight.

The fight for the three titles was sensational, fast and clean with barely a clinch. Jones was by far the better boxer, but he could not subdue the Londoner. Noted for his toughness and punching power, Ladbury battled on and gradually made up the leeway that the Welshman had gained in the early stages.

In the last six rounds Percy began to weaken, as the rigorous way he had got off those superfluous ounces began to tell.

Only his superb footwork, clever defence and accurate left hand enabled him to stay the full 20 rounds and secure the decision by a hairline margin.

The titles proved to be a mixed blessing. Although he successfully defended the World title against Frenchman Eugene Criqui, Percy was by now a natural bantamweight and had great difficulty getting down to the eight stone limit for flyweight contests. Seven weeks later he met Joe Symonds of Plymouth, in what was billed as a title fight with all the honours at stake. Percy scaled eight stone eight pounds. Symonds was keen to fight, thinking he stood a good chance of winning the titles, and the purse money was good. So he did not demand forfeit. The contest went ahead.

In the eighteenth round, Percy was put down twice and, as he had no strength left at all, his corner threw the towel in.

Of course, the NSC refused to recognise Symonds as champion because Percy Jones's failure to make the weight meant the contest could not be counted as a title bout. Under the rules set up a few years earlier, Percy still held the Lonsdale Belt.

However, he was soon obliged to forfeit belt and titles when, in October 1914, he again failed to make eight stone against Scotland's great flyweight, Tancy Lee. The fight was allowed to proceed, but as a catchweight bout rather than for the titles, and Lee won. It wasn't long though before Tancy Lee gained the flyweight crown.

When the First World War began, Percy lost no time in joining the Rhondda Bantam Battalion of the Royal Welsh Fusiliers and was sent off to do battle of an altogether different kind. He was blown up in January 1917 and his horrific injuries resulted in thirty operations and a leg amputation. He also suffered permanent effects from gassing, and trench fever.

Percy attended a charity show at the Cardiff Empire in November 1922. Tragically, the lad with the smiling chubby face who once had trouble making flyweight, now weighed little more than four stone two pounds. The story goes that his friends gently carried him in a blanket to his seat in a place of honour. 'If you're short of an exhibition bout, I'll take you on to show I haven't forgotten what you taught me,' he joked with Jim Driscoll.

Percy had been born on Boxing Day, 1892. He died on Christmas Day, 1922.

'It was a great pity Percy died so early,' said Jack Scarrott. 'Everybody in South Wales boxing felt very sorry and sympathised with his relatives.'

Jack Scarrott himself died at the age of eighty-four in 1947.

Chapter 4

Lord Lonsdale's Belt

'If ever a boxer epitomised the ideals, the dreams—even the purpose—of the National Sporting Club, then that boxer was Jim Driscoll.'

John Harding, *Lonsdale's Belt*

Some years before the First World War, it had become increasingly clear that British boxing would benefit from further regulation. In order to standardize matches between boxers for championship status, the National Sporting Club decided to act. In 1909 they laid down their new rules: for all decision contests there were to be seven different classes within strict weight limits (light-heavyweight was added in 1914), and the champion of each of these classes must defend his title every six months as long as there be a worthy contender. Prior to this boxers could, and often did, contest matches at any weight and call it a British Title Bout. A boxer could therefore claim to be the British 8 stone 4lbs Champion, while someone else could claim the equivalent at 8 stone 2lbs.

In truth the committee and club members were also anxious to keep control over the boxers who, realising their worth to the gentlemen of the club, were making ever increasing demands for higher purses. After a great deal of discussion (among the doubters on the committee was founder A. F. 'Peggy' Bettinson), they came up with the answer: the prize that every British boxer would want, the National Sporting Club Belt. It was soon dubbed the 'Lonsdale Belt' after the club's president; though it seems likely that Lonsdale himself had little to do with it, he did pay for the first belt.

National Sporting Club, Covent Garden, 1891-1929.

Interior old NSC Club at Covent Garden, c.1900.

Actually his portrait in the well-known front enamel panel did not appear until the British Boxing Board of Control took over the responsibility for the belts in 1936. The original NSC belts were made of nine carat gold with an enamel centre panel showing two boxers in fighting stance surrounded by a chased oak leaf border.

It took a little while for the significance of the Lonsdale Belts to sink in (intrinsically they did not have the same appeal as a bigger cash purse), but it gradually dawned on those in the boxing fraternity that the value of the Lonsdale Belt lay in the rule that the holder was the one and only official champion of England (Britain) in his weight class. Belts as prizes for champions at different weights, had been awarded, and defended, since the latter part of the nineteenth century, but had no 'official' status. The winning of the Lonsdale Belt meant that no other boxer could claim the title without defeating the holder in a contest for the title; that is the reason for its lasting appeal. Furthermore, under the new rules, two successful defences of the title meant that the champion got to keep his belt as the outright winner. Still further, a much-vaunted pension of £1 per week was to be paid to each outright winner from the age of fifty (though this part of the prize was such a radical idea that its funding was never properly worked out and, as the Board could not see any way of taking responsibility for the pension, the idea faded away with the decline and eventual demise of the NSC).

Three out of the seven first recipients of these new prizes were Welshmen: Freddie Welsh, Tom Thomas and Jim Driscoll.

Freddie Welsh was the first. Born Frederick Hall Thomas in 1886, Freddie adopted the name 'Welsh' to avoid embarrassment to his family in Pontypridd. He was the son of a local businessman and the family may well have thought that it was not good for business to be associated with boxing. It was probably for the same reason that, unlike most of his contemporaries, he preferred not to stick to the usual training ground of the boxing booth, but instead travelled to America at a very young age where he studied the art of boxing in a very serious and individual way. He devised his own strategies and diet and after a series of successful contests in Philadelphia, he returned to Britain in 1907

A trio of Taffies.
From left to right: Freddie Welsh, Tom Thomas and Jim Driscoll.

where he continued to beat opponent after opponent, including Seaman Hayes at the National Sporting Club.

Gilbert Odd for *Boxing News*, described him as 'A self-taught scientist with the gloves, who believed it was more important to avoid a punch than to give one.' His study of anatomy, however, enabled him to place punches where they would have the maximum weakening effect.

Freddie Welsh.

Ironically, when he returned home, his mother proclaimed her pride in him and his sister Kate took on the task of supervising his vegetarian diet.

Off he went again to America where he remained until 1909, beating Abe Attell in Los Angeles, among many others.

He made history in November 1909 when he beat Johnny Summers of Canning Town and originally from Middlesborough, to get the very first Lonsdale Belt and the British lightweight title.

But it was in July 1914 that Freddie Welsh reached the peak of his career, beating American Willie Ritchie at London's Olympia and thus becoming universally recognised as World lightweight champion. He kept the crown for three years before losing it to Benny Leonard in New York at the age of 31.

Freddie Welsh served in the US Army during World War One where he received a commission as captain and was assigned to the rehabilitation of wounded veterans in Washington DC in 1917. He also continued his boxing career through the war. In all he had 137 fights in US rings.

Sadly, he died penniless in New York in 1927, having unwisely invested his money in health camp ventures in America. He was only 41 years old. In 1931, Freddie Welsh's Lonsdale Belt was last seen being handed to the then current World lightweight champion, Tony Canzoneri, by Welsh's widow.

Tom Thomas, the second winner of the new Lonsdale Belt, was born in the Rhondda on 19th April, 1880. A farmer's son, he was something of a loner who fixed up a punchbag in the barn and undertook most of his training, including a lot of road work, on his own. Unfortunately, he also suffered from recurring bouts of rheumatic fever which dogged him throughout his short life. Despite his ill-health and probably due to his dedication to his solo training, he was tremendously strong and could hit very hard indeed.

At eighteen years old he decided to fulfil his ambition to box professionally. Up till then, he had watched and learned plenty from the boxers he saw in the travelling booths; now he offered his services as a boxer in the same booths, and had no trouble proving his worth.

Over the next two years he grew to middleweight, and became a popular figure as he fought and mostly beat opponents all over South Wales. It was a measure of his confidence that he entered a heavyweight novices competition at the NSC where they discovered, after he had been beaten on points in the first round, that despite his impressive physique, Tom weighed only 11 stone. The matchmaker told him to be sure to come back when they were holding the middleweight competition. He did—and beat four opponents to win the competition.

After that Tom was much in demand at the NSC and other London venues, and gained a reputation as a boxer who was able to stop his opponents inside the distance. In Cardiff, he beat Harry Dunstan in three rounds to become the Middleweight Champion of Wales.

Then, on 23rd May 1906, he met Pat O'Keefe in the by-now very familiar setting of the NSC, for the British title. Pat O'Keefe was the more experienced of the two boxers although three years younger than Thomas, and he started the favourite.

The contest provided plenty of excitement for the gentlemen, and went the full fifteen rounds. But Tom outfought O'Keefe close in and outboxed him at long range, putting his opponent down for short counts four times. It was a close thing, but Tom Thomas came out the worthy winner.

However, another crippling bout of rheumatic fever put him out of boxing for almost two years!

Eventually, still with stiff, painful joints, he climbed back into the ring to beat Mike Crawley in Marylebone with a KO in five rounds. Tiger Smith, fellow Welshman, suffered a similar defeat in round four, at the NSC. Thomas went on to gain a twenty-round points win over American middleweight Bart Connolly for the very substantial purse of £300 with £100 side stake. But in terms of his health it cost him dearly and he needed another long lay-off. Then in December 1909, still the recognised British middleweight champion, Tom Thomas was called upon to defend his title for the Lonsdale Belt. His challenger was Charlie Wilson of Kensington and the battle was savage but short. In his book *Welsh Warriors*, Fred Deakin described the fight:

> Wilson attacked hard as he tried to get in close where he could use his powerful short hooks to the body; those strength-sapping, rib-bending body punches could have been a match winning tactic for him. But Tom strived to keep the fight at long range with his heavy straight shots to the head. Both men took a lot of heavy punishment before Wilson was counted out in the second round.

There was more than a second notch on his Lonsdale Belt at stake when Tom Thomas defended his title against Jim Sullivan of London. The two were due to meet in June 1910 but Tom was suffering another bout of rheumatism and the fight was postponed until November.

A month earlier, World titleholder Stanley Ketchel, known as the 'Michigan Assassin' and ranked by Nat Fleischer as the all-time greatest World middleweight champion, had been gunned down and killed by a man named Walter A. Dipley. On his death, the title was claimed by Billy Papke, a German-American from Spring Valley, Illinois, because he had previously taken the title from Ketchel before losing it back to him in their return fight a couple of months later. As Tom Thomas and Jim Sullivan were ranked as possible contenders by British promoters, there was every need for Tom to be as fit as possible when they met. But in spite of an improvement in his health through the summer of that year, when he climbed through the ropes to fight Jim Sullivan he was certainly not fighting fit. According to *Boxing* magazine's correspondent, Thomas's self-styled training (he had rejected the services of his old trainer, Dai Dolling) resulted in him going up to London 'in flabby condition and was as slow as the proverbial cart-horse against the well-trained Sullivan'.

> It was a tremendous battle with Sullivan boxing carefully at long range and Thomas trying to end it as quickly as possible with short hooks to the head and body.
>
> Thomas attacked fiercely, bobbing and weaving his way skilfully at close quarters and battering his challenger about the ribs. Several times he had him on the verge of defeat but each time Sullivan managed to box his way out of trouble.
>
> At the end of twenty savage rounds the champion's corner men felt that he had done enough to win, but the referee gave the decision to Jim Sullivan and Thomas suffered his first defeat.

It was also the first unsuccessful defence of a Lonsdale Belt.

But Tom Thomas, who must surely have been one of the most courageous boxers ever, challenged Billy Papke directly, backing himself with £1,000 of his own money to beat Papke.

The American declined, saying he already had many lucrative offers in America and had signed contracts for a series of profitable Music Hall appearances. And so they never met. Jim Sullivan, however, fought Papke on 8th June 1911, and got knocked out in the ninth round.

Two months after that defeat, Tom Thomas walked home through the rain from an exhibition bout, was taken ill and died from pneumonia on 11th August.

Fred Deakin, summing up Thomas's courage, had this to say:

> Imagine the agony of trying to do your road work when your knees are stiff and swollen. Imagine trying to skip when you are bouncing up and down on torturous ankles. Imagine trying to work out when your wrists are so painful that you want to scream every time you strike the bag. Imagine trying to do all, or any, of these things when your shoulder is so agonisingly painful that you have to rest your arm in a sling. It doesn't bear thinking about.

Jim Driscoll.

'Peerless' Jim Driscoll was the golden-haired darling of Cardiff and he became the third Welsh winner of a Lonsdale Belt on St Valentine's Day in 1910, when he stopped seaman Arthur Hayes to confirm his status as British featherweight champion. He had first won the title in June 1907 by beating Joe Bowker. Much has been written about him, his outstanding boxing skills and his 'celebrity' status. Guy Deghy in his history of the National Sporting Club recalls John Bohun Lynch's opinion: 'Not at any weight nor at any time was the championship of England (Britain) held by a better boxer or a straighter man.' Nowhere was his popularity greater than at the NSC. It was said that he was the only pugilist to have had his portrait hung on the walls of the old Covent Garden club.

Born in Cardiff of Irish extraction, Jim Driscoll had spent his early boxing years in Jack Scarrott's booth where he quickly became the star attraction. Having boxed mostly in Wales until 1906, Jim was already twenty-nine years old when he won the Lonsdale Belt and thus far, he had been beaten only once in sixty-four recorded fights.

Later that year though, he lost to Freddie Welsh on a foul in a controversial and punishing contest that was the talk of Cardiff for a long time.

Jim Driscoll was the first outright winner of a Lonsdale Belt. He got to keep it after beating Spike Robson for the second time, for the featherweight title, in the New Year of 1911. It has been lovingly handed down through successive generations of Driscoll's family.

By 1914, Freddie Welsh, Jim Driscoll, Newport's Johnny Basham and Jimmy Wilde had all won Lonsdale Belts outright; a feat repeated by fellow Welshman 'Gentleman' Jack Petersen in 1933. It is more than likely that Percy Jones and Tom Thomas would also have been in their number had they not been prematurely robbed of their strength and their lives.

A. G. Hales, known as 'Smiler', a boxing writer and journalist from Australia, had started making trips to London during the 1890s, drawn to the excitement and atmosphere of the National Sporting Club. In this he was not alone, for the club's reputation for excellence also attracted admirers from all over Europe as well as America.

Hales got more involved in British boxing in the period just after the First World War. At the time, there were hardly any European titles in British hands, and although the NSC did not want British boxers to contest bouts for European titles, they were very popular with fans. Then the heavyweight champion, Joe Beckett, got knocked out within seconds by the magnificent Georges Carpentier of France. It was the final straw for British boxing fans and in a fine display of decisiveness, MP Horatio Bottomley decreed that 'Something must be done!' He also happened to be the owner of a very popular weekly magazine called

John Bull, which gave him the means to 'do something' and didn't do his circulation figures any harm either. Recruiting the help of A. G. Hales—in a blaze of publicity in his magazine, which was taken up by the press—he founded and financed the 'John Bull Boxers' in 1920. The idea was of course, to cast around in Britain for budding boxing talent, and young hopefuls were invited to apply. A camp was set up at Herne Bay on the Kent coast, where each applicant was given a chance to prove himself. Finally, it was hoped, Hales would be left with a troupe of decent boxers.

Exactly how A. G. Hales selected these boxers I do not know. But somehow or other his search led him to Ammanford; to Pontamman House in fact, where an early training gym for boxers, Ammanford Sporting Club, had been established for some years. A charming surviving photograph taken in the grounds of Pontamman House around the same time includes boxers Danny Rogers, Gomer Evans and brothers Idris and Idwal Jones (seated left to right). The Union Jack in front of the proudly displayed silverware and the boxer dog (innocently mas-

Members of Ammanford Sporting Club, c.1920.
Boxers seated, left to right: Danny Rogers, Idwal Jones, Idris Jones,
Gomer Evans. Young boy, 4th left: Tom Day (13 caps for Wales rugby).

John Bull Boxing Team, 1920.
Back row, left to right: Jim Prendy (London), Chris Langdon (Ystalyfera),
Billy Daniels (Llanelli), Jack Tirell (Cardiff), Jim Slater (Staffs.),
Jack Heathcot (Wigan), Steve Prendy (London).
Front row, left to right: Glyn Stevens (Pontardulais), Idwal Jones (Ammanford),
A. G. Hales, Idris Jones (Ammanford), Luther Thomas.

querading as a bulldog?) seems to indicate that the club had already established a connection with the 'John Bull Boxers'. Other boxers who trained at Ammanford Sporting Club were Alf and Chris Langdon of Ystalyfera, and Ivor Day. Tom Day is one of the little boys sitting beside the dog in the picture. Tom, of course, grew up to captain Swansea at rugby and had thirteen caps for Wales between 1931 and 1935.

A second photograph, from 1920, is of some of the 'John Bull Boxers' themselves. It shows no less than five local boxers, three of them from Pontamman House, among the chosen few: Billy (later 'Gypsy') Daniels, Llanelli; Chris Langdon, Ystalyfera; Glyn Stevens, Pontardulais; Idris and Idwal Jones, Ammanford.

Chapter 5

The Hungry Fighters

In 1927 Tirydail Colliery, Ammanford, sounded its siren for the last time. It closed for good in that year which was also the year that the United Anthracite Collieries Ltd merged into the much larger Amalgamated Anthracite Collieries Ltd.

My grandfather who had worked in Tirydail for many years and was also a safety officer, was 56 years old. Possibly the closure was not such a devastating blow for him as it was for his sons, Will and Emrys, and other younger men who must have scrambled for any work there may have been in other local collieries: not much, I would guess, in 1927.

But Stephen Jones, my grandfather, was a man of many talents. Having persuaded his second wife, my grandmother Maggie, that home-owning was the thing of the future he must have been one of the first people in Ammanford to put down a deposit on the newly-built houses in Talbot Road, near the park. They moved in around 1907 and he promptly set about some DIY, installing a flush toilet in the *Tŷ Bach* out the back. At some point he apparently rigged up some kind of bell system so that Maggie (in the kitchen) knew that Stephen (in the bath) was ready to have his back scrubbed. Pithead baths did not become commonplace until after the Miners' Welfare Act of 1921. My mother Iris was born in Talbot Road in 1910, Stephen and Maggie's fourth (and last) daughter.

One Sunday when Iris was very small, there was pandemonium in the house. It was a day she never forgot because Sunday was generally so well ordered: chapel in the morning, followed by lunch, followed by Sunday School, then tea and then chapel for the third time. My grandfather had walked along to the colliery with Tiny, the family's Airedale dog, whilst Maggie and the two older girls prepared the lunch. He was carrying out a routine safety check and was expected back in time for the meal which had to be prompt because of Sunday School starting at two o'clock. Suddenly, Tiny appeared at the back door alone. A quick look up and down the road confirmed there was no sign of Stephen. It could only mean there had been an accident.

Fortunately, Will was at home at the time. He immediately summoned help from neighbouring fellow-miners who left whatever they were doing, and ran 'full-pelt' to the colliery. There they discovered Stephen underground, lying on the floor. He had been gassed. He was carefully carried out and put to bed at home where the doctor, hastily summoned, confirmed the diagnosis. Although it took him some time to recover, he had been fortunate indeed as gassing incidents underground were often lethal. Tiny was now not only a much-loved pet but also a heroine!

In 1914 and again in 1920, *Kelly's Directory* lists my grandfather as a hairdresser (barber) in Talbot Road. No doubt this sideline stood him in good stead when he was made redundant from the colliery for, by all accounts, he had no shortage of customers. He was also well known locally as a pretty decent repairer of clocks and watches. My mother remembered the dustman bringing him a clock that had been thrown out, knowing that Stephen Jones would be able to do something with it.

Electricity was first commercially available in Ammanford in 1909. Poles and overhead cables were erected and the supply reached Talbot Road in due course. Naturally, Stephen took full advantage of this modern wonder and had an overhead light installed on a pulley system so that you could pull it up and down. Underneath this he would sit at the table to do his clock mending, sometimes calling out to Maggie while his fingers held tiny pieces of workings: *'Maggie! Tyn' y golau lawr!'* ('Maggie! Pull the light down!').

Yet another abiding interest of Stephen's was photography. He had built a shed with dark room in the garden, which I remember being full of big glass photographic plates, and he was a founder member of the Ammanford Photographic Society.

The closure of Tirydail Colliery followed a turbulent period in mining history in South Wales. In 1925, Ammanford found itself in the forefront of this industrial unrest when in April, the Anthracite Strike began in the collieries of the town and quickly spread to outlying mines. The main dispute was about the seniority rule: 'last in—first out', which miners had always considered sacrosanct, but which the managers of the United Anthracite Collieries had been choosing to disregard during periods of lay-offs. Four months of brass band-led marches, meetings, lockouts and riots followed, culminating in the so-called 'Battle of Ammanford' on 4th August.

The day had been tense; the threat of full-scale riot ever-present made the constabulary fearful that they may not be able to contain the situation as evening approached. It was decided that help should be summoned from the Glamorgan Constabulary, a large contingent of whom were billeted at Gwaun-Cae-Gurwen brewery, some five miles up the road.

A bus was quickly organised to bring the extra policemen to Ammanford. But it got no further than the narrow bridge at Pontamman, where it was ambushed by striking miners, and battle ensued. Between 10.30 p.m. and 3 o'clock in the morning the police struggled to contain the riot, eventually driving the miners back as far as Ammanford Square. The Riot Act was read and many arrests were made, resulting in nearly 200 prosecutions.

My Uncle Will made his way home that night, having escaped arrest, only to face the wrath of my God-fearing grandfather, which in some ways was worse. Their lives were never to be the same again. The relationship between father and son, collier and butty, had changed.

Fifty-eight miners were eventually jailed including a neighbour, Joe Rainford, who got twelve months. When they were released they were feted as heroes by their communities. Each one received a scroll and a medal from the International Class War Prisoners' Aid Association.

*ICWPA medal presented to future International
Brigader Sam Morris for his part in the Ammanford riots.*

Incidents of industrial strife such as the events in the Amman Valley, increased over the autumn and winter, amalgamating with varying degrees of unrest in many other industries throughout England and Wales.

1926 was the year of the General Strike.

If you were unfortunate enough to be an out-of-work miner then there were some advantages to living in close-knit communities like the South Wales valleys.

For one thing almost everyone sympathised with you; indeed many were in the same boat. Your neighbours would try to ensure you could get by somehow, preferably without your having to be entirely dependant on charity. The more enterprising, like my grandfather, found other ways of putting food on the table. (In our family we still have a footstool made by my mining neighbours who had set up a little enterprise of their own during the 1984 miners' strike.)

And then there was boxing. Tradition going way back into the nineteenth century and beyond meant that any young man could get into a ring—boxing booths abounded in fairs and carnivals throughout the country—and call himself a claimant to a title if he beat enough opponents.

Later on things got more organised, safer. But there was still plenty of opportunity for any youngster willing to have a go, to make a few bob and maybe a name for himself as a boxer. After the First World War boxing and athletic clubs sprung up throughout Britain with Wales getting a good share of them. These clubs promoted both professional and amateur boxing.

And so it was quite natural that young miners, energetic and hungry, should try their luck in the ring. Where family disapproval was expected they would sometimes fight under a pseudonym.

As far as I know neither Uncle Will nor Uncle Emrys ever did any boxing—being my grandfather's sons this was hardly surprising. As a deacon in the Welsh Baptist Chapel, it is likely my grandfather would not have approved.

Besides, by the time Tirydail Colliery closed, both brothers were in their thirties. Emrys, the elder, was married to Lizzie Jane Morris and they had a daughter, Margaret. He managed to find work in Cwmllynfell Colliery—Lizzie was from Cwmllynfell—and they settled in a house up there on the mountain. But Lizzie's brother, Llewelyn, did some boxing—probably as a fairground booth fighter as I have not been able to trace his record. My cousin Michael, Margaret's son, remembers that Uncle Llew taught him how to square up and how to punch.

Will was restless for change. Around this time he married Jenny Anthony from Tycroes. She had relatives in Gallup, New Mexico, including her brother Thomas, and an uncle who was the manager of the Gamerco coal mine out there. When Will was offered a job in Gamerco, it didn't take him long to make up his mind. It was just what he wanted. Unfortunately, it was not what Jenny wanted. Despite his entreaties and no doubt those of the family, Jenny refused to go. Will decided to go alone and he sailed on the *Aquitania* on 27th September

Will Jones. Died at Gamerco,
New Mexico, 8th August 1935.

1929, promising to come back for Jenny when he had found them somewhere to live and earned some money. And this he did.

He came back for what was to be his last visit to Ammanford in 1934. Jenny had not changed her mind. What tears and recriminations there must have been it is not ours to know, but Will sailed back to America, this time on the *SS Berengaria*, once again on his own.

On the morning of 8th August 1935, he went to work and was crushed to death between the wall of the mine and a dram full of coal, following a derailment. That afternoon there was an inquest before Justice of the Peace Ramon Chaved and a verdict of Death by Accident was recorded. His funeral service was held at the First Baptist Church where he had been a member of the church choir and a boys' leader in missionary work; his father's son after all.

My Aunty Jen never remarried. She worked all her life, devoting all her spare time to voluntary work in St John Ambulance and after retirement, to the Old Age Pensioners' Association. For her unstinting contribution to society she was awarded the British Empire Medal. She died on 21st September 1983.

Chapter 6

Johnny Vaughan, Boxer and Manager

'No Boxers Managed Unless Training Under My Personal Supervision.'
—Johnny Vaughan, letterhead of
Ammanford Athletic and Boxing Club.

Although I didn't know it at the time, in 1968 we bought our house in Ammanford seven doors away from the house Johnny Vaughan was living in when he died just four years earlier, and so his widow, Maud, became our neighbour.

Fate had once again brought me close to the man I had come to admire for his achievements in the boxing world, as it had at various times throughout my life, and yet I never got to know him.

I was brought up in Penybanc, outside Ammanford. Not only had Johnny Vaughan lived there as a boy some forty years earlier, but it was also home to the Rule family, including the famous boxing brothers Archie and Crad.

In fact, the two families lived in the same street and it was George Rule, Archie and Crad's father, who taught Johnny how to box. The Rule kids (there were twelve in all) would sit on chairs around the walls of the kitchen to watch the sparring; early inspiration for Archie, who later joined Amman Valley Boxing Club and went on to win amateur Welsh and European titles in the early 1920s.

Then as a boy myself, around 1955, I heard the boxing club was looking for sparring partners so I decided to give the gym a try. To my recollection it was Johnny himself who put me in the ring with a school-boy champion whose superior skills put me on the floor and dashed my ambitions to be a boxer!

Johnny Vaughan was born at The Bird in Hand public house, Llanedi, on 5th October 1894 to William and Rachel Vaughan. He was the fourth of thirteen children.

Around 1905-06, the family left Llanedi and went to live in Penybanc. He attended the National School in Tycroes for the statutory period, leaving within a few years to work in the local colliery with his neighbour, George Rule.

George's ambitions for Johnny's future were supported by his friend, Jack Jaggard, who had also undertaken some of Johnny's early training. On George's recommendation, Johnny at the age of nineteen, made his way to the Llwyncelyn Hotel in Porth in the Rhondda Valley where he continued his training at the gym there. It was 1913. By this time Johnny reckoned he'd fought about fifty contests, winning most of them.

It seems likely, because of the lack of records of these early fights, that the majority of them took place in boxing booths, probably the one belonging to Jack Scarrott.

After arriving at Porth his next contest was at Tonypandy, against Llew Edwards of Porth. Johnny lost over six rounds, but he and Llew got on well and became friends.

In 1915, Llew Edwards became the British featherweight champion and won a Lonsdale Belt, against no less a boxer than Owen Moran.

In true Lonsdale Belt tradition, there is a story to this particular belt —it was 'lost' not once, but twice.

The featherweight belt was held by Ted Kid Lewis when in 1915, the NSC declared the British featherweight title vacant and matched Llew Edwards with Owen Moran. This was because Lewis had not made a serious attempt to defend the title, mostly because he had not been in the country, but also because he was now boxing at a higher weight. John Harding in his book *Lonsdale's Belt* points out that:

> In 1915 he was claiming the welterweight World title, which he was to contest with Jack Britton and others for the duration of the First World War.

Johnny Vaughan and Llew Edwards.

More importantly, he had taken his Lonsdale Belt with him 'to charm the ladies', first of all to Australia, then to America. In early 1915, he jumped at the opportunity to appear in some preliminary bouts during the run-up to the much-hyped Jack Johnson v. Jess Willard World heavyweight championship fight in Havana, Cuba. Naturally, the belt came too and was proudly placed as part of a display in a shop window in downtown Havana.

After the historic contest had taken place (Jess Willard knocked out Jack Johnson in the *twenty-sixth* round), it soon became obvious that the fight organisers were bankrupt. Lewis didn't get paid for his fight, and in all the kerfuffle, he retreated back to the States, forgetting to pick up the belt.

When Bettinson of the NSC cabled Lewis to ask if they could have their Lonsdale Belt back, Lewis was in New York. He cabled a friend to pick the belt up for him, but in the meantime it had disappeared!

The police finally tracked it down two months later when they arrested the thief who had tried to pawn it. Although Ted Kid Lewis had to borrow the money to retrieve it, he always remembered heaving a mighty sigh of relief to get it back. However, the Edwards v. Moran fight, which took place on 31st May 1915, was over by the time the Lonsdale Belt arrived back in England.

It was a controversial bout to say the least, which had the crowd on its feet complaining about the behaviour of Owen Moran, who had put Llew Edwards down with low punching, and employed other dubious tactics such as 'heeling' with the edge of his glove and holding Edwards's head. The referee, Mr Douglas, was forced to warn him, between rounds, to obey the rules. But describing the tenth round, John Harding says:

> . . . both men went into a clinch, Edwards crouched low and covered up. Moran struggled to rip his gloves away, even wrestled with the younger man and finally landed yet another low blow—upon which Douglas rose, waved the men apart and disqualified Moran.

Moran, who was nicknamed 'Fearless', protested immediately, saying he had done nothing wrong and calling Edwards a 'quitter', who boxed covered up because he was afraid of being hit in the body. Nobody seemed to agree with him—his claim was belied by Edwards's display of speed and superior ringcraft in the earlier part of the contest —and he sadly finished a distinguished boxing career under something of a cloud. Among his opponents had been 'Digger' Stanley, Abe Attell, the World featherweight champion, whom he met in 1908 and 1910, and Jim Driscoll.

Astonishingly, the same Lonsdale Belt now held by Llew Edwards, arrived in Australia for the second time when Llew went there later in 1915. He must have liked it there for he continued boxing in Australia, successfully, until 1922. Clearly too far away to defend the title, Edwards did not actually return the belt to the NSC until 1918, when Charley Hardcastle had lost the featherweight title to Tancy Lee.

During these years, Johnny Vaughan won thirteen out of nineteen contests, mostly at Tonypandy.

Johnny stepped up a gear when he was matched with the likes of Nat Brooks at the National Sporting Club, London, and Frank Moody at the Queens Hall, Cardiff. He lost both these fights and although he won his next two contests, at Liverpool Stadium, he may have begun to consider his future. Maybe he wasn't going to get that coveted title.

It was about 1918 when Johnny decided to settle down in the Ammanford area. He was courting a girl from Llandybie, a couple of miles from Ammanford, Miss Sarah Maud Evans, an extrovert, bubbly young lady by all accounts, well-known for her recitation skills in *eisteddfodau*. But fate has a habit of intervening just when life seems sweetest. Johnny was scheduled to fight Idris Jones when he was struck down with appendicitis which put an end to his career as a boxer.

Nonetheless, he and Maud were married in August 1919, and settled down to married life in Iscennen Road, Ammanford. Their only child, Edgar, was born in 1920.

Although he was a miner through most of his working life, Johnny Vaughan's passion for boxing combined with a shrewd business sense ensured that he was soon involved in training others. The twenties proved to be the best possible time to start on this new career.

As detailed in a previous chapter, the General Strike and the industrial unrest leading to lockouts and widespread unemployment in South Wales meant that many healthy young men with strong muscles developed at the coalface were desperate for money.

Depending on how you looked at it, offering to get in a boxing ring and pit your skills against another desperate young man, was easy money. At least you got paid straightaway so your mother or wife could put a meal on the table. Anyway, along with the Rhondda and Swansea valleys as well as other areas in South Wales, the Amman Valley produced some very good boxers during the twenties and thirties.

It may seem strange to us in these days when most of us only watch professional boxing on the television, that a small town like Amman-ford (population almost 7,000 in 1920) staged boxing shows regularly for many years, attracting large crowds from miles around to watch what were often extremely good bills. During the period just after the First World War, a gym for the increasing number of boys presenting themselves for training was set up in an ex-Army shed on what is now a car park but was then the 'fair field'. It was purchased for the purpose after the war by 'Mr William Peregrine, Wil Jones, Aberdare, Ted Davies (boot shop) and Mr Parry'. Among notable local boxers who would have trained there at that time were Idris Jones and his brother Idwal, Ivor Day, Chris Langdon and probably Archie and Crad Rule. It's likely that Johnny Vaughan had a hand in training all of them. In 1923 half the shed was sold to the Salvation Army who took it away and erected it in Margaret Street where it was used for their services until the 1990s when they replaced it with a purpose-built hall.

Sometimes open-air boxing contests would be staged on the recrea-tion ground, a multi-purpose venue where horse racing was among the sports on offer. In the area where boxing events took place the venue was apparently enclosed by a fence of zinc sheets so that you had to pay to get in and see the action! Although incredibly popular, boxing was not universally approved of in the valleys and 24th May 1924 was the day chosen by the local chapels to stage a protest against this most barbaric sport. Welsh chapel folk were still gripped by the fervour of the evangelical revival of 1904. Preachers like Evan Roberts, who were among the greatest orators of their time, had been able to stir whole congregations, and their influence was still strong in the twenties, and for many years afterwards.

On this occasion in 1924, Idris Jones was to fight the World Scout-ing champion, Dick Harry from Trebanos. Some 300 protesters had gathered outside the recreation ground as the earlier bouts commenced. They listened as several chapel ministers spoke in turn, with increasing passion, and then finally began to sing the rousing hymn, *'O Agor Fy Llygaid i Weled'* ('Oh Open my Eyes to See').

Unfortunately, the singing was drowned out by the cheering of 1,000 sporting fans inside the fence who had just witnessed Idris Jones knock out the champion in ninety seconds!

Idris Jones was a favourite sparring partner of flyweight champion Jimmy Wilde who, throughout his incredibly successful career, would often call upon Idris's services.

Meanwhile, Johnny Vaughan was building a reputation as a trainer and masseur. In September 1927 he opened a gym at the Cross Inn, together with Edwin Evans. Over the next two or three years they trained a number of very successful boxers, both professional and amateur, including Arthur Rees, Arthur Davies, Idris Jones, Billy Quinlen, Ginger Jones, Steve 'Curly' Fay, Danny Evans, Crad Rule, Watt Phillips, 'Nipper' Thomas, Bertie Davies, Bryn Edwards and Cliff and Gwyn Peregrine.

Among their early successes was Arthur Rees, who stopped Con Moriarty in seven rounds in January 1928, and Steve Fay who out-pointed Tommy Hope over six rounds at Llanelli, in June 1928. When the latter two met again in December of that year, Fay knocked Tommy Hope out in the fourth round.

Arthur Rees, whose boxing career apparently lasted only a couple of years, had notable success over 1928/29, beating such opponents as Young Derrick, Billy Nicholas and Billy Green and holding Billy Fry and Jerry Daley to draws.

Steve Fay was with Johnny Vaughan for two or three years in the early part of his boxing career but, at some point during the 1930s, he went to live in High Wycombe, and boxed from there. In 1934 he beat Tuck Mason of Windsor convincingly, to win the Berks and Bucks welter-weight title, when his opponent's corner threw the towel in at the end of the fifth round.

He had a total of seventy-three contests in a career spanning over sixteen years, winning forty-three of them. His last contest was in 1945 when his opponent Billy Stevens of High Wycombe suffered an injury after falling in the ring.

Idris Jones.

Idwal Jones.

Idris Jones, together with his brother Idwal, belonged to the early school of boxing in Pontamman, which probably joined forces with the gym when it was set up in the Army shed on the fair field. The brothers were among the hand-picked group known as the John Bull boxers, who trained in Herne Bay, Kent. Idris was given the opportunity to box at The National Sporting Club, the Ring and Liverpool Stadium before the nineteen-twenties. During the early days of his career, Idris showed much promise, and had stopped a number of his opponents inside the distance when he joined the John Bull boxers. Writing in 1958, Jack Leyshon described Idris as 'a master of the game. He could punch from any angle and fought such top fighters as Charlie Hardcastle, Mike Honeyman and Joe Conn' (who lost to Tancy Lee in a contest for the British featherweight title in 1918).

'In my opinion,' said Leyshon, 'Idris Jones made a mistake when he refused Dai Dolling's invitation to accompany him to America.' Dai Dolling was a well-known athletics trainer, who trained runners as well as boxers. For a while he had been trainer to Lonsdale Belt winner, Tom Thomas.

As far as titles were concerned, Idris never fulfilled his potential, failing in two bids for the Welsh welterweight title, against Billy Moore of Penygraig and Billy Thomas, Deri. He was a favourite of Johnny Vaughan's, and also knew Joe Gess, for whom he did a lot of boxing in the late twenties. Idris had ninety-five recorded contests, winning forty-seven, with thirteen draws. He remained Johnny's friend and neighbour throughout his life, which turned out to be tragically short. He was killed in an accident in a local colliery on 22nd November 1935, at the age of thirty-seven.

His brother Idwal emigrated to Ontario, Canada, where he successfully continued his boxing career for a while. According to Jack Leyshon, he won seventeen out of twenty-three contests he had there.

Just before Christmas 1927, Johnny had finished working at Pontyclerc Colliery but was lucky enough to be taken on a fortnight later at Pantyffynnon, another local colliery and so, early in 1928, he was able to purchase the materials to build his own ring. The first recorded Johnny Vaughan Promotion took place in the open air on 28th July 1928; it was raining! Spectators were treated to an array of local talent: Arthur Rees drew with Arthur Davies and Steve 'Curly' Fay stopped Griff Griffiths in the fifth round of a ten-round contest. Cliff Peregrine beat Young Cullen. Johnny Vaughan pondered on the advantages of having a covered venue!

It was around this time that Cliff Peregrine duly turned up at the New Dock Tavern, Llanelli, one evening, expecting to top the bill with a boxer called Jackie Lewis from Aberavon. A good crowd had gathered to see the action, and Cliff was preparing for the fight in the dressing room when word came to him that his opponent had failed to arrive. The organisers were loath to disappoint the audience, not to mention having to pay them back, so after some hasty discussion, they approached

Cliff's brother, Gwyn, who had come to watch his brother fight. Reluctant at first, he was eventually persuaded to fight Cliff in the top-line bout. Someone was sent to tell Cliff, who had started dressing to go home, and had to get gloved-up again.

Under the assumed name of Billy Lewis, Brynamman, Gwyn climbed into the ring for this very unusual event—a contest between two brothers. It is to their credit that they managed to put on a very entertaining bout for the audience, and a draw was the inevitable result.

Arthur Davies was the first of Johnny's Welsh title hopes and to help with his training Johnny enlisted the aid of Evan 'Scwt' Williams, whom he had known from about 1911. According to the *South Wales Echo*, Evan Williams was known as Ianto Scwt in the Rhondda, and had had a notable boxing career in the army, joining the Royal Army Service Corps in 1914, and serving in France, Italy, Egypt and Salonica. Here he won a handsome belt decorated with the badges of the regiments whose champions he had beaten to gain the lightweight champ-

Arthur Davies.

ionship of the British Forces in Asia Minor. This distinguished gentleman arrived in Ammanford to begin the training regime the week before the arranged match between Arthur Davies and Gordon Cook, the reigning Welsh lightweight champion.

The pair met on 29th September 1928 at Bridgend. F. R. Hill, Welsh correspondent of *Boxing* newspaper, went to see it:

COOK RETAINS TITLE

Gordon Cook remains lightweight champion of Wales. He cleverly out-pointed a plucky and persistent opponent in Arthur Davies at Bridgend on Saturday night, the contest being witnessed by a packed house. One cannot say that the contest was anything out of the ordinary, but if it fell below championship standards there was much to sustain interest. Davies was always trying to make an impression on the champion but was not sufficiently speedy to counteract the southpaw method of Cook.

In the fourth round however, he cut Cook's eye rather badly. But two rounds later the champion returned the compliment so that afterwards each lad paid a deal of attention to the other's damaged optic. Cook all round was the more effective, but in the twelfth round Davies caught him with a right to the jaw and the titleholder looked to be in real diffi-

Cliff and Gwyn Peregrine, 1920's.

Back right: Edwin Evans with his boxers. including Cliff and Gwyn Peregrine.

culties; however, he kept his head and recovering quickly, never gave Davies the chance to repeat the dose. He showed the more intelligent anticipation of moves and at the full distance was a nice winner though Davies deserves praise for the fine fight he put up.

The gym, now at the Cross Inn, had built a thoroughly deserved reputation for good boxing, and could be relied on to provide value-for-money contestants for top, middle and lower down the bill. But it wasn't all plain sailing. There were obviously some disagreements over training methods, purses and so on. Notably, Edwin Evans who was co-trainer with Johnny, set up his own gym at stables behind the New Inn, later moving to the Cooper's Arms, Betws. He was joined by Cliff and Gwyn Peregrine. And I know that for a short time, there was another 'rival' gym at the Castle Hotel.

Johnny Vaughan's great strength was that he was able to bring business skills to add to his expertise in training methods, and was therefore a good boxing manager and later, a promoter too.

In the restless world of boxing, changes and upheaval were never far away and 1929 certainly brought some major changes.

Chapter 7

The Birth of the Board

'Anything produced by the Welsh Board is well worthy of consideration for it possesses the highest of records and has done endless good for boxing; not only in Wales but throughout the nation. Some of the outstanding boxers and champions of the world—in fact the majority of them—were Welsh.'

The Rt. Hon. The Earl of Lonsdale, K.G., *Handbook*, Welsh Boxing Board of Control, February 23, 1931

Previous abortive attempts to set up a body in overall controlling charge of boxing, both in terms of safety for the boxers and regulation of championships in weight divisions, came to fruition at last in 1929 when the British Boxing Board of Control, originally formed in 1918, was reconstituted.

The Welsh Boxing Association and Control Board had been set up in April 1928, and initially sought to remain independent of the British Board, with whom it had some disputes. By 1929, however, it amalgamated with the BBBC and thereafter Welsh boxing was managed by the Welsh Area Council.

The Welsh Board set about establishing a championship for each weight division. By a method of adopting some champions where it was agreed they merited the title and arranging title fights for the remaining divisions, all eight weights had a fully recognised Welsh champion by 1929. In that year the champions were Dick Power, Cwmfelynfach (heavyweight, adopted); Frank Moody, Pontypridd (light-heavyweight, adopted); Billy Green, Taffs Well (middleweight); Ben Marshall, Newport (welterweight); Gordon Cook, Penycraig (lightweight); Billy Evans, Rhondda (featherweight); Dan Dando, Merthyr (bantamweight); Phineas

John, Pentre (flyweight). From now on the title could only be won in a Board of Control designated championship contest.

Sadly, today the Championship of Wales is not held in the high esteem it had been for so many years—between 1st July 2005 and 30th June 2006 there was not one champion of Wales in any division. There are eight areas administered by the British Boxing Board of Control and Wales is one of them. But in the nineteen-twenties and thirties and later, the Welsh champions were regarded as representing their country, rather than just an area.

Frank Moody, the Pontypridd light-heavyweight, was one such proud Welsh champion, who went on to take British titles at light-heavy and middleweight. He was one of six boxing brothers, three of whom were very successful. A few months before his adoption as Welsh champion, Frank took part in the first of a number of popular boxing events on Cresci's field, Ammanford, on 30th June 1928. The Moody brothers, Glen, Frank and Jackie were all on the same bill. Glen beat Arthur Rees on points and Jackie beat Cliff Peregrine, again on points. Frank boxed an exhibition bout with Police Constable Harold Williams.

Frank Moody successfully defended his Welsh title once before re-linquishing it in 1930.

In 1931 the Welsh Board published their first *Handbook*, with a foreword by Lord Lonsdale. Here it is stated that the West Wales branch was chaired by C. F. Meyrick of Ammanford. Ginger Jones was the boxers' representative; managers' representative was Johnny Vaughan and the representative for the appointed referees was Jack Leyshon, boxer and rugby player for Ammanford during the early 1920s.

They had by now overcome several teething problems and bones of contention with the British Boxing Board of Control, not least of which was the Welsh 'referee problem'.

Writing in *Boxing* in October 1928, F. R. Hill reported that:

There have been some frightfully bad rulings in Wales recently, espe-cially down in the West. In each case it was a question of inexperience and I do think it is time that the Welsh Association proceeded with the work of weeding out the incompetents. These sort of individuals who return farcical decisions are naturally doing a great deal of harm to the game and they should be called upon to explain their actions, and if that explanation is not satisfactory then they should be suspended and not allowed to officiate again until they have satisfied the Council that they are really capable.

In accordance with the new regulations, Johnny Vaughan now had to apply for licences for training and managing his boxers.

A promoter's licence in 1931 cost two guineas for Grade 'A' championship, while Grade 'B' cost one guinea. Johnny Vaughan held a Grade 'B' licence.

Referees' fees (first and second class) cost one guinea. Third class (graduate) was half a guinea. Jack Leyshon held one of these.

Boxing managers' fees were two guineas, where a boxer earned a minimum of £20 in a single engagement. Where boxers earned less than £20 in a single engagement, the fee was one guinea. Johnny Vaughan held the latter.

All boxers had to be affiliated at a cost of half-a-crown each.

All travelling promoters had to be licensed.

In November 1928 Johnny had opened a second gym at the Farmers Arms, Cross Hands, noting that he had purchased ring posts, gloves and punchball for the purpose.

By this time it became apparent that some official organisation would need to be formed as more and more youngsters came forward for the chance to train under Johnny, whose reputation was growing. By the start of the 1929-30 season Ammanford Athletic Club was duly inaugurated with Johnny Vaughan as boxing instructor at the Cross Inn. The Rt. Hon. Viscount Deerhurst of Amroth Castle became Hon. President. It was affiliated to both the Welsh Boxing Board of Control and the Welsh Amateur Boxing Association and its aims were to promote both the professional and amateur codes of boxing.

In September 1929, Johnny had his first Welsh title success, when Ginger Jones, originally from Ferndale, outpointed Billy Evans, Rhondda, at Pentre, to win the featherweight title. It was a red-letter day for the Ammanford camp, and it gave Johnny much to think about.

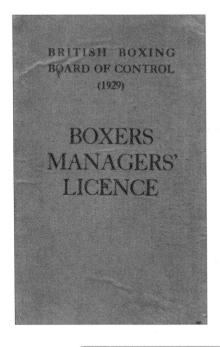

THE FOLLOWING BOXERS ARE UNDER THE MANAGEMENT
OF *Johnny Vaughan*   REG. No. *M.194*

A COPY OF THEIR AGREEMENT HAS BEEN FILED AT THE CONTROL OFFICE

Under this licence, unless the Manager has taken out a separate licence as Trainer and Second, the
Manager is only allowed to train and second Boxers as under:—

BOXER'S NAME	REGISTRATION NO.	REGISTERED WEIGHT	AGREEMENT EXPIRES
Don Chiswell	B 6342	Lightweight	Full
Tommy Davies	37042	Middle	Full
Benjy Price			
Danny Jones	B11755	9st. 7½lbs	
Sid Williams	B12459	9st. 4lbs.	Full
Tommy Davies	B7042	11st.	Full
Henry Jones	B 13661	11st 3lbs	Full
Ken Millard	B 13447	10st 4lbs	Full
Len Anthony	B. 15017	9st 9lbs	Full
Tommy Jones	B. 10731	9st 3lbs	Full

An idea that Johnny had been mulling over for some time to operate a covered venue for his contests could now be acted upon. His ring set up in the open air depended on fine weather (unreliable in Wales, so they say), and after several wet and abandoned fixtures he found a piece of land to rent at the back of the Cross Inn. There he oversaw the construction of a large timber frame and corrugated iron building capable of seating several hundred people plus of course, the ring. It was completed in 1929 and Johnny's accounts show that the cost was around £80.

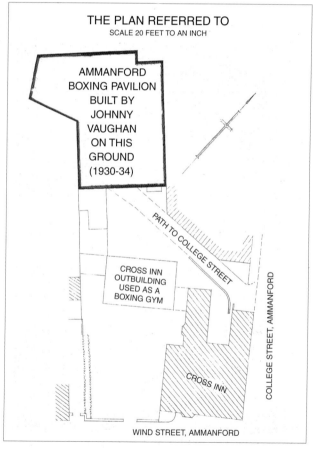

Plan for Ammanford Boxing Pavilion.

Over a span of four or five years, this pavilion played a major role in Welsh boxing contests and provided first-class entertainment for its patrons; some seventy shows were held in Ammanford during this period, about fifty of them in the pavilion. When fixtures were held benches would be hired for the spectators, and chairs for dignitaries and ringside guests, at a total cost of £2.19s.10d, including haulage. Printing and advertising costs were around £2.15s.0d. Entertainment tax was due on each fixture and was about £5-£6 each time, worked out on the cost and number of tickets sold. There was also a charge for police attendance.

Sometimes though, the pavilion was not big enough to hold the expected crowd and then Johnny Vaughan would use other venues, at Llanelli for example.

Five Welsh title fights were staged by Johnny Vaughan in Ammanford between 1930 and 1932:

> Ginger Jones, Ammanford v. Billy Evans, Ystrad Rhondda, on 27th December 1930.
> Ginger Jones v. Selwyn Davies, Caerau, on 16th May 1931.
> Danny Evans, Ammanford v. Billy Fry, Blaenllichan, on 19th September 1931.
> Glen Moody, Pontypridd v. Jerry Daley, Penycraig, on 28th March 1932.
> Billy Quinlen, Ammanford v. Alby Kestrel, Cardiff, on 7th May 1932.

We know from a first-hand account that the Danny Evans v. Billy Fry bout to decide the welterweight champion of Wales, was topping the bill in one of Johnny's shows in his pavilion on that September night in 1931.

> On this occasion the pavilion was packed to capacity while hundreds more lined the streets and filled the courtyard of the old inn. A casual passer-by may have been forgiven for thinking that this was a tremen-

dous crowd, even for a Welsh title fight. However, there was another attraction that night, and one which had been brought to Ammanford by Mr Johnny Vaughan himself.

What the fans and the merely curious had flocked to see was a real World champion, Panama Al Brown, making a much-advertised appearance in the pavilion's ring to be 'introduced' to the man he would be fighting a couple of nights later in Mountain Ash: Ginger Jones, then Welsh featherweight champion.

That night was talked about long afterwards. There were craned necks all round to see Al Brown as he stood in the ring, surrounded by his entourage and very dapper in his grey check suit with plus fours. Then the good-natured guffaws and finally roars, of laughter as Ginger, slightly built at five foot four inches, stepped up beside the six-foot World champion with his reputed seventy-six inch reach. The excitement was crowned when Ammanford's Danny Evans snatched the title from Billy Fry over fifteen great rounds of boxing. Financially, it turned out to be one of Ammanford Athletic Club's most successful evenings ever. The accounts show the takings as £124.8s.7d with a net profit of £32.1s.8d, a very healthy return in 1931.

Such comparatively large sums of money explain the main reason why there were so many young hopefuls willing to step into the ring. As part of its vigorous regime to prevent the exploitation of boxers, the British Boxing Board of Control now began to issue Articles of Agreement which were binding on the part of the promoter to pay the boxer a previously agreed sum. For example, an agreement drawn up between Billy (Gypsy) Daniels and Johnny Vaughan of the Ammanford Athletic Club shows that for his contest against Canadian Del Fontaine in 1932 his purse amounted to £15, or 25% of gross receipts, win, lose or draw. As a top-of-the-bill boxer his earnings were quite a bit more than many people could earn in a week. Set against this of course, the risks of lasting injury were quite high, and though boxers' careers tended to be longer then, it never could be a job for life.

First Annual Dinner, 1931.

Not all these hopeful youngsters were destined to be top-liners, but Johnny valued them greatly as second-liner and undercard boxers and gave them every encouragement. Among these boxers in his stable over the years were: Bertie Davies of Garnant, Handel Richards of Tycroes, Idris Davies and Dai Rickard (both of Pontardulais), Wattie Phillips, Saron, Dave Williams, Blaenau, 'Nipper' Evan Thomas, Ammanford, Dai Bowen and Don Chiswell (both of Penybanc), brothers Benny and Dai Price from Cross Hands, Billy Walker, Penybanc, Steve 'Curly' Fay, later of High Wycombe, Meidrim Thomas, Ike Lloyd, Crad Rule, Eddie Bach Thomas and Martin Fury, all from Ammanford.

The *Amman Valley Chronicle and East Carmarthen News* ran regular reports on the boxing in Johnny's Ammanford Pavilion. On 5th November 1931, an account of a fight between Cliff Peregrine and Percy Dexter of Sheffield was recorded:

The third of a series of international contests was held in Ammanford Pavilion on Saturday last, under Mr Johnny Vaughan's promotion, when Percy Dexter of Sheffield, a first-class flyweight, who has been opposed to the best men in his class in the country and recently defeated the German flyweight champion, met Cliff Peregrine; who by the way, is one of the cleverest flyweights in Wales and has qualified to box Kid Fielding of Wrexham, for the right to meet Fred Morgan for the championship of Wales. Dexter received a splendid reception when he entered the ring.

Both boxers sparred for an opening in the first round, Peregrine landing the first blow and having a shade the best of it.

After an evenly fought contest, Dexter won on points. A very similar result followed a little over a month later, when Cliff was outpointed by Kid Fielding in the eliminator for the Welsh title mentioned in the report.

Another very useful boxer was Bryn Edwards from Garnant, who did some training with Johnny Vaughan for three years at the beginning of the 1930s. He started off at bantamweight, and had some good wins, including one in June 1930 against Young Teddy Baldock of Treherbert.

He held Kid Kelly and Young Bull to a draw each in 1931 and 1932, and then moving up to lightweight by 1933, beat Paddy McGrath in the first heat of a lightweight competition before being outpointed by Len Wickwar in the second heat. Len Wickwar went on to beat Harry Mason twice, in 1935 and 1936.

Finally, Bryn Edwards met future British and European champion Ernie Roderick on 27th March 1933, but had to retire in the eleventh round. He pretty much gave up boxing after that, when his career still seemed to hold some promise.

By 1930 Johnny Vaughan had a straightforward but ambitious plan: to train as many Welsh champions as he could. Ginger Jones was his first, having got his title the previous September. If, Johnny thought, he was lucky enough to train some boxers with the potential to go on to eliminators for British titles, well, that would be a bonus. He was going to have a damn good try.

Idris Davies.

Dave Williams.

Eddie Bach Thomas.

Dai Bowen.

Chapter 8

The Jones Boys

It was a lucky day for both of them I think; that day in the summer of 1928 that Bryn Jones left his home town of Ferndale in the Rhondda and came to train at Johnny Vaughan's gym in Ammanford. Bryn had found the trainer and promoter who was to lead him to fight some of the best boxers of the thirties, and whose own reputation grew as a result.

Bryn shared a name with a legendary footballer and also a time in history. For at the same time as Bryn Jones the footballer, born in Merthyr, was making a name for himself at Wolverhampton Wanderers, later being transferred to Arsenal, our Bryn had become Welsh featherweight champion, a title he never lost in the ring.

Our Bryn, universally known as 'Ginger', was born in Ferndale in 1905. His parents, William Evan and Jane, had ten other children and his dad was a well-known mountain fighter and a collier. Dad had rigged up a gym in a stable in the garden so it was inevitable that the seven boys would start training at a young age. Ginger was about seven when he started to take a real interest; probably inspired by older brothers, Will Evan and Tommy. They both boxed in the Army in 1914 and Will Evan was a 1914 Army champion. At this time, around the outbreak of war, boxing champions, including some holding a British title, were used as part of the recruiting drive to attract young men to join up, and as P.T. instructors to shape up the raw recruits. During the war they would stage exhibition bouts for the wounded soldiers, and as morale-boosting entertainments for the troops. One amazing group of such boxers was 'The Famous Six', an elite corps of Army Physical

Training Instructors, under the command of Captain Bruce Logan: they were Johnny Basham, Jim Driscoll, Jimmy Wilde, Bombardier Billy Wells, Pat O'Keefe and Dick Smith. The first three were among the finest boxers Wales ever produced, while Bombardier Billy Wells, renowned for his magnificent physique, was later famously featured as the man who bashed the gong at the beginning of Rank Organisation films. They toured Britain on a kind of boxing booth basis, taking on all comers and winning the Army a lot of friends.

Around 1915, Ginger's brother Harold, fifteen years old, started doing a bit of boxing in scout camp and after a few local bouts, he stepped into the ring for a fifteen-round contest against Eric Jones, Tylorstown, on 15th December 1917. This punishing initiation went the distance but Harold stepped out the victor and went on to better things.

It was commonplace in those days for pubs or hotels in the Rhondda Valley to have gyms attached to them and Harold did his training at Gomer Perkins's gym at the Rhondda Hotel, Ferndale, under the guidance of Will Pearson, where he was shaping up as a useful bantamweight. They soon found him contests further afield, from Pembroke Dock to Liverpool and he showed remarkable promise, winning most of these early fights, while a couple were drawn. His first foray to the National Sporting Club at Covent Garden was in March 1918, when he outpointed Jack Wilkinson of Barnsbury over ten rounds. Harold's first win on a knockout was at Cardiff against Billy Ralph of Poplar, and this was followed by a draw with Frankie Ash at Plymouth in October 1918. The National Sporting Club invited him back for a contest against Andrew Newton, Marylebone to take place a couple of weeks before Christmas. Harold put up a great performance and had no trouble beating his opponent over ten rounds; the gentlemen of the club warmly applauded the plucky Ferndale bantamweight.

This was followed by a rotten New Year for Harold who lost his next three fights over the first three months of 1919, the last of these when he had to retire in the seventh against Billy Matthews of St James, again at the NSC. During the rest of the year though, his fortunes improved considerably and he recorded wins, among others, over Gus Legge, who had beaten him previously; Kid Harris of Canada, on a disqualification, and Jack Kid Doyle of Salford on points, at the NSC.

Harold, fired with success, now set his heart on winning the British bantamweight title and the beautiful Lonsdale Belt that went with it. Most of all as he readily admitted, he was interested in the money. After all, there were still many mouths to feed at home and his purse money had increased along with his skill and success. In an eliminator contest in December 1919, Harold scored a comfortable victory over Kid Doyle of Salford and was a step nearer his goal. The final hurdle was a contest with Scottish bantamweight champion Dave Willox at Liverpool. Although his opponent had him down twice in the early rounds, Harold knocked Willox out in the sixth round of a fifteen-round contest. He came home with the large sum of £35 and having secured his shot at the title.

The National Sporting Club seemed to have a soft spot for Welsh boxers. Just as they had taken 'Peerless' Jim Driscoll to their hearts, there was now a lot of support for the young Ferndale bantamweight Harold Jones. He had already fought within these hallowed portals five times and here, in February 1920, he expected to meet Walter Ross of Scotland to decide the Bantamweight Championship of Great Britain. However, at the eleventh hour, Walter Ross declared himself unable to make the weight and a substitute match was found: Jim Higgins, also of Scotland.

Later on Harold said: 'I had never heard of Higgins before, except as Ross's sparring partner.' Nevertheless, and in spite of the club's natural sympathy for the Welshman, Jim Higgins was 2-1 favourite to win when the contest started. Within minutes it became obvious that Harold was no pushover and by the third round it was evens.

The seventh round saw Higgins hit the canvas but he was saved by the bell with the count on nine. By the tenth, Harold was 15-1 on and 'a dead cert' as the *South Wales Echo* put it; Harold was almost unable to believe his luck in having one of the 'easiest fights of his career'.

When the bell sounded for round thirteen there were seven rounds left and it was clear that Higgins was losing badly ('Higgins did not land a punch on me the whole fight,' said Harold afterwards), but he caught the Welshman off-balance with a blow to the chest and Harold went down on one knee. He took the count in that position and was up at 'eight', covering up immediately. What happened next was described by Howard Rose, a Rhondda journalist: 'Higgins threw a wild right, hurting his hand on the top of the Ferndale boy's head.' But although Harold had started his left going again, referee Douglas stepped in to stop the fight in favour of the Scotsman. The crowd was in uproar; and according to Rose the odds at that point on Harold Jones winning the contest were 20-1!

It was reported that two hundred members wrote letters of resignation to the National Sporting Club expressing their outrage at this extraordinary decision.

He had been robbed of the Lonsdale Belt and the title but Harold returned to Ferndale with £100 and because of the controversial decision, a place in boxing history.

In the interests of impartiality it should be stated that there were some who thought the Scotsman won fairly. In a 1982 article for *Boxing News* about 'Little' Jim Higgins, Gilbert Odd described the end of the fight in rather different terms:

> By the thirteenth, Jones had only his great courage to keep him going. He showed the first signs of real weariness and immediately Little Jim leapt at him, hooked left and right to the chin and Harold hit the deck.
>
> He struggled up at eight but a right swished over to drop him again. Once more Jones stayed down for eight seconds, then retreated and stood with his back to the ropes, his arms criss-crossed in front of his face in an effort to stall off the impending doom. Higgins could scent the finish and punched away with both hands for a full minute at his helpless rival. Had Jimmy gone for the ribs he might have got Jones to lower his guard and leave his chin exposed for a finishing right, but the Scot punched so fiercely that eventually the referee called: 'That's enough', and Higgins had scored his first notch on the Lonsdale Belt.

Then again, could 200 punters at the NSC have been so wrong?

Harold carried on boxing intermittently, until the beginning of 1934, but with absolutely none of the enthusiasm or success he had enjoyed before the title fight. His penultimate fight was for Joe Gess in Ammanford just before Christmas 1933, when he outpointed Ammanford's Idwal Jones, brother of Idris.

Although he had shrugged dismissively and said he 'did it just for money', I know it went much deeper than that. He confided in his family that much as he appreciated the widespread support he received from the National Sporting Club members, he would rather have had the title he had longed for.

Undeterred, young Ginger decided to turn pro at the age of nineteen in 1924. 'Money was short,' he explained. He had no official amateur experience but his father's early training stood him in good stead when he started his professional training with Will Pearson in Ferndale and later, Dai Lodwick. His first manager was Teddy Lewis who arranged his mostly local early contests. Soon Ginger had a series of good wins under his belt: Emrys Jones, Johnny Haydn, Billy Meade and Evan 'Scwt' Williams among them, in contests usually over 10 or 15 rounds.

Ginger had gained a good name for himself by 1927, and more contests were coming his way. In October that year he went to Carmarthen to meet a former British champion, Billy Beynon, from Taibach:

> He was a pocket Hercules of a man with very short legs but the powerful shoulders of a giant. When I entered the hall he was sitting on a tip-up chair eating sweets, and swinging his little legs like a child.
>
> But in the ring, he was a monster. He constantly came after me; slow but irresistible, like a moving morass. Although I checked his progress each time with a left lead, he persisted in coming forwards and swinging punches—very hard ones too—to both sides of my body which I protected with my upper forearms, otherwise I should have had some broken ribs.
>
> Again I won this contest, but the following morning both my forearms were swollen to twice their normal size.

It just so happened that one of Johnny Vaughan's friends was the genial former British welterweight champion Johnny Basham of Newport. This giant among champions counted many boxers among his friends including Peerless Jim Driscoll, with whom he had shared many exploits in France during the First World War. Johnny Basham knew the Jones family from Ferndale and was an admirer of young Harold. So during a meeting with Johnny Vaughan in Swansea on 9th January 1928, Basham mentioned that Vaughan might like to take a look at Harold's younger brother, Bryn 'Ginger' Jones, who was due to box at Brynamman against Reggie Jones of Pontypridd on 18th January.

Johnny duly attended the evening's entertainment and saw Ginger win on a disqualification in the eighth. He must have been impressed because in due course he signed him up.

Ginger Jones's magnificent record under Johnny's guidance, during a period of the fiercest competition among British boxers shows one bout lost out of forty-one between December 1928 and March 1931; altogether he had about 130 recorded fights, winning over eighty with sixteen ending in a draw.

Ginger travelled to many famous venues from 1929 onwards. He fought at the National Sporting Club where he outpointed Jim Briley of Peckham over eight rounds in February 1929. No doubt he had his brother Harold in mind when he stepped into that famous ring, and how sweet the victory must have been!

He was a very popular figure at London's Premierland, Jack Kid Berg's favourite venue (Berg had fifty fights there). Premierland, founded in 1911 by Harry Jacobs, came to represent the pinnacle of boxing prowess. Boxers who fought in this converted warehouse were reckoned to be at the top of their profession and Ginger had six contests there during 1929. He beat ex-British champion, Johnny Curley of London, Jack Kirby of Birmingham and Jim Ashley of London on points over 15 rounds apiece. Contests against Jack Garland of Belfast and Tiger Smith of Birmingham, both at Premierland in September, ended in a draw.

Between March 1928 and September 1929, Ginger clocked up an impressive thirty-two fights, most of them punishing 15-rounders and two of them Welsh title eliminators.

One of the fights he had at Premierland in May 1929, was against Johnny Curley of Lambeth. Tears of laughter would come to Ginger's eyes when he used to recount this contest, many years afterwards:

When Johnny Curley came out—he was more or less a local boy—I discovered that he had ginger hair and at that time, of course, mine was really ginger too. I thought this was rather unusual; then, lo and behold, the referee, Mr Jack Hart (who also became a commentator) climbed into the ring and he was as ginger as a tomcat!

The mainly Jewish audience, always quick on the uptake, started laughing and yelling: "Go on, Ginger!" but we had no idea which one of us they meant!

Anyway, the little Welsh Ginger was top dog on this occasion!

Then on 21st September 1929, Ginger Jones found himself facing Billy Evans of Ystrad for the Welsh featherweight title. He had met Billy Evans on two previous occasions, losing to him in November 1928, but beating him on points two months later over fifteen rounds at Bridgend.

Stablemate Billy Quinlen travelled with Ginger to Ton Pentre for the big occasion as he was appearing on the same bill. It was a Saturday night.

Boxing newspaper's F. R. Hill reported the evening's events:

ANOTHER TITLE CHANGES HANDS

Four Welsh titleholders have been deposed during the last three months, the latest victim being Billy Evans, the featherweight champion, who was outpointed by Ginger Jones at Pentre on Saturday night. There was no fluke about the victory either for Jones proved himself a bundle of energy, lasting out better than the champion. Evans did well up to the seventh round, boxing stylishly, but from that point on Jones took a greater hand in the game. He scored with short hooks to the jaw as Evans came in and varied this with uppercuts. Continuing to take advantage of every scoring opportunity, Jones forged ahead and though Evans made a big rally in the eleventh, he had a very rough time in the twelfth when Jones cut him with a right to the jaw and then forcing him onto the ropes, scored heavily with both hands. This weakened the champion but he made another gallant effort in the fourteenth. However, Jones was also busy and getting the better of the last round, gained the decision.

Although he too came away a winner, Billy Quinlen, who was often billed as 'Quinlan', didn't get quite such a good press on this occasion:

> Many present thought that Oliver Cullen was unlucky to have the verdict given against him in his supporting bout with Billy Quinlan. Cullen who is undoubtedly an up and coming lad, boxed really well and appeared to at least hold his own against the West Walian. It therefore came as a surprise when Quinlan was named the winner.

Now quite used to boxing in London, Ginger was introduced to a Belgian boxer and a couple of Frenchman towards the end of 1929. In October he lost to Nick Bensa at The Ring, Blackfriars, when he was disqualified for fouling in the thirteenth. But he beat Jean Boireau at Premierland on a technical knockout in the second round on 1st December, and a week later, outpointed Georges Gourdy at Holborn Stadium.

In the winter of 1929-30 Ginger, accompanied by Johnny Vaughan, braved the Irish sea crossing to meet Belfast's Jack Garland at the Ulster Hall, Belfast. They sailed from Liverpool at 10 p.m. on Monday, 27th January, as Johnny wrote in his diary, having caught the train up from Ammanford and waited an hour and a half for their connection from Shrewsbury. They arrived in Belfast at 7.30 the following morning. There is no mention of what the crossing was like on that cold winter night but Ginger was fired with enthusiasm, and perhaps a little trepidation, at the prospect of the important contest ahead of him.

It was an eliminator for the British featherweight crown, currently held by Johnny Cuthbert of Sheffield. The fight took place on 29th January, and at the end of the fifteen rounds, referee T. Murphy declared Ginger Jones the winner. An earlier contest between Ginger and Jack Garland in September 1929 had ended in a draw, so Johnny Vaughan and Ginger were delighted with the Belfast victory.

Jack Garland's supporters and fans on the other hand were far from happy with the verdict, and demanded a return match.

There followed a little cat and mouse game between Johnny Vaughan and the Garland camp via the *Sporting Life* and the *Belfast Telegraph*. On 5th February, the *Sporting Life* ran the following paragraph:

> The offer of Jack Garland's supporters to back their man against Ginger Jones in a return match at the featherweight limit and lay £300 to £200, has brought an acceptance from Mr Johnny Vaughan who states that he will cover any deposit at once on the conditions named for Garland.

A few days later Garland's backers were pushing hard:

> As the featherweight eliminating bouts may last indefinitely, or at least into next season, Jack Garland's backers are of opinion that articles could with advantage be signed right away for the return match with Ginger Jones, deposits posted and purse offers invited.
>
> There is another eliminator to be boxed off, but nobody knows when or where, and until that information is forthcoming Jones is left high and dry. Here is a definite and an immediate match offered him —so why hang back? asks Garland's backer.

But on 12th February 1930, Johnny Vaughan makes it quite clear through the pages of the *Sporting Life* that he is not going to be bullied by the Belfast camp:

> Mr Johnny Vaughan writes to assure me and Jack Garland's supporters that Ginger Jones has several engagements on hand besides the feather-weight eliminator, but he is prepared to box Garland any time after May. In the meantime there is young Quinlen, and if Garland wants a match with him he has only to say so and put up a deposit with the *Sporting Life*.

In its edition of 15th February, the *Belfast Telegraph* reported the fol-lowing:

GARLAND–JONES FIGHT. PAIR TO MEET AGAIN.
BOXING BOARD BOMBSHELL OVER
LONSDALE BELT CONTEST

There has been a dramatic sequel to the recent Garland v. Jones contest at the Ulster Hall, Belfast, which was an eliminating contest for the Lonsdale Belt.

The British Boxing Board of Control has decided that the pair shall meet in a return contest. The contest is to take pace on neutral ground. Promoters are asked to make purse offers for this bout, and tenders must be received by the Control Board by the 28th February.

This contest, which was one of the best seen in Belfast for a long time, has ever since provided a great deal of controversy. Jones was given the verdict on points, and this decision met with a hostile reception. Nearly 90 per cent of the crowd considered that Garland had won, and a demonstration followed the announcement made by Mr T. Murphy, Newcastle-upon-Tyne, the referee.

'I think it is unfair that Belfast has not had an opportunity of staging the return contest,' said Mr Jim Rice, the promoter, to a *Telegraph* representative today. 'Arrangements for the last contest were all that could be desired, and I was assured by the managers of the rival boxers, especially Mr Jack Goodwin, Garland's manager, that they had no complaint to make.'

This decision came as a surprise in boxing circles, but there was satisfaction that Garland, who is a Belfast-born boxer, is to have another chance of making a bid for the belt.

It appears that this was a clever piece of reporting—or a bit of Irish blarney—rather than the fact that its headline would suggest: actually the return fight did not take place until 1932.

In spite of the Belfast win against Garland, though Ginger would have been fully justified in expecting a crack at the British title, it seems that British Boxing Board of Control passed him over as a contender to meet Cuthbert. The saga of the eliminators for the British featherweight crown dragged on. Piecing together the things Ginger told me years later and the terse notes in Johnny's diary, it appears that the two of them were in no hurry to be hustled into a return contest with Garland, particularly in Belfast, as they considered Ginger had already won this stage of his bid for the British title. Instead, Johnny considered it wiser for Ginger to prove his worth by taking on other formidable boxers in his division, including others who were themselves considered contenders. It may have been a decision that cost Ginger his chance—who knows though, what the outcome would have been had he met Garland again at this time?

Ginger was certainly feeling a bit rattled by all the hoo-ha. His next contest a few weeks later, against Jim Travis of Oldham, unfortunately resulted in his disqualification in the first round.

Johnny Cuthbert's defence of the British featherweight title, which he first won in 1927 by beating Johnny Curley, is a fairly complicated story in itself.

In March 1928, Harry Corbett of Bethnal Green took the title, beating Cuthbert on points. But a year later the title was once more in contention when the two met again. Although Corbett was knocked down twice, the fight was so close that the referee declared a draw, the first time this had happened in a British championship bout for the Lonsdale Belt. It was also the first championship contest to be decided over fifteen rounds, rather than the old NSC rule of twenty rounds. A ruling was made by the new British Boxing Board of Control that an immediate rematch be arranged, although Corbett was allowed to keep his Lonsdale Belt.

Less than two months later, Corbett and Cuthbert met yet again to decide the championship.

On this historic occasion—Olympia was booked by the NSC in order to recoup purse money by attracting a huge audience—Harry Corbett put in a disappointing performance and Johnny Cuthbert was restored to the Championship. Thus he became the very first boxer to win a Lonsdale Belt outright in a venue outside the National Sporting Club and to add to the sense of history, Lord Lonsdale himself presented the belt.

So the stalemate between Cuthbert and Corbett having been resolved, the way was open for others to challenge Cuthbert for his title.

NATIONAL SPORTING CLUB
AT OLYMPIA
On Thursday, 16th May, 1929, at 8 p.m.
3 CHAMPIONSHIP BELT CONTESTS
15-ROUND CONTEST at 11st. 6lbs.
**For the Middleweight Championship of Great Britain
And Europe and the Lonsdale Championship Challenge Belt.**

ALEX IRELAND   v.   LEN HARVEY
(EDINBURGH)   (LONDON, late of
Middleweight Champion   PLYMOUTH)
of Great Britain And Europe

15-ROUND CONTEST at 9st.	15-ROUND CONTEST AT 8st. 6lbs
For the Featherweight Championship of Great Britain And the Lonsdale Championship Challenge Belt	For the Bantamweight Championship of Great Britain And the Lonsdale Championship Challenge Belt
HARRY CORBETT	**KIT PATTENDEN**
(BETHNAL GREEN)	(BETHNAL GREEN)
Featherweight Champion and Holder of Belt	*Bantamweight Champion and Holder of Belt*
v.	v.
JOHNNIE CUTHBERT	**TEDDY BALDOCK**
(SHEFFIELD)	(POPLAR)
Ex-Featherweight Champion and ex-Holder of Belt	

AND OTHER BOXING (time permitting)

There was an abundance of good featherweights at this time in Britain. No doubt as part of a plan to sort out the ducks from the geese, a Grand Featherweight Competition was held at the Holborn Stadium Club in April 1930. Johnny had lost no time during his recent game of bluff with the Belfast folks, in putting forward both Ginger's and Billy Quinlen's names for the first series. The prize for the overall winner was £250 and competition was ferocious! The bouts consisted of three three-minute rounds and Ginger got through to the semi-finals, beating Young Clancy of St Georges to win his series. In a disputed verdict (Johnny Vaughan always maintained it was a bad decision) he lost to Jimmy Rowbotham of Birmingham in the semi-finals.

However, Ginger had settled into a training routine which enabled him to prove his worth in a second meeting with Jim Travis of Oldham, when he beat him over the distance at Belle Vue, Manchester. There followed a series of wins through 1930, including a knockout against Jim Crawford of Wrexham and a points victory over the French featherweight Dominique Di Cea. Throughout the year Johnny worked towards the goal of a chance at the British crown for Ginger, but though Cuthbert defended the title twice in 1930, Ginger was disregarded in spite of his win in Belfast. It was a rebuff he never forgot.

Cuthbert's defence against Dom Volante in May 1930 resulted in a good points win for Cuthbert, whose 'counters worked effectively. Volante was good in the twelfth, but was being chased all round the ring at the finish.' But when the champion met Nel Tarleton in November the result was a draw: 'Cuthbert advanced continuously, but was generally smothered. A hard right in the sixth knocked Tarleton's gumshield out. Cuthbert's consistent attack deserved better.'—*British Boxing Yearbook.*

Ginger Jones, undefeated Welsh featherweight champion.

It was December 1930. Events had moved on. The infant Boxing Board of Control was firmly in charge, but no doubt still encountering teething troubles. Johnny Cuthbert had put on weight and fought Al Foreman for the British lightweight title, an excellent contest that ended as a draw.

Ginger had beaten Jim Crawford of Wrexham in August, after their first contest in June ended quite controversially, with some of Crawford's followers suggesting that Ginger had cheated. He took it in his stride, however, and remembered Jim Crawford as being 'one of nature's gentlemen—really nice.'

There was no doubt about the verdict in the second contest, where Ginger was defending his Welsh title. The *Western Mail* and *South Wales News* reported it:

> A crowd of about 3,000 were present on the Wrexham Football Ground on Monday to witness a fifteen three-minute round championship fight between Ginger Jones, Ammanford, featherweight champion of Wales and Jim Crawford of Wrexham. The fight went the full distance, the South Walian being awarded the verdict on points. Jones was a worthy winner exhibiting much superior ringcraft all through. Using both hands to great advantage he had Crawford down twice in the third round for counts of six and eight, while in the fourth round, the Wrexham man took a further count of eight.

Ginger met Italy's Luigi Quadrini a week before Christmas at the Albert Hall and beat him when the Italian was disqualified on a foul in the fifth. Quadrini had been European featherweight champion.

On Boxing Day he gave Billy Evans of Ystrad another go at the Welsh title, but Ginger won easily over the distance.

It had been a year of mixed fortunes and dashed hopes; starting with the successful trip across the Irish Sea, the controversy, then the hard work which hadn't paid off. But still, Ginger reflected, it had been a pretty good Christmas. What would the New Year bring?

What it brought was a very heartening draw with Dom Volante in Liverpool on 8th January. So far, so good. There followed five points wins—three against old rival Billy Evans, with Sheffield's Tommy Dexter and Billy Buchanan of Hoxton getting the same treatment.

With his customary shrewdness, Johnny had secured Ginger's next fight with his eye still on the elusive British title. But, as it happened, there was very little chance for his man to recoup his strength. Just five days after beating Billy Buchanan, Ginger met Nel Tarleton at New Brighton on 26th March 1931.

Boxing ran two reports on this encounter:

NEL TARLETON DEFEATS GINGER JONES

Too Clever for Welsh Champion

There was another big crowd at the Tower on Thursday night, when Mr Best staged the fifteen rounds between Nel Tarleton, Liverpool and Welsh featherweight champion Ginger Jones. The Liverpool boxer was seen at his best and was always boxing like a winner. The Welshman proved tough; Tarleton's blows had not too much effect upon him, for Jones finished fresh, notwithstanding the peppering he had received from Nel's straight punches. It was a splendid contest, and delighted the crowd.

*

Tarleton surprised the Celt in the first ten seconds by landing a right to the jaw. Jones dashed in for the ribs, only to be met by stinging lefts and to be cautioned for the use of his wrist. It was Tarleton's round.

The local held on to his advantage in the second. Jones attacked in good style and tried rights and lefts to the head. Tarleton skipped away on elusive lines and scored several without return, swaying back across the ropes from the Welshman's rights.

There were several fast rallies in the third and both were seen to advantage. Jones grazed the local's jaw in the fourth but Tarleton had a superb defence against the vigorous attempts to land a KO. Tarleton was brilliant in the fifth, and a couple to the mark made the Welshman wince; the latter jumped back and had a 'bundle' but Tarleton again drove to the stomach. Jones fell to the boards and took a seven count. The local tore in, in the next round, but Jones proved capable of accepting all that the Merseysider handed out.

The Liverpool boxer was almost over the ropes in the seventh, in avoiding a fierce swing to the jaw. Tarleton took most of the honours to half-distance. He was spoken to by Mr Gamble, the referee, for heading, but it proved a very clean contest.

In the tenth, a couple to the mouth jarred Ginger's head right back. The Welshman, notwithstanding his heroic efforts, was falling further in arrears. It was plain that, barring a KO, Tarleton had the issue in safe-keeping.

In the twelfth, most of the Welshman's blows fell on Tarleton's arms and the latter tried a terrific swing to the jaw, but missed and came down.

Tarleton volleyed vigorously in the thirteenth and there was much excitement as Jones came back and mixed it furiously to the end. It was Tarleton's fight and the referee had no hesitation in awarding the local the decision.

Ginger was bitterly disappointed but he had put up a magnificent performance for his many admirers. However, this very significant loss probably spelled the end of his chance to be considered a serious contender for the British crown. In October of that year, plucky Nel Tarleton won the title from Johnny Cuthbert in front of a huge crowd in Anfield football stadium. I guess Cuthbert must have had to work hard to make the weight, but it was a contest that did not begin well for Tarleton. In the first round the referee unfortunately stepped on his foot. Cuthbert set up several busting attacks and Tarleton had to box his way out of trouble. But Cuthbert went down for a couple of counts. At the end, Tarleton, the local lad, had his hand raised to an almighty cheer.

It has to be said that Nel Tarleton was a notably worthy champion. He was one of Britain's most skilful defensive boxers, twice regaining the British featherweight championship, in 1936 and 1940. He also made two very creditable attempts at the NBA World title against Freddie Miller in 1934 and 1935. He retired as undefeated British and British Empire Featherweight champion in 1945. During the later part of his fourteen-year career, he fought with only one sound lung following an attack of pleurisy and pneumonia.

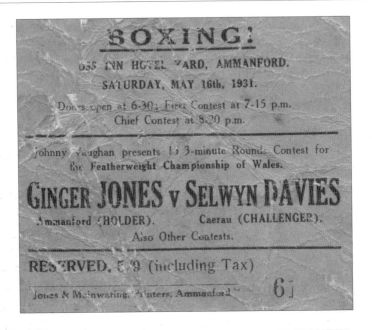

BOXING!

CROSS INN HOTEL YARD, AMMANFORD.

SATURDAY, MAY 16th, 1931.

Doors open at 6-30; First Contest at 7-15 p.m.
Chief Contest at 8-20 p.m.

Johnny Vaughan presents 15 3-minute Rounds Contest for
the Featherweight Championship of Wales.

GINGER JONES v SELWYN DAVIES

Ammanford (HOLDER).   Caerau (CHALLENGER).

Also Other Contests.

RESERVED, £9 (including Tax)

Jones & Mainwaring, Printers, Ammanford   6⌐

For Ginger there wasn't much time to reflect on this blow—he was straight back into training for another defence of his Welsh title against Selwyn Davies of Caerau on 16th May, in Ammanford.

Referee for the occasion was C. B. Thomas of Maesteg. Selwyn Davies started well, on aggressive lines, and for the first four rounds, took the fight to the champion. The pace was a lively one and though Ginger's left was not much in evidence at this point, he showed a good defence. From the fifth round, the champion began to dominate the fight, introducing greater play with his left. During the middle rounds, Ginger demonstrated his superior ring skills without actually doing much damage, and towards the close, the challenger realised that his only chance of victory would be to knock out his opponent. But Ginger frustrated his attempts by clever defensive boxing and by use of his quick prodding left, running out the winner at the end of an interesting contest.

On the same night, Cliff Peregrine and Dai Davies gave a no-decision display of boxing over six rounds, and Watty Phillips, Ammanford, was beaten over ten rounds by the famous ex-amateur champion, Ike Lloyd from Glanamman.

During the summer of 1931, Ginger had a good win over Paddy McGrath at Liverpool, when his opponent retired after the seventh round, but he lost on points to Moe Moss of Mile End. Most of his time and concentration was taken up at this time with training for a forthcoming event in September: Ginger was to meet the current World bantamweight champion, Panama Al Brown, who was touring Britain and taking on the best bantamweights the country had to offer.

Alfonso Teofilo Brown, Latin America's first ever World champion, was born in Colon near the Panama Canal, on 5th July 1902. He had his first professional fight in 1922 and his career spanned twenty-two years. After the first phenomenally successful seven years, which included many knockouts, Al entered a tournament in June 1929, which had been ordered by the New York Boxing Commission to find a successor to Charlie Rosenberg. No longer able to make the weight, Rosenberg had been deprived of his World title by the commission. Panama Al Brown became World bantamweight champion when he beat Vidal Gregario in the final bout of the tournament.

They said Al was too tall to be a bantamweight. But during the 1930s, the *London Times* described him as: 'A bantamweight, 71 inches tall, yet by some miracle of physique, perfectly proportioned.' He kept his World title for six glorious years, defending it nine times until he finally lost it to Spaniard Baltazar Sangchilli in June 1935. Panama liked coming over to Europe and particularly Britain, and did it as often as he could.

Ginger and Panama were scheduled to meet in Mountain Ash, but at a meeting of the Ammanford Athletic Club shortly before the encounter, the gentlemen were all agreed that the fight was also a golden opportunity for Ammanford to have some of the glory. They therefore invited Mr 'Panama' Al Brown and his manager Mr Dave Lumiansky, to meet Mr Bryn 'Ginger' Jones a few nights before the fight, at the boxing pavilion in Ammanford. It just happened to be the night of the Welsh title fight between Danny Evans and Billy Fry, at which big crowds were expected anyway!

ALL IN MY CORNER

It was a publicity stunt to be proud of. The local press reported it:

> For hours before the contest thousands of West Wales fans assembled at the centre of the town to welcome Al Brown (Panama), who is due to meet their fellow townsman, Ginger Jones, at Mountain Ash Pavilion tonight. Brown came in for a vociferous welcome and, with Jones and Mr Dave Lumiansky, was subsequently introduced from the ring.
>
> All three gave short speeches and Jones said: 'I promise to give Al something to go home with.' By way of response, Brown just gripped him firmly by the hand, and smiled!

I remember Ginger told me that the Mountain Ash Pavilion had been built to house the National Eisteddfod when it was held there in 1905, and was consequently large enough to house such a popular event. Even so, it was 'packed to suffocation' on the evening of 21st September 1931 for the big fight. Ginger peered across the ring towards Al's corner, and found it difficult to see him through the smoke haze that hung over everything. The crowd were in fine voice and belting out Welsh hymns to encourage Ginger at the start of the fight.

Round one saw Ginger in close and pummelling Al about the stomach, as he had agreed with Johnny Vaughan was the best way to start—'but his long arms came across my shoulders and he beat a tattoo on my buttocks.' Ginger found him a very awkward opponent because he was certainly almost six feet tall and had a 76-inch reach, while his legs were like long beanpoles. Ginger, who was about five feet four inches, had had to undergo a complete change of style during training. Nevertheless, he put up a great fight and reckoned he was ahead at the start of the ninth.

To be fair it was probably almost as awkward for this abnormally tall bantamweight to deal with so short an opponent and he was tending to bring punches up from low down to catch Ginger in the stomach. In the ninth, Ginger moved forward right on to one of these low punches, which caught him in the groin. Ginger collapsed on the canvas and referee W. E. Allen counted him out, in spite of the cries of 'foul' from the audience.

*Panama Al Brown, W. H. Allen, Teddy Lewis
and Ginger Jones, in Mountain Ash.*

Panama Al Brown floors Ginger Jones in the 9th round.

It was all over.

Panama Al Brown went to live in Paris in the late thirties. He owned several properties and a stable of racehorses and, it is said, used to send his shirts over to London to be ironed because in France 'they didn't know how to do a good job'. Paris took to Al, who was said to be fluent in seven languages.

Battling on, Ginger enjoyed the rest of 1931 as he chalked up wins against Albert Barker, Sheffield; Tom Bailey, Liverpool; Tommy Hyams of Kings Cross and George Williams, Treherbert.

The New Year of 1932 was also a joyous time for Ginger because he got married on the last day of January, to Olive Jones. In due course they had two children, Brian and Jayne.

In April 1932, *Boxing* reported that: 'The Welsh champion has been kept out of the ring owing to facial trouble, but returned, more brilliant than ever, and easily outpointed Boyo Rees.' That was on 2nd April at Merthyr, and the win was quickly followed up with a points win against Billy Barnham of Fulham:

> Jones boxed aggressively throughout, and would appear to have gained in hitting power since his return to the ring. The Welsh champion always had the fight well in hand after the third round, and as the contest proceeded his great skill and versatility became increasingly evident.—*Boxing.*

Tommy Lye of Acton was his third April victim, outpointed at the Mannesmann Hall in Swansea, and back in Merthyr on 25th April, Ginger triumphed again when Billy Peters from Bermondsey retired in the tenth round. Ginger had boxed 56 rounds in 24 days!

Sadly, there are often disasters waiting to follow on the heels of triumph, and a contest at Newcastle with Seaman Watson on 2nd May ended when Ginger's corner had to throw the towel in the tenth round because of a cut eye.

Worse was to follow though, when six months later Watson beat Nel Tarleton to win the British title; a blow that added to Ginger's intense disappointment about not getting a chance at the title himself. His claim to fight Nel Tarleton for the title had been turned down by the Board of Control in spite of a contention that Ginger should have been allowed to meet Seaman Watson in an eliminator.

The *Amman Valley Chronicle* had this to say:

GINGER JONES' CLAIM REJECTED

The claim of Ginger Jones, the Welsh featherweight champion, for a contest with Nel Tarleton of Liverpool, for the British featherweight championship has been turned down by the Board of Control. Seaman Watson of Liverpool, has been selected as a contender.

Jones and Watson met a fortnight ago and the former agreed to fight although the latter could not make the poundage. This being so, it was sheer bad luck for Jones that he was compelled to retire through a badly damaged eye. It is contended that Jones should have been permitted to meet Watson in an eliminating contest, and considerable disappointment has been caused in Amman Valley boxing circles as a result.

Another points win against George Morgan of Tirphil brought Ginger up to June 1932, when, at long last, a return match with Belfast's Jack Garland had been scheduled. A summer crossing this time, and more company too, for Ginger and Johnny were accompanied on this Irish sea voyage by Danny Evans and Glen Moody. After all the fuss and bother that followed their previous meeting, Ginger easily outpointed Garland over eight three-minute rounds at Belfast Windsor Park.

A month later he met Cuthbert Taylor at Merthyr. The fifteen-round contest was for £50-a-side and according to some reports, 3,000 fans packed the Merthyr Labour Stadium while a similar number were unable to gain admittance! Under the heading: TAYLOR GETS DOUBT-FUL VERDICT OVER JONES, *Boxing* reported the fight, finishing up with: 'The featherweight champion appeared to have won the fight and I think the most surprised person in the whole stadium must have been Taylor himself.'

Ginger resumed his training with a wry shrug; he'd been paid, life goes on and less than two weeks later he was back in the ring for a

*From left to right: Danny Evans, Ginger Jones
and Glen Moody, enjoying a stroll in Belfast.*

fifteen-rounder against Boyo Rees again, at Llanelli. This proved to be 'one of the most exciting contests ever witnessed in West Wales' according to *Boxing*, who described Ginger's win as 'brilliant'.

Tommy Lye travelled down to Swansea from Acton, to meet Ginger for the second time in four months and was stopped in the eighth round on 13th August.

Ginger was obliged to defend his Welsh featherweight title now, and the contest was with George Fielding of Wrexham at Llanelli Workingmen's Club, on 3rd September. In the fourth round Ginger was floored by Fielding and took a count of seven. The shock, however, seemed to have a very positive effect on him because he came back very strongly and reversed the situation by knocking out his opponent in the sixth.

As usual, takings and expenditure for the contest were meticulously recorded in Ammanford Athletic Club's account book, and showed that Ginger received £24.5s.7d, while George Fielding had £15.2s.0d. The hall cost £3.3s.0d to hire and advertising and printing came to £3.15s.0d. The takings amounted to £88.16s.11d, and after the expenses of the officials and timekeeper, and various sundry payments had been made, the club profited to the tune of £37.0s.1d—a very good night's work. And Ginger was still featherweight champion of Wales.

A couple of weeks later, at Pontardawe, he beat Billy Pritchard of Treherbert, who was disqualified in the seventh round, but Ginger had an enforced three-month lay-off following the fight, because of injury.

He was definitely under par when he took on the talented Len Wickwar of Leicester in December in Swansea and did well to hold his opponent to a draw. Six days later another draw was recorded against Evan Morris at Blaengarw. After Christmas and into the New Year, Ginger had three good points wins against Phineas John of Pentre, Norman Snow of Northampton and Tommy Hyams from Kings Cross.

Next he met George Williams of Treherbert in a contest at Trealaw on 3rd March 1933. The main purpose was to give Williams experience at boxing at championship level because he was the main contender for the Welsh bantamweight title. Ginger beat him on points but the experience must have done some good because in November of 1933, Williams outpointed Swansea's Len Beynon to get the Welsh title. He held it until the following May when Beynon took it back, at Swansea.

Two draws followed for Ginger before March was halfway through, against Douglas Parker of Sunderland and Frank McAloran of Belfast, and a week later he stopped Norman Snow of Northampton in the tenth round at Merthyr. Just to prove he was a much better boxer than the Belfast man he outpointed Jack Garland for the third time at Crystal Palace on 3rd April.

Four days after this satisfying encounter, Ginger set sail for South Africa, where he was to box South African champion, Laurie 'Non-stop' Stevens. Altogether he would be away for about three months, and it was quite an experience for the young man from Ferndale. On the ship training continued without let-up, under the guidance of Harry Little-john, who was also sparring partner to Ginger. Two days off Johannes-burg, disaster struck: Ginger's eye was badly cut during training. A few days remained before the fight, but despite the best efforts of his seconds, Ginger's eye was in a vulnerable condition when he stepped into the ring with Laurie Stevens on 6th May in Johannesburg.

Sure enough the cut was re-opened in the second round and Ginger had to concentrate very hard to keep his opponent's punches from inflicting further damage. It was very much to his credit that he staved off the inevitable until the seventh round (some reports state it was the eighth) when the referee stepped in to save Ginger's eye from more serious injury.

Three years later, Laurie Stevens beat Jack Kid Berg, to add the Empire lightweight title to his South African one.

Before sailing home, Ginger took on another South African boxer, Gerry Stone and got a points win.

I suppose every boxer knows when he has had his day—the end of 1933 was Ginger's time for realising that he was looking back on his boxing career rather than looking forward to the next fight. He lost three of the five fights he had during the rest of that year and relinquished his featherweight title in a somewhat half-hearted attempt to move up to the lightweight division. But a period of indifferent health meant he was unfit when he met Tommy Dowlais at Bargoed in March 1934. *Boxing* reported that: 'It was apparent that he has not yet recovered his old form.' He was outpointed by Dowlais over twelve rounds. Only one other fight is recorded after that; a draw with Swansea's Danny Thomas at Milford Haven Market Hall on 31st October 1934. Ginger had been undefeated as Welsh featherweight champion, having successfully defended it four times. He had fought every decent British featherweight boxer in his bid for the British title and missed it by a whisker. He had taken on his share of European boxers and beaten most of them, as well as giving a creditable account of himself against a World champion and a South African one. He had much to look back on, with pride.

Ginger kept a paternal eye on younger boxers in the valleys 'by helping in any way I could in the local gyms.' He also took part in other sports, notably fishing, golf and tennis. He worked for the London and Manchester Insurance Company and was in the Pioneer Corps during the war. He used to say that he wouldn't have changed a thing if he had to do it all again: 'I enjoyed every minute of it and made hundreds of friends for life.'

Of course, Ginger was an elderly man when I used to spend some time with him at the Swansea Ex-Boxers Club and at his home in Pontardawe. Like so many of the old boxers he was a gentle man, with a tremendous sense of humour and a store of interesting anecdotes.

He died at the age of eighty-one, in December 1986. The late Ron Olver paid a tribute to him on the occasion of Ginger's eighty-first birthday, when he spoke of 'the gratitude of all who remember your fine career with affection and who would like to pay tribute to your major contribution to British, and especially Welsh, boxing.'

Ginger's brother, Harold, died in the late 1970s, aged 76, after a career with Great Western Railways, and later British Rail(ways) until the closure of local lines in 1969. He was known as a 'quiet champion who made the name of Ferndale famous in the rings of Liverpool Stadium, the Ring, Blackfriars, the National Sporting Club and other famous boxing centres.'

Panama Al Brown left for the United States when Hitler invaded France, leaving everything behind. Though his reason for doing so is far from clear, he was reputedly gay, and lived with writer Jean Cocteau while in Paris.

By now he wasn't far off forty years old but, having very little money, he carried on boxing while living in New York, because he had been unable to find cabaret work—he had become something of a performer in Paris. Eventually, he was busted for using cocaine, and the judge deported him to his native Panama for a year, where he was welcomed as a great hero. However, boxing promoters there were keen to cash in on his celebrity status, and soon he was boxing ten-rounders instead of the four-rounders he was used to in New York, though still with the skill to knock out most of his opponents.

Eventually, when he was forty-four years old, the Panamanian authorities stepped in and took his licence away.

He tried some promoting and one of his protégés was boxer Simon Vergava, who many believed was Roberto Duran's father. Eventually, with things not going well in Panama, he returned to New York where he died from tuberculosis on 11th April 1951, after collapsing in the street.

As for the venue of the memorable encounter between Panama and Ginger, the Mountain Ash Pavilion, I am told that it has recently been demolished.

Bryn 'Ginger' Jones.

*Laurie Stevens
(South African champion).*

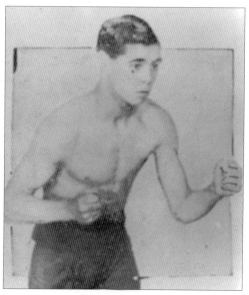

Cuthbert Taylor.

Chapter 9

Danny, Tiger and a Murder

Tom Evans is best remembered in the valleys as one of the greatest captains of Neath R.F.C. In the 1928/29 season he led Neath to the Welsh championship, when they set a Welsh record of 930 points and wing Dan Jones established a world record of 59 tries. But in the Amman Valley where he came from, Tom was also known as a fine amateur boxer. Big Tom won the Welsh heavyweight ABA championship in 1920, and then went on to gain the British title. In fact he was the first Welshman to achieve the British amateur title at heavyweight. They used to say about Tom: 'Talk about a puncher! And he was so strong that if he was underground the hauliers could do without a horse!'

He never turned pro; he preferred to use his sporting skills on the rugby field, but the success he had enjoyed as a boxer, and the admiration it had won him, had a big effect on his young brother, Danny.

When he was about fourteen, Danny began training as an amateur at the Amman Valley Boxing Club in the wake of Tom and another brother, Dai. He was boxing in the senior division by the time he was twenty, and in 1927 he got as far as winning the Welsh amateur welterweight title. A year or two after this success, he met Welsh amateur middleweight champion Frank Hatto, in a contest held at the old Palais de Danse in Garnant, a popular local venue which was full for the occasion. Danny lost on points by a narrow margin—Frank Hatto held the amateur middleweight title from 1926 until 1929.

It turned out to be Danny's last amateur contest. Unlike brother Tom, Danny eventually decided boxing was the life for him and besides, times were hard; work in the mines was short and insecure in the aftermath of the General Strike. He walked down to Ammanford and sought out Johnny Vaughan. 'I think I'm good enough to be a professional,' he told Johnny, and asked if he was willing to take him on. Johnny Vaughan, who kept a close eye on all young local boxers with potential, was only too happy to oblige. He decided to introduce Danny to the professional game by putting him in an exhibition bout of three 3-minute rounds with the gentlemanly Frank Moody. The venue was one of Johnny's occasional gala shows on Cresci's field; very popular events when boxers would be invited from a wider area to show their ring skills with Johnny's local boys. The three Moody brothers were always a good draw.

Danny's first pro fight for a decision was against Trevor (Tate) Evans from Maesteg. It took place on 29th June 1929 in Ammanford, over ten rounds, and Danny managed an easy points win. Over the following two months he scored points wins over Bertie Rees of Pontyberem and Dave Watts, Llanelli; both in the six rounds. Three more fights went the distance with three more wins for Danny, two of them against Billy Nicholas of Blaengwynfi. The second of the bouts against Nicholas (at Aberavon) was fairly remarkable for the fact that Danny fell out of the ring in the second round and landed on his head, only just beating the count.

They had reached the New Year of a new decade. Johnny Vaughan stepped up the training and put Danny in with Gordon Cook of Penygraig, who was the new Welsh Area Council's first designated Welsh lightweight champion. Later on, Gordon Cook would become cornerman for Freddie Mills during the early part of Mills's career.

He and Danny met in Llanelli on 1st March 1930 over fifteen rounds. Although Danny lost to Cook, the result was gratifyingly close and Johnny Vaughan was pleased with Danny's performance.

A likely contender for the Welsh welterweight title at that time was Billy Fry of Blaenlichan and Tylorstown. Already in his thirties, Billy was an experienced and talented boxer but his one fault was that he didn't take his training seriously enough. He had started his boxing career around the beginning of the First World War and by the end of it had notched up an impressive record of victories. He became quite a favourite at Liverpool Stadium and among his opponents was Tancy Lee.

In 1921 Fry was able to claim the lightweight championship of Wales by beating Danny Morgan of Tylorstown over 20 rounds. But after campaigning unsuccessfully during 1922/23, he seems to have dropped out of sight for a while.

By the time Danny Evans was in contention for the welterweight title, Billy Fry was back with a vengeance. He had beaten Danny Evans's stablemate, Idris Jones, on two occasions and more importantly, scored a points win over Gordon Cook, Penygraig. A few months later though, the tables were turned when Cook beat Fry on points. Those two fifteen-round contests were so hard-fought that they were described by Hedley Trembath as 'a Rhondda epic!'

Johnny Vaughan next put Danny Evans in with Ashton Jones of Trealaw, who was also an opponent of Billy Fry at this time. On 24th March 1930, Ashton Jones held Danny to a draw in Shrewsbury. A month later in Llanelli, Danny beat Jones over 15 rounds. The match between Fry and Danny Evans was made.

They first met in Ammanford on 24th May 1930. Johnny Vaughan recorded in his diary that the result was a draw.

Seven days later Billy Fry was in the ring again, but this time he was up against Danny's other recent opponent, Billy Nicholas, who had been trained as an amateur by Jim Driscoll. The ten-round contest took place in Cardiff but was almost called off because Nicholas's infant son had double pneumonia. His doctor persuaded him that, there being nothing practical he could do at home to help the child, the best thing for both of them was for Billy to go ahead with the contest.

Oscar Rees, recounting the story in the *South Wales Echo*, wrote:

> As he entered the ring one of the crowd shouted, 'We'll see the old master making a monkey out of this boy.' One of Billy (Nicholas)'s supporters Patsy Powell, then licensee of the Wyndham Hotel, Treherbert, shouted back: 'I've got a few pounds here says he won't.'

In this keen atmosphere and with his thoughts wandering back home to the sick bed of his young son, Billy Nicholas entered upon one of the greatest nights of his life. As the boxers entered the ring Billy Fry commented: 'It's a mug's game, Billy,' and Nicholas replied: 'I don't know—you've not done so badly.'

Something that was part observation and part instinct on Nicholas's part guided him that night. He later recalled: 'Billy Fry liked his opponents to come to him. I decided to try in the first round to box him. It worked, so I continued.'

There was a disconcerting muddle at the end of the ninth when the referee, having miscounted, thought the fight was over and had moved towards Nicholas to raise his hand as the winner before his error was pointed out to him. Showing remarkable coolness under fire, Billy Nicholas surmising that he just had to avoid a knockout to win, decided to change his tactics in the last round: 'I gave Billy Fry another surprise . . . I stopped boxing and made a fight of it.'

For this textbook points win, Billy Nicholas received the sum of £3.

After the fight, sporting Billy Fry confided that his young opponent had discovered his secret: 'I thought you would come out and fight,' he told Nicholas, 'You beat me because I didn't think you would have the confidence to box me.'

Happily, Billy Nicholas Junior made a full recovery from illness and might have followed his father into boxing after becoming an ATC champion. But Dad thought it more important for him to carry on with his studies.

The next contest between Billy Fry and Danny Evans in November 1930 was for the vacant welterweight championship of Wales, and it resulted in a definite win for Fry over the distance of fifteen 3-minute rounds. Although, as *Boxing* reported, Fry did nothing specially sensational, he had a nice lead at the end of five rounds. Evans made a big effort in the sixth but was well-met, and sustained a bad cut over the left eye which may have handicapped him a bit, though he did not ease up at all and kept Fry busy. But Fry maintained his mastery of the situation and, if he did not display any marked superiority over his most persevering opponent, he had done enough by the close to earn the verdict.

It was a disappointing result for the Ammanford camp and it would be another ten months before Danny got another crack at the title. Meanwhile, a strict training regime was adhered to. The following April, an eliminator contest for the welterweight title was arranged to take place in Llanelli between Danny and Arthur Rees. Danny came out the winner by a long chalk over the distance.

His next opponent was Bill Hood from Plymouth. He was a tough fighter for Sam McKeowen's boxing booth in the West Country, twenty-one years old, whose real name was Sidney Dawson. He travelled to Ammanford for a contest with Danny on 2nd May 1931, and got roundly beaten on points by his Welsh opponent. Not long afterwards, Hood went to try his luck in America but there wasn't much luck around for him, and he came back to Plymouth after a few months. 'I was broke when I arrived and I was broke when I left,' was how he summed up his sojourn to the States. Undeterred, Hood resumed his boxing in Britain, where he enjoyed great popularity. After a few successful years, his boxing career declined, coming to an end during the Second World War. Bill Hood became a dustman for Plymouth Corporation. He had had over one hundred and fifty recorded fights and many unrecorded, in a career he thoroughly enjoyed. 'Boxing was my life,' he would say, 'I have only kind thoughts about the sport.'

The date had been fixed for Billy Fry's defence of the welterweight title against Danny Evans. As he sometimes did for such occasions, Johnny Vaughan had engaged the services of another champion to help with his man's preparations for the fight. This time it was Ben Marshall, former Welsh welterweight champion, who had had three successful defences before he was deprived of the championship in June 1930, probably because he was unable to make the weight.

Marshall was passionately proud of the strength of his chin and jaw. And he could demonstrate it. While he was staying in the Amman Valley, the travelling fair had arrived at Glanamman and there were the usual crowds around for Fair Day. Ben Marshall, Danny Evans and a group of onlookers had gathered at the local forge. The blacksmith's name was William Davies. As he had a ready-made audience, Marshall saw an opportunity to perform one of his party pieces. Spying an enormous wheel from a *'gambo'*, or hay wagon, standing against the wall of the forge, he asked some of the men to lift it and carry it to a space in the middle of the room, where he promptly lay down.

'Now, keep it upright,' he told them, 'and balance it on my chin.' The men cautiously did as they were told, slowly withdrawing their hands but keeping them close enough in case the thing overbalanced. The whole crowd held their breath for the long seconds that Marshal took the whole weight of the steel-rimmed wheel on his chin, and broke into applause when the ordeal was over. Danny hoped he would get half such an ovation from the audience when he and Billy Fry got in the ring together for the third time.

Ben Marshall and Johnny Vaughan supervised the last days of Danny's training and hours of sparring with close attention. On 19th September 1931, a huge crowd had gathered to watch this important return match. The Ammanford boxers lower down the bill did not fare well that night: Ivor Drew (Trealaw) beat Dai Davies, Dai Rickard of Pontardulais beat Morris Jones and Idris Davies was beaten by Glyn Day (Pontardulais).

The main bout began as the two protagonists touched gloves in front of the biggest crowd Johnny had ever had in the pavilion. Jack Leyshon was the referee.

The first few rounds went Danny's way and he built up an early lead. Although Fry revealed some of his old-time adroitness in defence by the way he took Evans's blows on his gloves, there was little zip in his punches. It was not until the seventh that a glimpse of Fry the Champion was seen.

Fry kept close to Evans and his leads were superbly judged as they sped on their way to Danny's face. But in the eighth, ninth and tenth rounds, Fry took some severe punishment and needed to draw on his vast experience to survive the onslaught of his more youthful opponent.

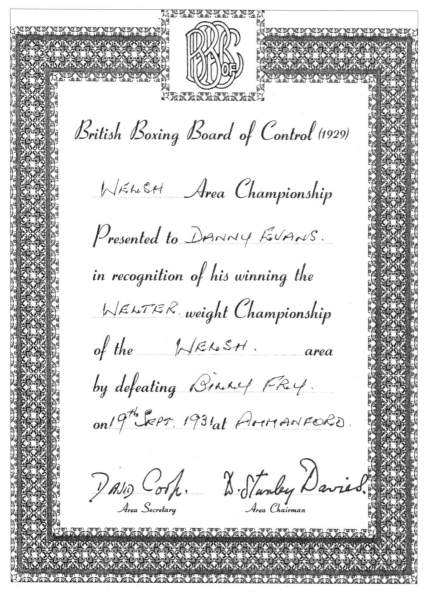

British Boxing Board of Control (1929)

WELSH Area Championship

Presented to DANNY EVANS.

in recognition of his winning the

WELTER weight Championship

of the WELSH. area

by defeating BINNEY FRY.

on 19th SEPT. 1931 at AMMANFORD.

David Cook.
Area Secretary

D. Stanley Davies.
Area Chairman

Danny Evans, BBBC Certificate.

In the thirteenth Fry had recovered enough to take the initiative and slip some clever lefts to the contender's face. But Danny's extra training showed in a storming finish which had the crowd gasping their surprise that the old champion was still on his feet as the final gong sounded. The thunderous applause was for both men.

Danny showed his respect for his opponent in the time-honoured way. Fry was nearing the end of an impressive career as 'one of the greatest glove artists produced in the Rhondda.' Indeed, *Boxing* reported that 'some surprise was caused in South Wales circles when Billy Fry of Tylorstown, lost his title of Welsh welterweight champion to Danny Evans of Ammanford,' and went on to say: 'Yet it was not really surprising that the 35-year-old champion should lose his title to a man of Evans's speed and ability, for the Ammanford lad boxed in tip-top form to win by a clear margin of points over 15 rounds.'

The evening was also a great financial success, with receipts of almost £125. After the boxers had been paid and other expenses accounted for, Ammanford Athletic Club made a net profit of £32.1s.8d, a tidy sum in 1931.

In November 1931 Herbert Jacques, a boxer from Sheffield, travelled to Ammanford to box Danny Evans. As it turned out he was well out-boxed by Danny and the local press sent a reporter who used the nom-de-plume 'Right Cross' to record the proceedings:

> The fight opened in a sensational manner, both men exchanging punches rapidly, and it was evident from the outset that both men meant business. However, towards the end of the round Evans boxed cleverly and gained the honours.
>
> In the second round Evans again showed up with a beautiful straight left, while his opponent swung wildly, very rarely connecting . . . In the third and fourth rounds, Jacques was again outpointed and towards the end of the fourth took a count of eight.
>
> Fifth round—Evans made the mistake of mixing it with Jacques whose swinging blows were dangerous; the round ending more even. Evans boxed like a real champion in the sixth and easily won the honours; the seventh round was fairly even, Jacques doing better than in any of the previous rounds.

Eighth round—Evans again boxed splendidly and Jacques went down for a count of seven. In the ninth round Jacques was down on three occasions for counts of nine, the gong saving him the last time.

Effective covering in the tenth saved Jacques, who appeared leg-weary; Evans again winning this round. Evans again went for his man with determination in the eleventh and after several hard body punches Jacques, who had put up a plucky display, went down to be counted out.

In his comment, 'Right Cross' referred to Danny's 'lovely left hand which will gain for him many points', a prediction which proved to be wholly accurate.

That same evening was successful for another of Johnny's boxers, Handel 'Handy' Richards, who beat Young Willie Piper of Swansea in one of the minor bouts over six 2-minute rounds.

Dai Rickard of Pontardulais knocked out Bryn Jones of Swansea in the ninth round.

Another encounter with Billy Nicholas resulted in a points win for Danny but he lost on a foul in the fourth to Jacky Moody on Boxing Day 1931. A couple of months later Danny sustained a cut eye at Newcastle against a local boxer, George Willis.

It was fortunately not as bad a cut as at first feared, because Danny's defence of his Welsh title had been arranged to take place on 19th March 1932, against Myrddin Ellis Davies of Ystradgynlais. Myrddin, who boxed under the names Young Ellis and Tiger Ellis, also had the formidable nickname 'The Mad Mullah', probably because of his rather manic boxing style. A couple of months before his bout with Danny Evans, Ellis had been matched against the South African welterweight champion Barney Keiswetter, and held him to a draw over 15 rounds at Ystradgynlais.

'Ellis forced the fight from start to finish in his usual bustling manner,' the local press reported. 'He piled up points by his clever attack. Keiswetter had to clinch to save himself from Ellis's vicious two-handed barrages. There was too much hugging in the clinches which tended to spoil the effect of the clash.'

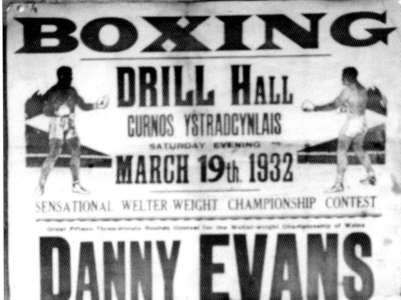

Referee Mr J. R. Smith from Cardiff announced the verdict as a draw, to the disgruntled booing of the local crowd.

Going through the pre-fight formalities in the ring, Young Ellis was unimpressive beside the athletic figure of Danny Evans. But as the contest took place at Ystradgynlais Drill Hall, Ellis's fans were all there and the crowd was generally with him.

Perhaps Danny was a little rattled from the start; perhaps he was nervous about his still-tender eye. Whatever the reason, for the second time in three months he was disqualified for a foul blow, this time in the fifth. What worse way can there be to lose a title?

Danny was downcast on the short journey home, but Johnny was philosophical and already engaged in making plans for Danny to meet George Rose of Bristol in May. At the end of March he outpointed Pembrokeshire boxer, Ocky Davies, in Milford Haven over fifteen rounds, but the contest with Rose in Swansea resulted in a draw.

Meanwhile, Danny had been selected—along with Ginger Jones and Glen Moody—to take part in a boxing show in Belfast featuring bouts between Welsh and Irish boxers. The three of them travelled together with Johnny Vaughan at the beginning of June 1932.

Danny fought six 3-minute rounds against Carl Peterson, winning on points, and Ginger was something of a star for the Welsh contingent when he outpointed Jack Garland of Belfast in a repeat of his meeting with Garland over two years previously.

But the highlight of the trip for Danny was watching the great Primo Carnera boxing his exhibition bouts. It was one of his favourite memories. 'What a man!' he would tell me many years later: 'Over twenty-two stone and nearly seven feet tall! He had hands like shovels and his gloves were enormous, but he had the gentle nature of a mouse.'

Although Danny's description may have been a little exaggerated, Carnera was certainly a giant of a man, weighing in at well over 19 stone; everything about him seemed enormous including his wide, friendly grin.

Carnera had been in London in May, where he lost to Larry Gains over ten rounds. It would be another year before he beat Jack Sharkey for the World heavyweight title.

Back home again and Danny had to steel himself for another contest with Tiger Ellis. He was going for the Welsh title again and had less than two months to prepare.

The day, 30th July 1932, duly arrived and Danny had worked hard. There was a good crowd at the 'neutral' venue in Llanelli, for both boxers had a sizeable following.

Danny and Tiger glared at each other across the ring.

The contest was strenuously fought, with Evans refusing to be hustled by Ellis's persistent onslaughts; Evans accurately delivering both left and right crosses to his opponent in the early rounds. One particularly good cross brought Tiger Ellis down but he was up again on a count of six. The fight was marred by some rather wild punching, mainly on Ellis's part, though in the sixth and seventh round it improved, but with Evans tending to hit more cleanly.

The pace had become so furious by the twelfth that both men fell through the ropes, fortunately both of them clambering back unhurt! Then in the thirteenth round it was Danny's turn to get caught off guard and he went down, but sprang back quickly to his feet. Although the last two rounds were more even, Danny was the clear winner overall.

He smiled for the first time that evening—he was the Welsh welterweight champion once more.

Had he had a crystal ball, Danny may have been even prouder of his achievement: a little over seven weeks after this encounter with Danny Evans, Ellis actually beat Tommy Farr when the referee stopped the fight in the fifth round because of Farr's cut eye. Thereafter, Ellis was known for many years in the Swansea valleys as 'the miner that once licked Tommy Farr'; a finer reputation it would be hard to find!

It was with his confidence fully restored that Danny met his next opponent: South African welterweight champion, Barney Keiswetter, held to a draw by Tiger Ellis six months earlier. Barney Keiswetter was an exceptionally clever boxer and his ring work 'was a delight to see,' said the local reporter. An attractive contest at Plasmarl, Swansea, resulted in a win for Danny Evans. The local press recorded the fight, I suspect with more than a little prejudice in favour of Danny:

Keiswetter opened the exchanges, smiling and brimful of confidence, by taking the fight to the Welsh champion who, fixing his opponent with his hawk-like eyes, easily avoided the dangerous blows, countered well and followed up with two rapier-like straight lefts which rocked his opponent.

Keiswetter who looked bigger and more powerful than his opponent, maintained his aggressive attitude in the second round . . . scoring with a lightning straight left to the head, but a moment later was forced to take a dose of similar medicine himself. The Welsh champion . . . was landing consistently and solidly to Keiswetter's face in the third and fourth rounds, with a perfectly timed left delivered at lightning speed, while his inside work was the more effective.

A furious toe-to-toe rally occurred in the fifth after the Springbok had missed with a terrific right to the jaw, the Ammanford boxer giving back as much as he received. From then on, Evans gradually assumed command, the South African champion relying almost on defensive measures except for an aggressive spurt in the eleventh. He did little during the last four rounds, appearing diffident to go in to the attack . . .

Evans continued to follow up his opponent, scoring effectively.

After the fight, Danny was presented with a silver cup by Jackie Picton-Phillips, son of the well-known Chief Constable of Carmarthenshire Constabulary; both father and son were enthusiastic fans of Welsh boxing. He had promised the cup to the first Welsh boxer 'to lower the colours of the South African champion.'

The two had a second contest in November of 1932 at Bristol, and were so closely matched that the result was declared a draw. A great deal of interest had naturally been aroused by such 'exotic' visiting sportsmen in Wales, although boxers from other nations, and their managers, had been attracted to the National Sporting Club in London for many years.

In 1932 several South African boxers met opponents in South Wales, including Keiswetter, George 'Panther' Purchase and Dave Burger; the last a tiny man of 7st.2lbs who gave 'pretty displays of fast boxing'.

'Panther' Purchase was a particular favourite in Wales. He liked the place and the people so much that he made his home in Roath, Cardiff,

Danny Evans.

Tiger Ellis, Ystradgynlais.

between 1931 and 1937, when he thoroughly got into the swing of boxing in the valleys. Not only did he draw appreciative audiences at many venues, but also had a go at taking on all-comers in the boxing booths, so much a part of life in the valleys. Twice, in 1936, he even fought for the Welsh welterweight title—how did he qualify for that, I wonder?—but lost to Ivor Pickens, who held the championship from 1934 until 1937.

Purchase had been a previous winner of the South African lightweight crown; his manager was his wife, Kit, which must be quite unusual. Among his British opponents were Jack Kid Berg, Harry Mason and Jake Kilrain. He also fought Danny Evans in 1935.

After returning to South Africa he became a referee and then a trainer.

The October between his two contests with Keiswetter was an outstanding month for Danny and must count as a highlight of his glittering boxing career. In the space of four weeks he had a points win followed by no less than three consecutive knockouts.

He beat Albert Danahar of Bethnal Green on 8th October over fifteen rounds at Llanelli, then he and Johnny went down to Bournemouth where he met Reg Travell of Northampton. The result was a knockout to Danny in the tenth round. Back in Ammanford five days later, he knocked out Harry Vaughan from Porthcawl in the seventh and on 31st October, Albert Johnson of Manchester was the latest recipient of Danny's awesome left hand when he went down for a knockout in the sixth round! The sheer number of fights in a short space of time that these 'hungry fighters' had is mind-boggling. They certainly earned their few quid!

After a couple more points wins, one against Battling JoJo from the Gold Coast, West Africa, Danny was defeated in Leeds by Scotland's welterweight champion, Willie Hamilton.

It was February 1933 and Danny had taken a break over December and January. The long journey to Leeds only to get beaten was enough to persuade him back into serious training. Although a week later, he beat Dixie Cullen of Chelsea over fifteen rounds at Shrewsbury, it was May before he and Johnny Vaughan were confident that Danny was ready to embark on his new and more ambitious campaign. Over the next two months, he chalked up six points wins, his opponents including Jackie Phillips from Canada at Crystal Palace and Tommy Taylor at Liverpool. Three others were boxers from Lancashire: Jack Marshall of Accrington, Tommy Marren, Burnley, and Jack Lord from Bolton, who would later wrest the Northern Area welterweight title from Chuck Parker.

Jack Lord was an opponent that Danny could never forget.

From boyhood, Jack had taken a keen interest in boxing. He started as an amateur in the local club, but a World middleweight title fight on 30th June 1927, when British boxer Tommy Milligan was stopped by America's Mickey Walker, inspired Jack Lord to take up the sport professionally. According to Jack's daughter, Patricia, speaking to Ron Olver in 1988, there had been a total eclipse of the sun on the following day, when the newspapers were full of critics lamenting the dearth of British boxers who could beat the Americans. To her father 'it seemed as though British boxing too had been eclipsed from the world scene,' she said, adding that the taunts of the journalists '. . . prompted Jack to turn professional, if he had ever needed any prompting.'

He made his winning professional debut over six rounds at the age of seventeen and went home with £1 'thinking I was Rothschild!' In November 1930, he topped the bill for the first time against Sam McVey, but the following year suffered broken bones in both hands during a bout with Jim McAllister and had a lengthy lay-off. Apparently though, this time was not wasted as the sporting Jack obtained a position as golf professional at the Copenhagen Golf Club and actually taught the finer points of the game to Queen Alexandrine of Denmark.

Returning to boxing, he had a long run of success through 1932 although his first meeting with Chuck Parker brought defeat. He had a particularly notable win over 15 rounds against Billy Bird of Chelsea which prompted the alliterative *Boxing* headline:

'BOLTON BOY'S BRILLIANT BOXING AGAINST BILLY BIRD'.

On the strength of this win Jack bought himself a car, only to crash it swerving to avoid 'a cow coming out of a field', and the damaged ribs sustained caused him to retire in round seven of a contest with Willie Hamilton.

Jack Lord and Danny Evans met in Swansea on 8th July 1933. Jack was well-known as 'a kind and gentle man'. Certainly he did not intend to cause Danny any permanent injury, but the unfortunate fact is that a punch to Danny's throat during the bout left him with damage to the vocal chords which condemned him to speaking in a soft, hoarse voice for the rest of his life. In spite of this injury Danny won the fight over twelve rounds.

A week later, Danny married his sweetheart, Mildred Jones, of Quay Street, Ammanford, whose parents owned a bakery and provisions shop.

The local paper, announcing the wedding, stated that 'On Saturday next, the bridegroom is due to appear in a charity boxing tournament,' but makes no mention of the fact that Danny's 'I do' must have been rather hard to hear.

By this time Johnny Vaughan understandably had high hopes of a British title for Danny.

After a short period of rest, when the young newlyweds enjoyed their honeymoon, training began again in earnest, for the next contest was a big step up for Danny. At least it took place in Cardiff, which meant many of his supporters were able to make the journey. Danny Evans met Harry Mason of London, on 4th September 1933.

Harry Mason, though originally from Leeds, had a similar background to Jack Kid Berg having been brought up in the East End of London. He 'fancied himself as an all-round entertainer.' Before a fight, he would jauntily enter the ring smiling, in an 'exquisite silken robe', having just put down his violin which he was in the habit of playing loudly in the dressing room area, presumably to rattle his opponent. Actually, Mason was quite an accomplished musician and had apparently received offers to play professionally, though it's unlikely the other boxers were appreciative of his virtuosity. Jack Kid Berg, who was virtually Mason's stablemate and who had come close to meeting him in the ring to challenge his British lightweight title, thoroughly disliked him, as did others. Mason would boast that his carefully parted hair had never been disturbed in a fight and, like Muhammad Ali so many years later, he was never at a loss for words. He had even been known to recite his own 'rather haphazard' verses in the ring; I can only imagine the antagonism this must have aroused in the supporters of his opponents. Gilbert Odd wrote of Mason:

> He was definitely a boxer and a very clever one at that. But Mason could incite trouble. I've seen him leaning over the shoulder of an opponent, winking at the audience while throwing kidney punches! The referee was always on the blind side of course, and the more the crowd booed, the better Mason liked it.

Conversely of course, Mason's supporters (and he had many) loved his mind games, and were amused by his antics.

Harry Mason had been British and European lightweight champion in the twenties, as well as gaining the welterweight title in November 1925 by beating Hamilton Johnny Brown. He had subsequently lost the welterweight title to Jack Hood. When he met Danny in September 1933, both of them were building up to be in for a chance at the British title. This was the formidable opponent that Danny faced on that late summer night in Cardiff.

'Rhyswg', reporter for the *South Wales Evening Post*, took his ringside seat along with many other interested newshounds:

> It was a thrilling contest which put the Welshman right in the front rank of welters, for his left hand was at its best and he also used an occasional right cross with deadly effect.
>
> The bout was a battle of men who were each striving to force the other to employ his own tactics. Evans wanted the bout decided at long range, while Mason, whose speed was phenomenal, sought to force his opponent to in-fighting.
>
> Mason possessed an exceptionally sound defence, and needed it in the first three rounds which were won by the Welshman, who used both hands with equal facility. But in the fourth, Evans went to the boards from a right swing, jumping to his feet before the referee, Mr Bob Hill of Cardiff, could start the count. Mason did well in succeeding sessions and was ahead on points at the end of the tenth, but the next round saw Evans land the best punch of the fight—a perfectly timed straight left to the jaw.
>
> ### MASON TIRES
>
> The Londoner showed signs of tiring and Evans brought over some deadly lefts which could not be countered effectively. When the last round opened it was evident that the winner of that would take the spoils.
>
> Both fought desperately and Mason called on his reserves to launch a strong two-handed attack. He was unable to maintain the pace

and the Welsh champion replied with left swings. Mason made his last great effort, cornering his opponent, and the final bell went with both men fighting madly and the crowd cheering excitedly. So great was the uproar that the bell could not be heard, and both men had to be separated by the referee.

It was one of the cleanest contests seen between welters and Evans's stock has jumped a couple of points as a result of his performance.

Bob Hills, taking the line of least resistance so popular with referees in Wales at this time, declared a draw. But as Danny's performance was hailed as one of the best of his career, there were no long faces in the Ammanford corner. Danny himself took an impartial view of Mason's histrionics and pronounced him: 'The best boxer I ever fought.'

Meanwhile, Johnny made arrangements for a return contest with George Rose at Bristol. The contest took place on 20th October and this time Danny was successful over twelve 3-minute rounds.

So far, so good. Danny's superb form continued. Jerry Daley was his next victim, getting knocked out in two rounds at Ammanford, the day before Christmas Eve.

The New Year of 1934 was less than a week old when Danny travelled to Merthyr to fight Jack Ellis from London. He found this Ellis a lot easier to deal with than 'Tiger'. Danny dictated the exchanges from the outset with his left lead. Ellis worked to close quarters, and his rights were damaging, but Evans's footwork minimised their power, and his left continued to dominate the situation.

In the seventh round, Ellis introduced some variety to his delivery, scoring with rights to the jaw and a well timed uppercut, while Evans pinned faith in left swings to the body. But Ellis could not cope with Evans's left and the Welshman won well, over fifteen rounds.

In February, Danny met Willie Hamilton for the second time. The contest, which took place in Llanelli, was part of an elimination series to decide who would go forward for the British welterweight title, vacant because Jack Hood had relinquished it. This time there was no mistake on Danny's part. Hamilton was counted out in the second round. A second contest with Dixie Cullen, in March, went the distance, and once again, Danny's hand was raised.

But into every life a little rain must fall. Along with the April showers, Harry Mason travelled to Swansea for the final eliminator with Danny on the 21st. The showdown went the distance and the referee announced the winner—Harry Mason. He went on to win the British welterweight title for the second time, on a disqualification against Len Tiger Smith, just two months later.

Danny was devastated, and convinced he had missed his one chance to be British welterweight champion. And he was to be proved right.

In the meantime, worse was to come. Setting aside his hopes for the British crown, Danny defended his Welsh title against one Ivor Pickens of Caerau. The contest took place in Swansea over fifteen rounds, almost exactly a year after his marriage to Mildred. His old demon came back to haunt him that summer night, when he lost on a foul in the fifth round. I think it's fair to say that Danny lost heart after that. The foul got him into trouble with the Welsh Area Boxing Board of Control, who fined him £5. This in turn led to a deterioration in the productive relationship Danny had enjoyed with Johnny Vaughan, which was never quite the same afterwards.

None of this misfortune meant that Ivor Pickens was any the less worthy a Welsh champion. He successfully defended his title four times, finally losing it to Frank Moody's brother, Jackie, in October 1937.

Towards the end of the year Danny attempted the slow climb back up the ladder towards the British title by travelling to London for two contests against another Jewish boxer, Moe Moss of Mile End—Danny drew one and lost the second—and a battle with the popular Archie Sexton, who beat him on points.

Looking back, if Danny could have derived any comfort from his disappointment over the British title, it may have been from Archie Sexton's record, and the parallels in their careers.

Sexton was an outstandingly successful and popular boxer, one of three professional brothers whose father was a prizefighter. His workrate was phenomenal; at one point in the twenties he was averaging over twenty fights a year and winning nearly all of them. He boxed at all the big London venues and built a large band of loyal followers by beating men like Johnny Cuthbert, Glen Moody, Germany's Franz Kruppel, Bill Hood and Jim Cater of Glasgow (the last two by knockout). Significantly though, Sexton also lost to Harry Mason.

Although he had previously beaten Jack 'Cast-Iron' Casey from Sunderland and held him to a draw on another occasion, when Archie met him in October 1932 in an eliminator for the British middleweight title, he was knocked down and counted out in the seventh round. When the two met again the following year, Sexton beat Casey 'by a wide margin' of points.

This entitled him to a title fight with British champion Jock McAvoy but, though he 'gave everything he had' according to Ron Olver, Archie was knocked out in the tenth round. Just to rub salt in the wound, in April 1934 he was beaten for the Southern Area title by Edward Pearce who boxed under the name of Al Burke. Battling on despite his disappointments, Archie had a lot more successful fights over the following months, until the jinx struck again in 1935 when Jack Hyams outpointed him in another eliminator for the Southern Area championship!

Ironically, his last year of boxing, 1936, brought him even greater success and much critical acclaim, with *Boxing* praising his performance against Frank Hough in July with the words: 'Never have we seen Sexton display better skill and ring craft than he did here to gain a winning margin.' But no title came his way.

Sexton too received a permanent injury in the ring—in what was to be his last fight, again against Frank Hough, to whom he was conceding eleven pounds.

Caused by the lace of a glove, the injury was to one of Archie's eyes. He was operated on at Moorfields Hopital where they were unable to save the eye and later fitted him with a glass one. By an extraordinary quirk of fate, as though he was repaying the care he had received there, Archie had another encounter at Moorfields Hospital in 1944. He had become a War Reserve policeman, whose duties took him to places where terrible damage had been inflicted on London and its people by German bombs. One night he pulled two men and a woman to safety from a smoke-filled waterlogged shelter beneath Moorfields Hospital which had been bombed.

In an entirely unexpected way Archie Sexton finally got an award for his efforts—the George Medal for bravery.

Well, you don't always get what you want, as the song says, and I guess one inescapable if unpalatable lesson for both Danny and Archie was that Harry Mason was a worthier champion on the day.

There was another experience that Danny and Archie Sexton had in common: they both fought, and beat, the ill-starred French-Canadian boxer Del Fontaine. Danny knocked him out in the third round at the Drill Hall in Swansea when they met in 1934. Archie had outpointed Fontaine in 1932, and he beat him again early in 1935 in what was to be Del Fontaine's last fight. On 29th October of that year, Del Fontaine, having been convicted of murder at the Old Bailey, was hanged at Wandsworth prison. Danny would sometimes talk about Fontaine. 'He was a crazy man,' I remember him saying, shaking his head sadly.

Perhaps the shock of the Canadian's fate proved to be the final straw for Danny as far as boxing was concerned. Although he had once more secured the Welsh middleweight title in April 1935 by beating Billy Thomas of Merthyr on points, he decided to call it a day the following year, retiring as undefeated champion. Possibly Mildred thought it was a good time for Danny—now a family man—to settle down to steadier work. He returned to mining at Maerdy pit.

The *Carmarthen Journal* paid him a warm tribute: 'Evans has been one of the prettiest boxers in Wales and held the welterweight until beaten on a foul, by Ivor Pickens, Caerau . . . His left hand was remarkably good, and he won his way to a British title eliminator against Harry Mason . . .'

I remember Danny best in his seventies and eighties. He would greet me in his hoarse whisper, and we would while away some happy hours with him reminiscing and me listening. 'I'm still my fighting weight you know,' he would tell me, 'And look at this . . .': he would hold out an arm horizontally in front of him and lift up his leg till his toes touched his hand. 'Not bad, is it?' he'd grin.

Danny Evans died aged 87 in July 1993. I was proud to call him a friend.

Billy Fry died in Ferndale in 1958, aged 63.

By some strange twist of fate, 'Panther' Purchase was the victim of a similar crime to that suffered by little Jimmy Wilde. As an elderly man he was stabbed and beaten by muggers. He died aged 73, having suffered several strokes, in Cape Town.

Gentle Jack Lord went on to greater success, finally meeting Jake Kilrain for the British title in a very dramatic fight held in tragic circumstances. Having been postponed and re-arranged a couple of times, the bout took place in February 1938, a few days after Jack's baby daughter died from pneumonia. Deciding between them that the fight should go ahead, Jack's wife, parents and brother were all at ringside in mourning, and Jock McAvoy lent support in his corner. During an epic battle, both boxers were knocked down in round six, Jack Lord in rounds seven and nine, and Kilrain went down again in round eleven. Kilrain finally got the decision, but the sympathetic crowd cheered Jack Lord even louder than the champion.

Lord continued to box in the army after volunteering when the war started, and his last fight was in 1946, when he lost to the future British middleweight champion, Dick Turpin. He became a bus conductor for Bolton Corporation—a fact passed on to me by Miles Templeton, boxing archivist, whose uncle was Jack Lord's driver. Lord also became a Board of Control referee in 1952 and was involved in boxing for another twenty years. He died in April 1976.

Archie Sexton also became a Board of Control referee, thus sparking a mostly good-natured debate (prompted by the complaint of a French boxer's manager) about the advisability of having one-eyed referees. Needless to say, Archie's unflappable fair-mindedness won the day and he continued to referee fights into the 1950s. His son, Dave, carrying on the sporting example of his father, became manager of Manchester United.

*Billy Fry, Blaenllichan
and Tylorstown.*

*Harry Mason (British & European
lightweight champion and
British welterweight champion).*

Danny, Johnny Vaughan and Barney Keiswetter.

Chapter 10

Randy Jones and the Cruiserweights

By May 1932, Johnny Vaughan's gym had had three Welsh champions to advertise Johnny's effectiveness as trainer/manager. (Although Danny Evans had lost his title to 'Tiger' Ellis on 19th March 1932, he regained it four months later.)

Whether Johnny approached the up-and-coming young Randy Jones from Pentre Road, Pontardulais, or whether it was the other way round, is not recorded. However, Johnny would have seen him box at Gess's booth at Ammanford and Pontardulais and he signed him up in 1932.

In January 1932 Johnny Vaughan recorded Randy Jones's weight as twelve stone twelve pounds 6ozs; well within the heavyweight division. Here was something different for Johnny as a trainer; he had been used to training featherweight to welterweight boxers. For a start finding sparring partners for this big lad would be harder than for his smaller boxers, let alone contests. It was a challenge, but Johnny liked a challenge.

After an uninspiring early career—his latest bout against Irishman Pat McAuliffe at Bournemouth, had ended in him being disqualified — it was clear that Randy Jones's boxing would benefit from a change. He had had a couple of good wins, including a knockout against Swansea's Harry Davies, but had then lost on points to Wattie Phillips from Llandybie.

When Johnny Vaughan took him on, having spotted the potential in the twenty-year-old Randy, he had a plan in mind. To start off with, welterweight Danny Evans might be called upon as a sparring partner, he thought. Johnny was a shrewd judge and always kept a close eye on

Jack Petersen.

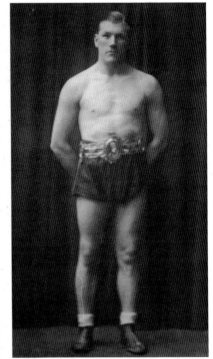

Tommy Farr.

the opposition. At the back of his mind was an interesting situation that had arisen in Welsh boxing then.

Extraordinarily, Jack Petersen, young Tommy Farr, and a couple of other notable Welsh boxers were bordering on heavyweight in 1932. But at the very time that Randy became part of Johnny Vaughan's stable, these promising youngsters were opening up the light-heavyweight, or cruiserweight, division to produce some very interesting competition, and Johnny Vaughan saw Randy Jones as a contender for the Welsh light-heavyweight title. Maybe the heavyweight championship might follow.

Welsh boxers over twelve-and-a-half stone are historically uncommon, although between 1928 and 1983, Wales produced twelve Welsh and/or British titleholders at heavyweight.

Heavyweight champions of Wales were Dick Power, Cwmfelinfach, adopted champion; Jack Petersen, Cardiff, 1932; Jim Wilde, Swansea, 1935; Tommy Farr, Tonypandy, 1936 and 1951; George James, Cwm, 1938 and 1939; Dennis Powell, Four Crosses, 1949; Carl Gizzi, 1961; Dennis Avoth, 1971; Neville Meade, Swansea, 1976 and David Pearce, Newport, 1983. Of these, Jack Petersen, Tommy Farr, Neville Meade and David Pearce went on to become British heavyweight champions; Johnny Williams and Joe Erskine won British heavyweight titles but never held the Welsh championship. Dick Richardson from Newport was a European champion,

When Randy Jones went to train with Johnny Vaughan, no less than four of the contenders for those titles were boxing at that time.

Among this elite band was Charlie Bundy of Treherbert. A contender at both cruiser and heavyweight, 'Square-shouldered Charlie', as *Boxing News* called him, was Jack Petersen's sparring partner. He 'was another Welshman who would have gone a great deal further if he had made boxing a full-time instead of a part-time job'.

Nonetheless, Charlie was up there with the best of them. Over his career he had contests against Tommy Farr, Jack London, British cruiser-weight champion Eddie Phillips and Midlands heavyweight champion Alf Luxton to his credit. He also fought for the Welsh heavyweight title against Swansea's Big Jim Wilde (not to be confused with little Jimmy Wilde, the flyweight 'ghost with a hammer').

An interesting comment was made in the nineteen-fifties about this Welsh phenomenon, when British heavyweight boxing was enjoying a period of success and great popularity, and *Boxing News* lamented the fact that Randy Jones, Big Jim Wilde and Charley Bundy were on the scene twenty years too early!

> There's no doubt about it, modern Welsh promoters would be rubbing their hands with joy if they had tough and rugged boys like Big Jim Wilde and Charlie Bundy as well as George James, Randy Jones . . . to pair against Richardson, Erskine, London, Cooper, Bygraves . . .

On 25th March 1932 Randy Jones met Charlie Bundy for the first of four encounters he had with him; he won on points over ten rounds at

Swansea's Mannesmann Hall. Six weeks later he outpointed Jim Wilde himself at Ammanford Pavilion, again over ten rounds.

Boxing reported the fight on May 11th:

> Never have I seen such excellent progress . . . as that made by the Pontardulais light-heavyweight Randy Jones, whose affairs are now being managed by Mr Johnny Vaughan, manager of Ginger Jones and Billy Quinlen, the respective featherweight and lightweight champions of Wales.
>
> A month ago, Jones's fighting at Swansea was slow and uninteresting, but on Saturday he boxed like a champion when he gave Jimmy Wilde, the Swansea heavyweight who recently defeated Peter Jackson of Australia at the Albert Hall, London, a terrific lacing. Jones has obviously taken a few leaves out of that delightfully scientific boxer, Dan Evans's, book, for he has indeed made wonderful progress since he joined Johnny Vaughan's school and started sparring with the ex-welterweight titleholder.
>
> He showed considerable boxing ability against Wilde and varied his perpetual motion attack with excellent judgement.
>
> ENDURANCE AND PLUCK
>
> Wilde had little defence but he showed he possessed endurance, pluck and stamina in no ordinary degree.
>
> During the whole ten rounds, Wilde never looked like a winner and when he was not absorbing terrific punishment, he was hanging on to his man like a leech to prevent himself being knocked out. The referee had a difficult time separating the men.
>
> However, in spite of this it was an excellent fight to watch. Wilde showed wonderful pluck and Jones, boxing ability above the average.
>
> J.W.P.P.

It would be another three years before Jim Wilde beat Charlie Bundy over fifteen rounds for the Welsh heavyweight championship after the title was relinquished by Jack Petersen.

As anticipated by Johnny, there seems to have been a shortage of opponents for his man to work his way to the title. This is apparent in the record, in the number of Randy's contests that were return bouts. Between September 1932 and January 1933, he met George Smith of Tonyrefail three times, finally outpointing him at Bargoed Coliseum after the first two contests ended in a draw.

During this period he also beat Phil Green of Bath and Cyril Edwards, Mansfield; the latter in the preliminary round of a heavyweight competition when the referee stopped the fight in the second round. Randy went on to lose in the first series of the competition to Seaman Atkey at Crystal Palace on 5th December. The Navy was a good source of opponents but, to tell the truth, Randy Jones found the big seafarers a bit of a tough proposition. In a total of three bouts with Seaman Frank Stubbs of Portsmouth, the first was lost on points while the other two ended in a draw.

By the New Year of 1933, Jack Petersen had relinquished his light-heavyweight crown, having gained the Welsh heavyweight title the previous year.

Randy's second encounter with Charlie Bundy was scheduled for 21st January 1933 at Bargoed Coliseum. It was a 15-rounder and ended with another points win for Randy Jones.

A delighted Johnny Vaughan saw that his chance had come, and he contacted the Boxing Board of Control to sanction a contest to decide the light-heavyweight championship of Wales between his man Randy Jones and Jerry Daley of Penygraig. The fight took place on 11th March 1933 and *Boxing* reported it:

A NEW TITLEHOLDER

Randy Jones Wins the Vacant Cruiser Championship

In spite of a plucky display, Jerry Daley (Penygraig) failed to lift the Welsh cruiserweight championship at Merthyr on Saturday night, being defeated on points by Randy Jones (Ammanford) after fifteen hard rounds. Thus West Wales can now claim a nap hand of champions, the four other titleholders being Len Beynon (Swansea), Ginger Jones, Billy Quinlen and Danny Evans, all of Ammanford—truly a record of which to be proud . . . Jones was fully entitled to the award but tribute was paid to Daley's pluck and determination under handicap. Firstly he was giving something near a stone of weight away (he is little more than a middleweight, for which title he battled successfully on four occasions) and, second, a cut eye in the fourth round did not improve his chances. Jones boxed well at times, but at others he was inclined to be a bit wild. He scored the more often to the head, while Daley's main target was amidships. In the end Jones was adjudged the winner.—F. R. HILL

Although he was quietly modest about it, Johnny Vaughan must have been 'over the moon' after this win. Of the 'nap hand' that F. R. Hill refers to, four of the boxers were managed and trained by Johnny.

Following his championship success, Randy had a drawn decision against Seaman Frank Stubbs at Bristol before travelling to Crystal Palace to meet Tommy Tucker of Preston.

It was a ten-round contest which Jones fought cleverly, keeping Tucker at a distance with his greater reach. Tucker was slow by comparison and had difficulty penetrating the Welsh champion's defence. At close quarters Tucker was more effective but Jones made him miss repeatedly with rights to the body. Randy Jones was the clear winner.

He followed this with another good points win over twelve rounds against Jack Marshall on 17th April.

By the end of July 1933, Johnny Vaughan would have had a complete nap hand of his own when another of his boxers, Bobby Morgan (Abertridwr) beat Billy Hughes of Maesteg on 29th July for the Welsh flyweight title. Unfortunately, this was scuppered by Tommy Farr who took the cruiserweight title from Randy Jones on 22nd July at Tonypandy!

NEW CRUISERWEIGHT CHAMPION

After seeing Tommy Farr beat Jerry Daley so roundly a little while back I predicted it would not be long before he wrested the Welsh cruiserweight title from Randy Jones. Well, Farr accomplished this when the pair met over fifteen rounds at Tonypandy with the Rhondda lad winning nicely on points. Jones fought well and there were times when some of his punches might have caused trouble had Farr been less alert, but the latter was undoubtedly the better boxer and well earned the decision.

Boxing, 26th July 1933

The *Amman Valley Chronicle* recorded that 'Randy Jones was slow, but always a trier, and even in the last round caught Farr on the jaw with a right that staggered the challenger.'

This was the second time Randy Jones faced Farr in the ring. A couple of months earlier on 6th May, he failed to go the distance, retiring after the sixth round in a non-title bout.

> Randy Jones, the light-heavyweight champion, figured in a surprise result at Merthyr where he was beaten by Tommy Farr, Clydach Vale, the fight ending at the beginning of the seventh round. The Ammanford boy had sustained a leg injury in the previous round and was unable to answer the bell.
>
> Until this point the contest had been an excellent one with both men showing their best form, but Farr was ahead on points when the fight ended. There was little in-fighting during six fast sessions, both men preferring long-range tactics in which Jones was more aggressive. Farr however, was the faster, and was more astute in taking advantage of scoring opportunities. His left was seen at its best, continually snaking through Jones's guard to establish contact with the champion's face, while his footwork kept him out of danger when Randy started effective countering.
>
> *Amman Valley Chronicle*, May 1933.

It was hardly a disgrace to lose against a man whom many would say was the greatest British heavyweight of all time, but as far as I can ascertain, Randy had only four more fights after the title fight with Farr; the last being an eliminator for another crack at the cruiserweight title, still held by Farr.

The eliminator was his fourth contest against Charlie Bundy, and again took place at the Mannesmann Hall in Swansea, on 17th February 1934. *Boxing* reported the fight under a heading which turned out to be over-optimistic:

RANDY JONES TO MEET FARR

By outpointing Charlie Bundy . . . over fifteen rounds, Randy Jones earned the right to meet Tommy Farr, the Welsh cruiserweight champion in a title contest. It was from Jones that Farr wrested the title some time ago. Though beaten on Saturday night, Bundy put up the best performance of his career. Jones was taller and longer in reach but did not get into his stride until the eighth round. Up to that point Bundy had forced the issue and scored heavily to the body. He was generally the stronger, but Jones boxed much better from the ninth round on, using the ring cleverly and timing his leads better than Bundy to gain the verdict by a narrow margin of points.

By way of contrast, the *Amman Valley Chronicle* was unusually damning in its report of the bout.

Randy Jones, Ammanford, earned the right to fight Kid Farr, Clydach Vale, for the cruiserweight championship of Wales, as a result of his points victory over Charlie Bundy, Treherbert, at the Mannesmann Hall, Swansea, but the fight, though a title eliminator, never rose above mediocrity.

Really, the least said the better, for neither man did well enough to justify him appearing in a championship bout, there being so much that was amateurish in their work, while neither of them made a fight of it. There were more yawns during this contest than any other Mr Johnny Vaughan has put on.

The decision of Mr Ben Hardwicke in giving the fight to Jones was not popular with a section of the crowd.

Randy Jones never did meet Tommy Farr in the ring again.

Following the eliminator contest with Bundy and the local press comment, he and Johnny had a heart-to heart; no doubt weighing up Randy's future moves. Johnny does not record what his advice was and maybe Randy thought he'd gone as far as he wanted to go with his boxing career; in any case he just seems to have given up after this.

He may already have set his sights on completely different horizons because to my recollection he emigrated to Australia after the war and became a policeman.

Randy Jones.

Tommy Farr.

Tommy Farr, who had been boxing since the age of thirteen, relinquished the Welsh light-heavyweight title in 1935 and went on to take the Welsh heavyweight title in August 1936 when he beat Jim Wilde. Relinquishing this title in1937, he became British and Empire heavyweight champion in March of that year. After that his boxing career scaled ever-increasing heights peaking in his fight with Joe Louis for the World heavyweight title in August 1937. Farr was one of only three people to go the distance with the Brown Bomber during his reign as World Champion, and American fight fans were mightily impressed by him.

In America, the radio commentator made a point of saying that he rarely interviewed a loser after a fight and inviting Tommy to speak to every British fan glued to their radio set at home. As Tommy answered questions about the two cuts to his eyes, back in Wales one young hospital patient had listened to the fight wrapped in a blanket. Dennis Powell, aged twelve-and-a-half, had been given special permission from the ward sister to sit up in the day room to listen to the fight, relayed from America at three am British time! It was something he never forgot, and his boyhood hero inspired him to take up boxing himself. Like Tommy Farr, he grew up to be a heavyweight but he never dreamt that fourteen years after that night in the hospital he would be swapping punches with Tommy himself for the Welsh heavyweight title!

Bobby Morgan of Abertridwr was not managed throughout his career by Johnny, nor did he stay in training at Ammanford after he won the Welsh flyweight title in July 1933.

It was indicative of Johnny's reputation that Morgan had apparently come to him specifically to train for the Welsh title. And it was proof that Johnny deserved his reputation that Morgan won the title!

Morgan went on to have a total of around eighty-six contests, winning fifty of them. Among his opponents was Douglas Kestrell who beat him in December 1932 in a fight described by the *Western Mail* as 'Kestrell's best victory in a short but brilliant career.' However, Bobby Morgan outpointed Kestrell and then drew with him the following February. Morgan had a crack at the Welsh bantamweight title in 1934, but lost in an eliminator contest against Terence Morgan of Newport at Merthyr.

Charlie Bundy returned full-time to mining when he finished boxing, working as a collier in Llanharan. Interviewed in the 1950s by Hedley Trembath, he said: 'I am happily married, in regular work, and I always have a couple of shillings in my pocket. I've no regrets. Life has been good and I enjoyed my boxing.'

Jerry Daley retired from boxing in his prime because of an injury sustained whilst carrying his disabled father. He left Wales and moved to Bath where he worked on the railway. He was killed by a train in 1954.

An interesting footnote to this chapter is my memory of being told that in at least some of his contests, Randy Jones boxed with what I thought would be an almost impossible handicap: he had lost part of all four fingers on his right hand in an accident, being left with a thumb and knuckles only! Perhaps this was the reason he stopped boxing.

Chapter 11

The Redoubtable Ma Quinlen and Sons

When Billy Quinlen's hand was raised as lightweight champion of Wales in May 1932, he may well have offered a silent prayer of thanks for mothers.

For like many a mother, Mrs Quinlen worried that her son would get hurt, but unlike most she was always willing to lend a practical hand when it came to training, once she saw that Billy had made up his mind that he wanted to box. Thus it was that on many an evening in the kitchen of the Quinlen home in Garnswllt, near Ammanford, you could find Ma with the parlour clock, acting as timekeeper for Billy, who would be sparring with his pretty sister, Cissie! Mind you, in a valley where every other house held a would-be boxer, perhaps the neighbours didn't turn a hair.

The Quinlen family were part of the community in the tiny village by the time Billy was growing up. They had moved to Garnswllt from Fforestfach, Swansea, where Billy had been born on 6th August 1911. It was a Sunday, which Ma thought was the best day of the week to be born.

He was one of a family of four boys and four girls and he attended the village school in Garnswllt, but Billy was the first to admit he 'was never much of a scholar.'

'I remember pretty clearly that if there were any hidings to be handed out, then Billy Quinlen was usually the "goat",' he remembered. Then, with a grin, he claimed he got one hiding after the teacher asked him who wrote Shakespeare's plays and he replied: 'I don't know Miss, but it wasn't me!'

As a teenager, Billy was drawn to the gaudily painted boxing booth belonging to the Taylor family when it visited the area. The barker was shouting for challengers for the boxers who stood, arms folded, sternly surveying the crowd.

'I'll have a go!' said Billy.

'Oh no, you won't!' said his mother who was standing nearby. Somehow she was persuaded to let him get into the ring and with anxiety and pride mixed, watched her son earn a few bob by stopping his chosen opponent.

Billy's little brother Reg was named after Uncle Reg Marley who had been a handy boxer in his day—one of his opponents was Archie Rule.

Billy couldn't wait to tell Uncle Reg about his success at the fair. Ma was still worried.

'Don't fret, woman,' said Reg, 'If he wants to box, I'll sort him out —he can start sparring with the Peregrines, Cliff and Gwyn, both good boys—they'll see he's alright.'

Surrounded as they were by a community where boxing was a part of life, it was natural for the Quinlen boys to take an interest in, and then to have a go themselves at the fistic art. In the end it was Billy and Reg of the four brothers who made the grade and became professional boxers.

But when Billy had his first proper contest—an amateur bout against Tich May from Swansea—Reg was still an infant, being almost fourteen years younger than Billy.

It was Boxing Day 1928 and Billy was seventeen.

Unknown to Billy, the contest, held at the Llanelli Pavilion, was watched by Mr Johnny Vaughan from Ammanford, on the lookout as usual for promising newcomers. Billy convincingly beat young Tich, and was feeling pretty pleased with himself as he made his way was back to the cloakroom, where Johnny introduced himself. His proposition was clearly enticing enough for Billy to make his mind up. Never one to hang about, he decided there and then to 'turn pro'.

Whether his name was misspelt on a boxing bill or whether it was a deliberate decision, he seems to have boxed under the name 'Quinlan' from quite early on, but I have decided to stick to his real name 'Quinlen'.

Meantime, Billy had found work in Wernos Colliery, Ammanford, where his Dad and Uncle Reg also worked. And so whenever work and wages allowed, Ma would put plenty of good food on the table, to build her son up for the challenges ahead.

I remember Mrs Quinlen when she was in her nineties—she was still playing darts if my memory serves me right—talking about the cooking she used to do.

'Billy had plenty of good packing,' she told me, 'Steak? yes . . . he always liked it rare.'

But those were difficult times in the valleys and miners were often on short-time.

There was a surprise waiting for Billy when he got news of his first professional contest, to take place in Swansea on 12th January 1929. He had been matched with none other than Tich May, who had also made the decision to join a rival professional gym. It made no difference to the result; at the end of the six rounds, Quinlen was declared the winner.

A fortnight later he took on Jackie Lewis of Aberavon over ten two-minute rounds. Billy, feeling his way but growing in confidence, put up a good performance and there was general satisfaction in the Ammanford camp when the result was a draw. A third bout with Tich May, over ten rounds this time, resulted in another points win for Billy.

By mutual agreement between Johnny Vaughan and Taylor's and Gess's booths, Billy was sometimes loaned to one or the other for a couple of weeks, as they were often short of a boxer. Billy was always glad of the extra money even though it was a hard night's work sometimes:

> I got £1 a night—take on all comers. Sometimes it was easy and I won my quid by beating three or four . . . always bigger than me. Other times it was hard—seven or eight would claim me in the course of an evening. They were on for five bob if they lasted the distance with me.

Joe Gess presented Billy Quinlen with a cup,
still prized by the Quinlen family.

Even the decision contests were for small purses. Billy would fight ten rounds for thirty shillings. 'I was so hungry in those days that it didn't matter. Why, if Mr Johnny Vaughan, the best trainer of boxers Wales ever saw, said: "Billy, there's a meal in the pantry or you can go to Newcastle to fight" . . . it was Newcastle for me, so that the others could eat.'

Over the next three months, Billy got wins or drawn decisions against Ammanford's Peregrine brothers, Cliff and Gwyn, Dai Morris of Treherbert and Billy Granelly from Pontypridd.

On 18th May he travelled to Llanelli to meet Teddy Baldock of Treherbert over ten rounds and Billy was cock-a-hoop when he knocked Baldock out in the sixth. A couple of weeks later he was able to repeat the achievement when he knocked out Emlyn Jones of Tumble at

Carmarthen Fair in the third of a six-round contest. I think it was around this time that Joe Gess presented Billy with a large silver cup, in appreciation of his sterling efforts for the booth, which remained among his proudest possessions.

A few days after that Gwyn Peregrine went down in the fifth; the result was a technical knockout to Billy Quinlen.

'Right, Billy,' said Johnny then, 'How do you feel about meeting Stan Jehu?'

Billy had heard about Jehu, a more experienced but still up-and-coming boxer from Maesteg, who had done his share of booth fighting but had stepped up to decision contests a year or so before Billy. By all accounts Jehu was good and Johnny Vaughan had had him earmarked as a likely opponent for Billy for a while.

They met in Ammanford on 29th June in a Johnny Vaughan promotion which featured a 15-round contest between Steve 'Curly' Fay, another of Johnny's boxers, and Bryn Evans of Caerau, as the main bout. The *Amman Valley Chronicle* gave prominence to the Fay-Evans fight where the Ammanford man, Fay, 'showed much the better form' and got his opponent down twice before the referee stopped the contest in Fay's favour. But Billy and Stan Jehu got a mention: 'The meeting of Billy Quinlan (Ammanford) and Stan Jehu (Maesteg) over ten rounds resulted in a bright exhibition, which ended in a draw.'

Billy Quinlen didn't get the chance to resolve that stalemate, for he never fought Jehu after that. In February 1930 Jehu outpointed Cuthbert Taylor to win the Welsh bantamweight title but by then Quinlen was boxing at featherweight; by the time Jehu moved up to take the Welsh featherweight title from Evan Morris in December 1933, Billy had held the Welsh lightweight title for a year and a half. It must have been Ma's steak dinners!

On 27th July 1929, the Johnny Vaughan stable had another successful event on Cresci's field, Ammanford, when Ginger Jones outpointed Glyn Mainwaring of Pontardawe after putting him on the canvas in the sixth; Danny Evans beat Bert Rees from Pontyberem and Billy completed the treble with a win against Young Derrick of Llanelli.

An impressive succession of eight wins followed for Quinlen, in just over two months, including knockouts against Teddy Ward of Trealaw and Jackie Moody.

After a points win over Tommy John of Gelli in October 1929, Billy had a couple of months rest—though not from training and 'sparring' on the booth. Then in December he met Oliver Cullen of Treherbert for the second time, having beaten him in September:

> The other main event came to an unfortunate end with Billy Quinlan (Ammanford) having to retire to Oliver Cullen (Treherbert) in the third round with a badly injured eye. Quinlan worked his way to close quarters with both hands while Cullen, at an advantage in height and reach, kept his opponent at bay with long lefts. But in the third round Quinlan emerged from a bout of in-fighting with his eye cut, and the referee was obliged to intervene.
>
> In minor contests, Dave Davies (Penybanc) was beaten by Bryn Edwards (Garnant); Les Duggan (Penygraig) retired in the fourth round to Nipper Evan Thomas (Ammanford); Bob Roberts (Pentre) defeated Billy Phillips (Ystrad) on points.
>
> *Amman Valley Chronicle*

Johnny Vaughan noted in his diary that Billy sustained 'a severe gash', but he grinned at the young boxer's assertion that he would get even with Cullen, and arranged a return bout. So it was that on 18th January 1930, Billy Quinlen outpointed Oliver Cullen of Treherbert in ten rounds at Ammanford.

So far Billy's contests had been local—he was keen to follow in the footsteps of so many Welsh boxers, who had become popular, and been better paid, in venues throughout Britain. Johnny agreed, and found a fight for Billy with 'a much-fancied cockney lightweight', Billy Boulger of Canning Town. They caught the train up to London the day before the contest.

On the bright but cold afternoon of Sunday, 23rd March, a slightly apprehensive Billy arrived with his small entourage at the famous Ring at Blackfriars; there they were greeted by Archie Rule, who was living in

London by then and working for Westminster Council. What a relief it was to see another familiar figure—and such a useful one too! Billy, who loved to recall the incident, said: 'The most important thing for a fighter then and today, is to have people in the corner who have been through it. This Boulger was a southpaw and I knew little about wrong-way-round fighters, but Archie did: "Just show him the left hand and get him used to it", I was told, and I did just that.'

During the fight, the instructions came from the corner in Welsh—whether or not that could be considered an unfair advantage I cannot say. After all, an English (or Welsh) boxer would probably not understand instructions shouted from a French or German opponent's corner. At a crucial point in the tenth, Billy received the message: *'Torri o dan!'* (Cut from underneath!). According to the *South Wales Echo*: 'Billy Quinlan showed his opponent a series of left hands before pick-axeing his man with a mandrill swing with his right to the solar plexus. Boulger disappeared, an anguished flurry of arms and legs, between the top and middle ropes.' The referee intervened and Billy had won.

For good measure he beat Ted Cullen on the way home the following day, at Shrewsbury.

A week or so later Billy and Ginger Jones were back in London for a featherweight competition at Holborn. Billy got through the first series of the competition by beating Tom Cowley of Rotherham and Liverpool's Joe Humphries, in the preliminaries. In the second series on 16th April, he outpointed Les Burns of Bowes Park but met his match in the semi-finals when he lost to Tommy Lye of Acton on points.

Another trip up to Shrewsbury in May resulted in a win for Billy against Gran Jones of Wrexham, over fifteen rounds.

Over the summer of 1930 Billy's contests were all local ones; he was after all, first and foremost, a miner throughout his boxing career, which sometimes curtailed his ability to travel to distant venues (road and rail travel took a lot longer in those days and very few people had cars). But he always kept up his training and gym work.

Johnny Vaughan would have regular meetings which all his major boxers were expected to attend. Being a stickler for keeping a record of his boxers' weights, Johnny would weigh them all on the gym's scales which were frequently tested. Then he would advise the men on such things as diet, and work out with them how their training could be adjusted to suit any forthcoming contests.

Billy had six contests in Johnny Vaughan's pavilion during that summer and autumn, outpointing Billy Pritchard of Treherbert, Dan O'Connor of Pontypridd, Selwyn Davies, Maesteg, Tom Thomas, Merthyr and Dick Thomas of Ferndale. But he was beaten by Billy Evans of Ystrad, the former Welsh featherweight champion who had lost his title to Ginger Jones in September 1929.

Another good win over fifteen rounds on 1st November at Aberavon against George Williams of Treherbert, left Billy Quinlen enough time to fit in two bouts against Phineas John from Gelli before Christmas. He won them both.

Phineas John was remembered in the valleys with much affection as a fine sportsman. When he met Billy in 1930, Ted Broadribb had recently become his manager, so Phineas became one of 'Snowball's Sensational Star Scrappers', as Broadribb called his boxers. (In his fighting days, Broadribb had boxed under the name 'Young Snowball'). Ted Broadribb had marketing ideas way ahead of his time. His boxers all wore shorts with a big 'S' logo on the left side and were thus instantly recognisable.

Phineas moved his family up to London in 1931 and centred his boxing career there; an immediate improvement in his record showed it had been a good move, as he recorded nineteen wins that year, with three draws and only three defeats. In 1933, the *News Chronicle* and the *Sporting Life* put up a gold belt to be contested by the best sixteen featherweight contenders in Britain, the idea being to match the winner with the champion Nel Tarleton. Phineas won the competition, outpointing Benny Sharkey in the final, but as Phineas and Nel Tarleton were both managed by Ted Broadribb, that title fight was never on.

Phineas John boxed until 1940. His last appearances were exhibition bouts for the armed forces. The family moved back to Wales in 1946 and Phineas was a founder member of the Welsh ex-Boxer's Association when it was started in 1976. He died in 1985.

January 1931 brought another trip away for Billy—up to Shrewsbury, where he had become quite popular. This time his contest with Roy Beresford of Burslem ended in a draw, on 5th January. The following day, he caught a train down to Bristol, where he met Young McManus from Plymouth at Bedminster Arcade Hall on 7th January, but Billy lost to him over ten rounds. After this one defeat Billy had a brilliant year, recording seventeen wins and three draws up to December, including two very satisfying wins over the distance against Tommy Lye from Acton, who had defeated Billy in the previous year's featherweight competition. He beat Harry 'Kid' Berry of Bethnal Green at Ilford, Jack Glover of Barnsley, twice, at Newcastle and Tom Bailey, Liverpool, at Ammanford.

On 14th September, Billy knocked out Tom Thomas of Merthyr in the ninth round at Ammanford and he won a return match with Billy Boulger at Whitechapel in October when Boulger retired in the sixth round.

Perhaps he was resting on his laurels a little after another win at Newcastle, this time against Teddy Brown of Forest Hall, because he only had one fight scheduled for November. He quite easily outpointed Harold Ratchford from Oldham at Sheffield on 3rd November, but then lost a comparatively straightforward contest with Walt Saunders of Clydach at Trealaw on 5th December. Billy finished up the year with a repeat performance: a good win against Birmingham's Bert Taylor at Leeds Brunswick Stadium followed by a defeat at Dowlais by Nobby Baker of Trealaw on 18th December.

He lost no time in compensating for this last defeat however, by beating Nobby Baker over fifteen rounds on New Year's Day, 1932.

Christmas should be a period of 'good will to all men', but in 1931 that desirable state unfortunately did not include Billy Quinlen and Johnny Vaughan. Following his usual practice, Johnny had arranged for a return match between Billy and Walt Saunders, because Billy had lost to the Clydach man. However, he and Billy were unable to agree on the terms for the fight which had already been advertised for Boxing Day. Billy dug his heels in and refused to fight, to the fury of Johnny

Vaughan who was forced to spend part of Boxing Day pasting 'cancelled' stickers over the posters advertising the event.

The bad feeling remained between them well into the New Year, and Billy never did get in the ring with Walt Saunders for a return contest.

As luck would have it, there was even more controversy surrounding Billy's next fight, scheduled as a contest with Al Foreman at Sheffield Drill Hall, but this time the boot was on the other foot, so to speak. It was Billy's opponent who pulled out of the contest, arranged for 26th January.

The *Carmarthen Journal* quoted a letter from 'well-known boxing critic, Mr F. P. Ward, to *Boxing, Racing and Football* regarding the absence of Al Foreman . . . from his arranged fight with Billy Quinlen':

WHY THE QUINLEN-FOREMAN FIGHT WAS CANCELLED

BOMBSHELL OF UNPLEASANT KIND

A bombshell of a very unpleasant kind was hurled at the promoters of the big boxing programme to be staged at the Drill Hall, Sheffield. The principal contest was to be between Al Foreman and Billy Quinlen of Wales—the contract had already been signed and considerable expense incurred in special publicity. The first shock for the promoters was the receipt of a telegram late on the evening of January 20th which read: 'Al injured. May not be able to box'.

On Thursday last, one of the promoters ……….. was told Foreman had hurt his hand in training, and although not serious, it was thought inadvisable to try it out on such a first-class man as Quinlen.

(The promoters) sent the following telegram: 'Seeing you refuse to box Quinlen, have obtained substitute and shall claim forfeit'.

The substitute was Johnny Kid Clarke who, according to some reports, was the Army featherweight champion in India. However, though he put up a courageous fight he never looked like winning:

In every round Clarke absorbed an avalanche of terrific two-handed blows to the face, Quinlen going in relentlessly. Before the end of every round, it could only have been his tremendous will-power that kept him on his feet. Well into the sixth round these lads fought toe-to-toe, Quinlen ripping in scores of blows, yet Clarke kept on doggedly. It was not until the sixth round that Quinlen's fusillade of blows crashed Clarke to the mat for the full count.

WARD'S IMPRESSION

Summed up, my impression of Quinlen is this: if Foreman wants a real test, with the probability of being more than fully extended then Billy Quinlen is his man.

Some weeks went by before Billy resumed his training in Johnny's gym. With confidence fully restored on both sides, Johnny was keen to tell Billy that he was now the main contender to meet Alby Kestrell for the Welsh lightweight title, and to begin his training regime straight away. First there were a couple of engagements to honour. They travelled up to Sheffield again, by way of Middlesborough, where Billy outpointed Teddy Brown again at their second meeting. At Sheffield he met a new opponent, Sonny Lee of Leeds, and beat him over fifteen rounds.

Eighteen days later, Billy stepped confidently into the ring to face Alby Kestrell.

Under the heading 'Another Welsh Boxing Title Comes "West"', the *Carmarthen Journal* ran the following report:

. . . Quinlen punched with crispness, and as most of these were delivered from short range it is possible that their effect may have been lost on the audience, but few were prepared for so summary a victory. At that stage, the bout had reached interesting lines, and much of their work was well up to championship standard.

Kestrell, following his usual custom, cut out the pace with fast leads to the face, using the ring carefully and having an excellent guard for the chin with his right. Quinlen relied mainly on short, swinging punches, and fast footwork in order to secure position to put power behind his punches.

Kestrell took toll of Quinlen's face in consequence and had obtained a slight points lead by the end of the third round. Quinlen was improving gradually however, and it was noticed that Kestrell faltered towards the end of this session when Quinlen changed feet like lightning and caught Kestrell with a short left hook to the stomach.

Before Kestrell could recover, Quinlen brought over his right to the jaw and followed with a fast uppercut. Kestrell resumed the fourth round with respect stalking his every move. He did not now attempt to carry the fight to Quinlen, but seemed content to allow Quinlen a little more scope. If he meant to learn something of Quinlen's methods and general skill, he certainly succeeded; but it was a costly experience. With Kestrell's left temporarily aside, Quinlen brought his own shorter reach into play, and he not only got plenty of accuracy and sting into these leads, but contrived to vary his targets and weapons. Kestrell was obviously alarmed by the change of events, for he fell back on the ropes for support, while he countered with rights. It seemed at the end of the sixth round—by which time Quinlen had taken over the points lead—that Kestrell had shot his bolt.

The pace had been unusually hot, though not to an extent as to disturb Kestrell, but his feet lagged when he got out of the corner in the seventh session. He shot a number of excellent lefts to the face and steadied Quinlen with a hard right to the body, but Quinlen had engendered great confidence by now, and forced Kestrell into a neutral corner. Quinlen feinted with his left, and Kestrell lurched forward as if to clinch before getting away. Quinlen instantly stepped back and brought up a right uppercut. The glove seemed to land on Kestrell's shorts, although the blow did not appear to be particularly heavy. Kestrell 'hung suspended' in mid-air for a brief second and a cry of 'Foul!' disturbed the atmosphere. A moment later, Kestrell dropped to the boards, and without hesitation Mr Will Bevan proceeded with the count. It was a clever victory for Quinlen because he was travelling like a certain winner when the end came, but the knock-out did not give that all-satisfying thrill associated with it.

Randy Jones (Pontardulais) defeated Jimmy Wilde (Swansea) over ten excellent rounds. Hartley Griffiths (Glanamman) defeated Jim O'Flaherty (Swansea) on points over six rounds.

Jubilation, nonetheless, was brought to the Ammanford camp by this victory: Billy's lightweight title was the third Welsh championship for Johnny Vaughan's stable. Again it was followed very quickly by a defeat, at Merthyr by Norman Snow of Northampton, when Billy was dis-qualified in the seventh round.

He enjoyed a series of six wins during the summer of 1932, notably over George Kelly in Dublin and Douglas Parker of Sunderland at Middlesborough. Parker was 'a terrific hitter' according to Billy, 'and I doubt if I ever met a fighter with a more vicious punch.'

Billy was to beat Parker three times in all. A friend of Billy's later described the encounters between the two: 'When Billy and Doug used to meet at the St James' Hall in Newcastle, they used to knock sparks off each other, like a blacksmith off an anvil!'

He scored a knockout against Glyn Mainwaring of Pontardawe in the fourth round. But October brought less good news.

After losing to Scot Johnny McMillan on a technical knockout at Glasgow, Billy had been matched with a very fine boxer, Ernie Roderick at Liverpool. Roderick was to become Nel Tarleton's brother-in-law, and had only just started on his successful career when he and Billy met on 20th October 1932. He was eighteen years old to Billy's twenty-one.

The contest took place on the opening night of Liverpool's posh New Stadium in St Paul's Square as part of a Johnny Best promotion, with Alf Howard and Stoker Reynolds top-lining in a welterweight contest. Johnny Best was the managing director of the New Stadium.

In his book *Lonsdale's Belt*, John Harding described Roderick as: 'An extremely clever boxer, he would exploit a stiff left lead with a superb right cross that ended many of his early contests inside the distance.'

This being the case, perhaps Billy did very well to last the full ten three-minute rounds, but it was the younger man's hand that was raised at the finish, after what the *Liverpool Evening Post* described as a narrow points victory.

Although Ernie Roderick did not get a title chance for another seven years,when he KO'd Jake Kilrain in March 1939 to lift the British welterweight title, he already had a very impressive record. He held the British welterweight title until 1948, successfully defending it four times and winning his Lonsdale Belt outright. He also won the British middleweight title, outpointing Vince Hawkins in 1945, and the European welterweight title in 1946, beating Omar Kouidri.

Following a couple of draws, in Manchester with Jim Learoyd, and in Leeds with Johnny Britton, Billy Quinlen beat Jack Davies of Ashton-under-Lyne, over twelve two-minute rounds.

On 2nd December, he successfully defended his Welsh title by out-pointing Alby Kestrell at Trealaw, cementing his earlier victory over the previous champion. The *Western Mail* reported the fight:

> The contest was too keen to be spectacular, but the contrast in styles kept the audience on tip-toe of excitement.
>
> Quinlen was always threatening to bring the bout to a premature close, and at the end of the seventh round Kestrell took so much punishment that he was expected to go down any moment, the bell coming to his assistance.
>
> Kestrell kept his left lead going and Quinlen had to take this punch in order to get to close quarters. Once he got there he was easily superior.
>
> Quinlen was much the stronger from the eighth round, and Kestrell slipped to the floor from sheer weakness on three occasions. He made a fine start in the thirteenth round, but was out on his feet in the last session. Quinlen was a clear points winner.

He finished up the year with a points win over Nobby Baker, at their third meeting which came about because Baker was substituting for Young McManus of Plymouth.

1933 began badly for Billy with two losses, one on a disqualification against Tommy Little of Notting Hill, in January. Then after losing on points to Jim Learoyd of Leeds in February, Billy didn't have another contest until 14th May, when he drew with Nipper Cooper of Leeds, at Middlesborough. A week later, the two met again and this time Billy outpointed the Yorkshireman. A period of ill-health seems to have dogged Billy during this time and resulted in fewer contests and a falling off in form in 1933.

A new challenger for Billy's Welsh title appeared: Evan Lane of Tre-orchy. The contest took place at Llanelli Working Men's Club on 6th June 1933, and it went the distance with Billy retaining his lightweight championship.

The *Carmarthen Journal* reported:

> There was a distinct contrast in styles, Quinlen favouring the inside position while Lane was more at home with long range. Both were cautious during the first five rounds; Lane appeared to be doing well in the matter of tactics and Quinlen, while punching with more power and precision, had to confine himself to countering until the tenth round.
>
> Lane continued to do well and appeared to be ahead slightly on points till the twelfth round. But Quinlen was much stronger afterwards and punched Lane more accurately in the last session in order to acquire the narrow margin of points that enabled him to remain lightweight champion of Wales.

In July he travelled to Liverpool Stadium to fight Chester's Jimmy Walsh but Billy was disqualified for fouling his opponent after six rounds. In 1936, Jimmy Walsh was to beat Jack Kid Berg to take the British lightweight title, later defending it successfully against Harry Mizler.

Just over a week after his encounter with Walsh, Billy Quinlen stopped Billy Pritchard in the fourth round at Ammanford.

Some good news arrived at the Ammanford Athletic Club: the Board of Control had sanctioned an eliminator contest for the British lightweight title between Billy Quinlen and Tommy Spiers of Glasgow, to take place on 23rd September, and Ammanford Athletic Club was chosen as offering the best purse for the fight. On 30th August, Johnny Vaughan sent contracts out to both boxers.

The fight was held at Llanelli, with the *Western Mail* looking forward to a 'clash of Celts' and giving both boxers a good build-up, though mentioning that Quinlen had:

> . . . not boxed as frequently as some would have liked since his illness. On the other hand, he has the capacity for taking hard punches without getting duly upset and his unorthodox style and fighting qualities at close range are the kind that put a good boxer off.

BOXING!

PAVILION, LLANELLY
SATURDAY, SEPTEMBER 23rd, 1933

Doors open at 6; First Contest at 7 p.m. prompt
Chief Contest at or about 8-20 p.m.

British Eliminating Light-weight Championship

Great 15 3-minute Rounds Contest—

TOMMY SPIERS v. BILLY QUINLEN

(Glasgow) Official Light-weight
Champion of Scotland.

(Ammanford) Official Light-weight
Champion of Wales.

Also other Contests

RESERVED, 5/9 (including Tax)   76

Jones & Mainwaring. Ammanford

However, the dice seems to be loaded in favour of Spiers if form is accepted as a true guide, and should Quinlen emerge the victor, we might reasonably expect the championship to come the way of Ammanford.

In front of a crowd of almost 4,000 fight fans, and contrary to expectations, Billy proved superior. Very few of the audience agreed with referee Jim Kenrick's verdict of a draw.

About a quarter of them staged a protest after the decision, refusing to leave for about ten minutes.

The Scot's defence was reduced to a right-hand parry and a curious lunge with head down in order to smother Quinlen's attacks, and his left, only in real evidence after the ninth round, assumed a downward flight of chopping character that was of little value because Quinlen's head work was so well-timed.

Spiers had no style to speak of, and here the difference between them was most emphasised. Spiers kept his feet so close together that he was

144

unable to regain his poise after he missed his target. For the same reason he was sent floundering, into the ropes, and on four occasions he slipped to the boards when, with a deft body twist, Quinlen avoided his attacks. Quinlen made . . . profitable use of the corners and ropes where his footwork was much superior. Had (Quinlen's) attack been as fine as his admittedly superior defence, Spiers would hardly have lasted out because the latter gave the impression he was not certain of his stamina. Spiers revealed how apprehensive he was in the last session when he swung blows from all angles, every one of which earned the description of haymaker, and in my view, did not belong to championship class.

In supporting contests, Len Williams, Llanelli defeated Llew Edwards, Ammanford, on points; Don Rees, Swansea, was forced to retire in the fifth round, to Idris Davies, Pontardulais and Reg Owen, Dafen, boxed a draw with Dave Williams of Blaenau.

Another strong contender for the British title towards the end of 1933 was the twenty-one year old Harry Mizler, of St Georges, in the heart of the East End. His parents had a fish stall in Watney Street Market off the Commercial Road, where Harry (known by his friends as Hymie), worked alongside his brothers, Moe and Judah. When he wasn't doing that he was training at the gym at the Ring, Blackfriars. In contrast to the flashier Jack Kid Berg, he was quiet and thoughtful, a neat conservative dresser who took his purse money straight home instead of going out to celebrate after a fight.

As an amateur featherweight, he had been chosen for the Olympic Games in Los Angeles in 1932, though he was surprisingly defeated in the first round.

A strange quirk of fate now intervened in Billy's career: his next two fights were both eliminators for the British title and he won both of them on disqualifications!

The first was a decider—because they had previously drawn—between Billy and Tommy Spiers on 13th January 1934 at Swansea's Mannesmann Hall; it ended when Spiers fouled Quinlen in the eighth round. Spiers had started well in the early rounds, but Quinlen got going after the fourth and his right did a lot of damage.

145

In the eighth and last round, Quinlen had got home some telling punches and had more than levelled the points when in a mix-up he was struck low and went down. He was scrambling to his feet at the end of the count, when the referee, Mr Dohy, Watford, had no hesitation in stopping the fight and giving the verdict to Quinlen.

Douglas Parker was his opponent on 5th February at Newcastle, for the final eliminator, when in the sixth round, the referee disqualified Parker for fouling. Mixed blessing though it was—after all it meant he got through the eliminators—this painful episode may have been a factor in Billy's apparent lack of enthusiasm during the following weeks.

In the meantime, Harry Mizler had become British lightweight champion by beating Johnny Cuthbert on 18th January at the Albert Hall:

> The Londoner repeatedly stabbed back Cuthberts' head with his im-maculate straight lefts, although the champion never stopped trying to unload with powerful rights.
> The pattern was maintained and by the last third of the contest, Mizler had gained the ascendancy which he was to keep.
> —Barry Hugman

Showing commendable generosity, Cuthbert was reported as saying: 'This is the way I have always wanted to go out of the game. We have a grand fighter to take my place.'

Victor Berliner, Mizler's manager, sent a telegram to Johnny Vaughan stating that arrangements could be started for his man Mizler to meet Billy Quinlen in a contest for the British title.

But the two did not meet until 4th August.

Billy had a very poor run-up to this vital chance to make a name for himself and attract the bigger purses he had always thought he deserved. For one thing, relations between Johnny and Billy seemed to have soured again. There are indications in the diaries that Billy's training was not as intense as it certainly needed to be at this time, though Johnny Vaughan was in constant negotiations to ensure the best purse and venue for this important contest. It seems that some of Billy Quinlen's backers were also in dispute with Johnny.

In April 1934, Billy lost two fights; he was outpointed by Liverpool's Frankie Brown at Leeds over twelve rounds, and he was forced to retire in the fifth round against George Bunter of West Hartlepool. He did not have another contest until 11th June, when he met Norman Snow—also a strong lightweight contender—for the second time, and lost to him on points.

Things were not going well.

In the mine, Billy was now working on the coal-face and was probably drawing a better wage. Perhaps that, together with family commitments, had given Billy a new perspective. If so, it was a shame that he chose this never-to-be-repeated time of opportunity to seemingly put less effort in.

Fortunately, when it was almost too late, Billy found someone to step in, to train and advise him: Dai Nancurvis, father of Cliff and Brian Curvis, who both grew up to become British and Empire (Commonwealth) welterweight champions in the fifties and sixties, respectively. Dai was already a very respected trainer in Swansea, when Billy joined his training camp and was given the opportunity to spar with boxers like the great Len Beynon.

It meant that Billy was fit and in the right frame of mind to meet the British champion, and at their pre-fight meeting and later at the weigh-in, it was a confident-looking Billy who smiled into the camera as he shook Mizler's hand.

Climbing into the ring on 4th August, Billy looked around for Johnny Vaughan's face in the crowd. It wasn't there.

For a British title fight, the crowd on the Vetch Field, Swansea, was disappointing—around 6,000.

Trying to overcome his mixed emotions, Billy sprang up at the sound of the bell for round one of fifteen.

Programme

One—10-Round Feather-weight Contest
IVOR DREW v. TERENCE MORGAN
(Trealaw)   (Newport)

Two—12-Round Contest
HARRY BROOKS v. FRED CARPENTER
(London)   (Merthyr)

Three—15 Rounds 3 Minutes each.
The Light-weight Championship of Great Britain
Weigh-in 9st. 9lbs. at 2 p.m. on Day of Contest

HARRY MIZLER
(London) Official Light-weight Champion of Great Britain

BILLY QUINLEN
(WALES) Official Challenger for the Title

Four—8-Round Bantam Contest
RONNIE JAMES v. FRANK SWEETMAN
(Swansea) W GsF   (Mountain Ash)

First Contest 7.15 p.m. prompt ;   Championship Contest 8.30 p.m. prompt

*At the Vetch Field, Swansea, Harry Mizler defended
his British title against Billy Quinlen.*

QUINLEN BEATEN

As a British championship, said the *Western Mail*, it was very mediocre. But it is to be said in the Welshman's favour that he gave a far better display than expected. After the first five rounds, Quinlen brought all his energy to bear on bustling tactics and, on more than one occasion during the middle of the bout, Mizler was in 'Queer Street'. Indeed, had he been a little steadier in the seventh round when Mizler sapped at the knees, the Welshman might even have been champion. It was not until the opening of the fourteenth round when Mizler adopted tactics best-suited, that he made victory certain, because Quinlen had practically wiped out the points he had made up till the fifth round.

There was an angry demonstration from a section of the audience when the verdict was known, hundreds running across the field from the cheap bank to demonstrate their disapproval. They crowded round the ringside seats and booed the champion.

Boxing had only a slightly different slant on the fight:

CRISP PUNCHES

Although he [*Mizler*] won on points over the championship distance, his form was disappointing. Harry started brilliantly and the contest began to develop a one-sided atmosphere but the Londoner was not punching hard and gradually lost the initiative. He looked stale or over-trained and fought back only in patches while Quinlen gradually mounted up his score.

In the last round Mizler suddenly realised his position and walked in determinedly and confidently. He scored with fine, crisp punches to the head and had the Welshman in a bad way. But if the rally had come earlier in the contest his victory might have been more decisive. Fortunately for him, many of Quinlen's punches were nullified because they were delivered with the open glove.

Mizler explained afterwards that he was handicapped by an extremely soft ring floor which affected his footwork. But the lack of fire in his performance could not be attributed to just that.

In spite of everything that had gone before, Billy's late efforts and brave performance brought him within a whisker of winning the British title. That was certainly the view of most, and some thought he had had it stolen from him. The most notable exception to that opinion was of course, the referee, whom I believe was W. Barrington Dalby. For the second time in his bid for the British title, Billy experienced the heart-felt support of his fans as they objected loudly to the referee's verdict.

Billy himself felt the decision was dubious: 'I finished up so fresh,' he said, 'that I felt I could go another fifteen. I was told by my corner that all I had to do was stay on my feet and I had won . . . but Mizler got the decision.'

He bore no grudge in later life. 'I'd like to meet Harry again—he was a good fighter. There couldn't have been much in it but he got the decision.'

Two months later, on 29th October 1934, Mizler lost the British lightweight title to Jack Kid Berg. Now if things had turned out differently at the Vetch, that would have been a fight my Dad would have loved to have seen: Billy Quinlen against Jack Kid Berg!

A sequel to this fight was a story that was doing the rounds: Jack La Rue, a well-known American film actor, who usually played a bad guy in the gangster films that were popular then, made a personal appearance at the Ring, Blackfriars. In pantomime tradition, the audience booed him, whereupon he feigned indignation and wise-cracked: 'If youse guys don't quit yellin' I'll fetch my friend Harry Mizler!' A voice from the crowd came loud and clear: 'Bring Billy Quinlen and we'd be frightened!'

For this memorable fight, Billy received £125—which he said was by far the most he ever got paid. Yes, it was a lot of money in those days, but considering he often got paid as little as £12, and bearing in mind that he fought the best boxers at his weight in Britain, you could understand Billy's point of view that the purses were often not enough for the men who took the punches.

In October he lost his Welsh title to Boyo Rees at the Mountain Ash Pavilion by a knockout in the ninth round.

The contest was part of a countrywide campaign to boost the funds set up after the Gresford Colliery disaster in North Wales, which had occurred a month earlier, on 22nd September 1934. Twenty percent of the takings were donated to the funds.

The Gresford disaster was one of Britain's worst ever mining accidents; 266 men died in the most horrific underground fires following a massive explosion. Sir Stafford Cripps, the miners' legal representative, cited the disaster as a reason for nationalising the mining industry, which was eventually achieved in 1946, with The Coal Industry Nationalisation Act.

On the same night, Jack Petersen boxed an exhibition at a tournament in aid of the fund, and presented a souvenir handkerchief to be auctioned to add more to the coffers.

Along with fellow miners, the length and breadth of Britain, Billy mourned the terrible loss of life. The loss of his Welsh title added to his despondency.

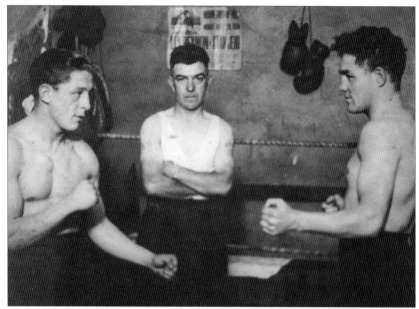

*Billy Quinlen spars with Len Beynon in preparation for his British
title fight under the supervision of Dai Nancurvis.*

After this contest, there were five more recorded fights up to February 1935 but only one win: against his old adversary Douglas Parker at Newcastle.

Before the spring and after his daughter was born, Billy 'hung up his gloves' for good.

As the years went by, he took less and less interest in boxing, but after a mining accident in 1941 he expressed the view that if he had his time over again: 'I would go in for boxing in preference to coal-mining. They never carried me out of the ring, but they did carry me on a stretcher out of the pit. These scars,' he would say, touching his flattened nose, 'are nothing compared to those I got underground. It happened in 1941 when I was working in the East Pit, Gwauncaegurwen. I was knocked out by a fall of rock, broke both legs, damaged my left hand and received back injuries which meant I had to be switched to light duties on the surface when I finally returned to work.'

A few years before he died in 1982, I remember asking Billy if he'd watched last night's fight on TV. He showed little interest and said he never watched them: 'Fighters are not hungry any more,' he'd say. 'They're not as good or as tough as in the old days and there are too few in the game looking after the youngsters. If you've done it, you can teach it—if you haven't, all you can do is talk about it . . . and there's too much talk these days.'

Nine years after big brother Billy's last fight, Mrs Quinlen was more resigned to it when young Reg went into the professional game.

It was wartime—February 1944—and Reg was eighteen years old. He had been given the opportunity to appear at the Queensberry All Services Club at the London Casino. This Club was the brainchild of the Marquis himself, who used his influence to persuade commanding officers to release their best boxers now and again to appear at the Club. It became an effective and popular way of ensuring that professional boxing was kept 'alive' during the war years. Reg appeared on a bill where the top-liner was a light-heavyweight contest between Freddie Mills and Bert Gilroy of Airdrie.

Both Ron Olver and Gibert Odd, later of *Boxing News*, were there to see it.

> During a spot of leave in the early part of 1944, I managed to slip into the Queensberry Club . . .
>
> . . . On the same bill, an eighteen-year-old Welsh Lad from Ammanford named Reg Quinlan was making his pro debut against Tommy Foxall.
>
> Immediately my mind flashed back to another boxer who bore that somewhat uncommon name—a certain Billy Quinlan—whom I remembered seeing Harry Mizler meet at Swansea ten years earlier.
>
> I never found out why Reg should come all that way, especially in wartime, when travelling wasn't easy. However, he gained a commendable points win over Tommy, and looked a useful prospect.

After this impressive start to his boxing career, Reg had only three other contests in 1944 and only two in 1945. The first of these ended in a draw with Harry Cartwright in April 1944 at Walsall—a situation resolved in July when he beat Cartwright on points over six rounds at Tipton. But the other four contests were all wins for Reg, including KOs against Dave Williams up in Brynamman, and Jack Todd of Sunderland in Walsall.

The latter fight, in November 1945, was an even more impressive performance by young Reg. *Boxing News* reported that he had knocked out his opponent in the first round: 'A right to the jaw quickly floored Todd for nine, and a terrific left, followed by a right uppercut, dropped him again to be counted out. It was all over in 95 seconds.'

After that, he became popular with the Walsall crowd, and was back there for three more excellent wins in the early part of 1946. On 7th January, he stopped Jimmy Anderson in three rounds; it took him four rounds to stop Hughie Smith in February, after flooring him three times. At 9st.10lbs., Reg was conceding nearly five pounds in this contest.

A month later, again in Walsall, he knocked out Jimmy Jury in six rounds.

Meanwhile, back in Trealaw, he had had a good points win over Wally Downes. *Boxing News* reported: 'Wally was undefeated as a pro, and in his Service life had boxed in America. Reg demonstrated that a straight left is the shortest and quickest way to travel to a given point, and his left glove found an easy target!'

If Reg thought he was almost invincible after his early success, he was brought down to earth by a run of four losses, three of them in a disastrous three weeks in May. Again conceding weight, he made his Liverpool debut against tough Irishman, Dan McAllister, on 9th May and got knocked out in the first round. Angry with himself over his first defeat, Reg pleaded for a quick return and got it a fortnight later, when he was half a pound lighter than at their first meeting. However, he put up a huge fight and narrowly lost on points: 'these two hard-punching boys put up a great show and thrilled the audience by their game display,' said *Boxing News*.

The effort had taken a lot out of Reg and it would have been wiser to leave the return with McAllister until a later date because, on 31st

May 1946, he entered the ring at Trealaw to fight Vernon Ball of Cwm-parc, in an eliminator for the Welsh lightweight title.

According to Vernon Ball, in his autobiography, *For the Love of the Game*, he had suffered a bout of influenza in early May and had been weakened by it, but:

> . . . on Saturday, May 25th, I did my last shift in the colliery before the fight with Reg Quinlan By the following Wednesday I had wound up my training, and had a day's rest. I had never had it so good; the purse was to be £100—£60 for the winner and £40 for the loser.
>
> . . . the day before I fought Quinlan, Mr Davies, the promoter, and the inspector of the local police station called in and wanted to know what kind of physical shape I was in for the fight, as they had covered all the bets that the Ammanford Police Station had put down. They wanted to know what I thought of my chances—but I always went in with the same attitude, that I'd be there at the end.

Reg Quinlen was outpointed though for once he had the weight advantage. He had made the mistake of letting Ball set the pace from the start of the contest, with the result that he began to drop behind in the point scoring, although his counter-punching enabled him to make up some leeway. At the end of the ninth there was not much in it and Ball came out in the tenth and last to set about his man. Reg joined in and they had a terrific spell of in-fighting that had the crowd thrilled. Coming away, Vernon caught his man with a wicked right hook to the jaw that almost had him down.

By using the ring, Quinlen managed to avoid Ball's efforts to score a knockout, but he was on the defensive most of the time and the referee made him the loser. At least the Ton Pentre policemen were pleased!

Tired and dispirited, Reg had a couple of months lay-off before meeting Merthyr's Eddie Thomas at Aberdare. Thomas was a young lightweight then, and Reg was the favourite at the start of the six-round bout, but Thomas also 'set the pace from the start' according to Gilbert Odd:

. . . but if he thought he had an easy job that night at Aberdare, he was very much mistaken. In Quinlan he found an opponent very much of his mettle, whose stinging left hand played havoc with Eddie's nose in the early rounds.

When they came up for the last it looked as though Thomas was going to come unstuck, but he saw a momentary opening in the Ammanford man's defence and whipped over a right to the jaw that dropped Reggie for eight. It looked as though the Merthyr star was going to score a knockout victory, for he had Quinlan on the boards again for seven from a left hook, and in a bad way, when the bell came to his rescue.

Thomas was given the verdict, though it was generally agreed that it was by a very close margin.

Eddie Thomas found a good source of boxing opponents in Ammanford, beating Don Chiswell in 1946, and Billy Walker in 1947.

It was October 1946 before Reg finally got another win, and it was in his 'lucky' town of Walsall again that he stopped Wally Davis in two rounds.

Incredibly, like brother Billy five years earlier, Reg was involved in an accident in his work as striker to a colliery blacksmith, and badly injured. He had to have eight months away from boxing to recover and rest, and so it was 6th June 1947 that he met Jimmy Jury at West Bromwich. Reg must have fully recovered by then because, true to his old form, he knocked out Jury in the fourth round after flooring him four times.

There followed four points wins and a knockout that year. Reg beat Billy Barton over eight rounds at Liverpool on 14th August, and, less than a week later, scored a win over Ivor Simpson at Bristol, whom he also outpointed two months later in Birmingham. In November he beat Billy 'Kid' Brookes over eight rounds at Gloucester, finishing up the month and his boxing year with a knockout in three rounds against Johnny Fitzpatrick.

The winter months wore on, Christmas 1947 came and went quietly with Britain still suffering austerity after the war, and 1948 arrived. The long evenings were often whiled away in the Quinlen household with sparring sessions. Now Reg benefited from the support of his mother, just as brother Billy had, but now there was a new sparring partner: Billy and Reg's sixteen-year-old brother, Roy.

And nobody cheered louder than he when Reg scored two more points wins in the New Year, against Ernie Thompson over eight rounds at Willenhall, and Johnny Carrington, again over eight rounds, in what was to be Reg's last contest in his favourite venue, in Walsall.

A probable reason for Reg Quinlen's fights being mostly outside Wales is that he did not opt for a local boxing manager—through most of his career he was managed by Jack King. It seemed to suit Reg very well, though not being seen much in Wales could have been the reason why it took him so long to get a Welsh title fight.

In the spring of 1948, he had two defeats on the trot: Ben Duffy of Jarrow stopped him in the fifth round and a trip up to Walworth, London, ended in a defeat at the hands of George Daly. Known as 'The Last of the Mechanics' because of his skills, Daly got the verdict over eight rounds, although Quinlen had put his man down briefly in round six.

Back in Wales in July, Reg had no problem with his first eliminator in a new bid for the Welsh lightweight title. After serious training he outboxed Tommy Jones to win on points over twelve rounds at Llanelli. A month later at Liverpool—not the luckiest of places for Reg—he was knocked out in the third round by tough Bert Hornby, who was rated No. 6 in Britain at the time.

While a final eliminator for the Welsh championship was being sorted out for Reg, he travelled over to Belfast in late September and stopped Harry McMurdie in five rounds.

Then on 22nd November, in front of a crowd of local fans in Ammanford, he met Bryn Davies who took him the full twelve rounds, but it was Reg Quinlen's hand which was raised at the end, to win him a crack at the Welsh lightweight title.

He had clearly enjoyed fighting in front of his local audience, because he requested that the return with Ben Duffy should take place in

Reg Quinlen.

Ammanford too. Unfortunately though, the crowd, in festive mood on 20th December, saw Reg get narrowly beaten on points by the Jarrow man.

Boxing News reported that: 'Quinlan, who did most of the leading, fought a very courageous fight and the decision in favour of Duffy, although well-merited, must have been by a very narrow margin of points.'

Perhaps surprisingly, Reg had only three fights in 1949. In April he ventured no further than Neath where he stopped Tommy Daley of Hamilton in the seventh round. In October he went up to Watford and was part of a memorable night when four brothers local to the area, the Buxtons, appeared on the same bill. All four of the brothers won that night, including Laurie who beat Reg Quinlen when the referee stopped the fight in the third because of Reg's cut eye.

The Buxton brothers' father, Claude came from Antigua, and according to Allan Buxton, was the first black man to settle in Watford. They were a popular family in the area and brother Alex later won the British light-heavyweight title by beating Dennis Powell of Four Crosses in Mid-Wales, in 1953. He lost it in 1955 to Randolph Turpin.

Quinlen's third contest in 1949 was for the Welsh lightweight title. It was seventeen years since his brother Billy won it.

Reg's opponent was Warren Kendall, who had held the title since 1944 and the fight took place in Hereford on 16th November. If someone in the audience had blinked, they'd have missed it, because Reg took 75 seconds to see off the champion, having floored him twice before the referee intervened. Apparently, Kendall did not get the chance to land a blow on Reg.

For his performance, Reg was awarded a 'Boxing News Certificate of Merit'.

Adding to the sweetness of this victory was the fact that Reg's old opponent, Vernon Ball, having got his chance at the Welsh title by beating Reg, had been defeated by Warren Kendall in February 1948.

A Canadian, Solly Cantor, was Reg's next opponent, in January 1950. *Boxing News* reported: 'Reg Quinlan surprised the prophets by forcing a draw with Solly Cantor . . . Quinlan stormed his man throughout the last round and there were moments when the Canadian looked apprehensive and certainly unsettled.'

Reg outpointed Johnny Hazel at Carmarthen in May.

In July an open-air event took place at the Coney Beach arena in Porthcawl. Topping the bill for the crowd of holidaymakers was Eddie Thomas v. Gilbert Ussin. Supporting bouts were provided by Charles Humez v. Cliff Curvis (grown up since Reg's brother Billy was trained by his dad), and Reg Quinlen v. Cliff Anderson.

Eddie Thomas was a points winner, Cliff Curvis lost to Humez, and Reg was unfortunately kayoed by Anderson, after having had the better of the opening rounds.

Also on the bill that day was Johnny Vaughan's boxer, Tommy Davies, who knocked out Joe Hyman in the second round.

I think the travelling, which had been a constant feature of Reg's boxing career, was beginning to pall for him by now. He had been a well-above-average boxer, with a knockout punch, but he had probably seen all he wanted to see and taken as many punches as he wanted to take, though he had dished out a lot more!

It was time to settle down, perhaps, and concentrate on his other interests, which included soccer, cricket and racing pigeons.

There are four more recorded fights for Reg Quinlen.

After ten years inactivity, Tommy Farr started his comeback in September 1950 in Pontypridd, and sharing the bill with him was Reg Quinlen. Farr knocked out Jan Klein and Reg outpointed Selwyn Evans over ten rounds. Reg had held Chris Jenkins to a draw at the same venue two months earlier.

Tommy Farr was on the bill again when Reg defended his Welsh title against Ron Bruzas in Carmarthen at the beginning of December. In the tenth round of his defence, the referee stopped the fight in Reg's favour after Bruzas had taken a count.

Tommy Farr lost on points to Lloyd Marshall.

In the New Year of 1951, Reg's resolution was to give up boxing. He had one commitment to honour and it meant travelling all the way to the Town Hall in Leeds to meet Ronnie Latham. *Boxing News* recorded the fight: 'It was midway through the eighth and last round that Quinlan landed a hard punch just above Ronnie Latham's right eye, causing the referee to stop the fight and award the decision to the Welsh champion.'

Still the champion, and certainly not past his peak, but Reg had made his mind up. He let the Board know that he was retiring un-defeated as Welsh lightweight champion, and he officially retired on 15th June 1951.

Chapter 12

'The Gypsy Who Never Was'

It isn't often that *Boxing News* gets things wrong—I have found it to be a mine of accurate information over the years and thoroughly enjoyed reading it over a lifetime. But one biographical error which seems to have been in common circulation, was carried on by O. F. Snelling in an article for *Boxing News*—that Gypsy Daniels was born Danny Thomas in Newport. I knew this was wrong as I had met some of 'Gypsy's' family and so I was able to point out the error in a letter to the editor.

Billy Daniel was born in February 1903 in Llanelli. They used to joke that his father was anticipating a full rugby fifteen, but in fact Billy was one of thirteen children. His father was D. J. Daniel, who played rugby for Llanelli and was capped eight times for Wales between 1891 and 1899. He was a forward in the famous Welsh team led by W. J. Bancroft in January 1899 which beat England at St Helen's, Swansea, by 26-3 points:

> A crowd of more than 25,000 saw Willie Llewellyn make a spectacular debut and score a record four tries on the left wing. He was to play 20 times for Wales. It was also the debut match for Jehoida Hodges who figured in 23 games for Wales and was to score three tries as an emergency wing against England in 1903.
>
> The brothers James returned for Wales after an absence of seven years and upset the English captain, Arthur Rotherham. Evan James and David provided the quick possession for the Welsh four-threequarter system to pile up the first big score against England. One report said: 'No international team England put in the field had ever been more routed.'
>
> —*History of Welsh International Rugby*, John Billot

WCN 095206

CERTIFIED COPY of
COPI DILYS O
Pursuant to the Births and

an ENTRY OF BIRTH
GOFNOD GENEDIGAETH
Deaths Registration Act 1953

Registration District
Dosbarth Cofrestru
} Llanelly

Birth in the Sub-district of
Genedigaeth yn Is-ddosbarth
} Llanelly   in the County of Carmarthen
                                     yn

No. Rhif	When and where born Pryd a lle y ganwyd	Name, if any Enw os oes un	Sex Rhyw	Name and surname of father Enw a chyfenw'r tad	Name, surname and maiden surname of mother Enw, cyfenw a chyfenw morwynol y fam	Occupation of father Gwaith y tad	Signature, description and residence of informant Llofnod, disgrifiad a chyfeiriad yr hysbysydd	When registered Pryd y cofrestrwyd	Signature of registrar Llofnod y cofrestrydd	Name entered after registration Enw a gofnodwyd wedi'r cofrestru
278	February 1903 32 Swansea Road Llanelly U.D.	William	Boy	David John DANIEL	Frances Ann. DANIEL formerly ROBERTS	Plasterer (Jammy man)	F.S. Daniel mother 32. Swansea Road Llanelly	Twenthieth February 1903	A.D. Davies	

Certified to be a true copy of an entry in a register in my custody.
Tystiolaethwyd ei fod yn gopi cywir o gofnod mewn cofrestr a gedwir genyf i.

CAUTION: THERE ARE OFFENCES RELATING TO FALSIFYING OR ALTERING A CERTIFICATE AND USING OR POSSESSING A FALSE CERTIFICATE ©CROWN COPYRIGHT
GOFAL: MAE YNA DROSEDDAU YN YMWNEUD Â FFUGIO NEU ADDASU TYSTYSGRIF NEU DDEFNYDDIO TYSTYSGRIF FFUG NEU WRTH FOD AG UN YN EICH MEDDIANT ®HAWLFRAINT Y GORON

WARNING: A CERTIFICATE IS NOT EVIDENCE OF IDENTITY.
RHYBUDD: NID YW TYSTYSGRIF YN PROFI PWY YDYCH CHI.

Superintendent Registrar
Cofrestrydd Arolygol

Date
Dyddiad
} 19th May 2009

Copy of Gypsy Daniel's birth certificate.

Known as 'Willie' in the family, Billy Daniel grew big and strong and soon showed an aptitude for pugilism. His first manager was his uncle, Alf Wheeler. He may well have had some early fights in the booths around South Wales, but his first recorded fight ended in a draw with Harry Higgins on 28th August 1920. This was the start of what proved to be a long record to be proud of: 155 contests, won 94, drew 12, lost 49.

Along with the confusion about his birth, he seems to have picked up an 's' on his surname early in his career, usually being billed as 'Young Daniels'.

It must have been very soon after this that Billy was selected for the elite John Bull Boxers, by Australian A. G. Hales, because he showed prodigious talent.

He went to the John Bull camp in Herne Bay on the Kent coast as a welterweight and, although losing his first bout to Jack Kid Davis on points, he quickly notched up four wins, including a knockout in three rounds against Bill Johnson, Drury Lane.

On 26th November 1920, the 'John Bull Boys' were introduced to the public at a tournament held at the Royal Albert Hall. Unfortunately, they lost the tournament overall, but Billy Daniel had no difficulty with his points win over Joe Davis of Newcastle.

Boxing newspaper picked up on his talent:

> This youth of 18 has only been introduced to boxing some eight months. He has the fighting spirit in his bones and this is the greatest of all assets. He appears to be the one with the most promise.

I guess all that seaside air and the fact he had just turned nineteen gave him a huge appetite because in 1921, he was boxing at the upper end of middleweight. In November of that year he actually entered a competition for heavyweights at Blackfriars Ring and *beat* his first series opponent, Guardsman West of Fulham.

A fortnight later he lost in the second series of the competition to Douglas Warner. Both of them must have been boxing above their weight, because the following March Billy met Douglas Warner again, this time in the third series of a competition for a middleweight belt and this time he beat him on points. Billy then went on to win the belt by beating Ernie Milsom in the final, 'well outpointing him' in his first 20-round contest.

Some six months later Billy was on his way to America, like many other British boxers before and after him. By now he was twenty years old and boxing at light-heavyweight.

Billy was a well-proportioned young man with a swarthy complexion, dark eyes and dark hair. He had secured an introduction to New York boxing manager, Jimmy Johnston. The story goes that Billy walked into his office; Johnston looked at him and, taking a fat cigar out of his mouth, said: 'Say, son, are you a gypsy?', which Billy indignantly denied, saying he was a proud Welshman.

But the idea had taken root in Johnston's entrepreneurial mind. He whisked Billy across the street to Woolworths, bought him a brightly coloured bandana to tie around his head and two large brass curtain rings to serve as earrings, and pronounced that he would promote him as Billy 'Gypsy' Daniels, King of the Gypsies. Next stop was the photographers for some shots of Billy in his new apparel, to be distributed to every sports editor in New York with a press release to say that he, Jimmy Johnston, had imported the King of the Gypsies from Wales and that he was going to be the heavyweight champion of the world! Whether he was amused, or just bemused, Billy sported a wide grin in the photographs. But when news of the incident reached his father he was not so happy about it apparently.

Wonderful though this story is, it is probably apocryphal. Gilbert Odd of *Boxing News* pointed out in an article in 1979, that Billy had adopted 'the addition to his name' before going to America. There is, however, a photograph taken in America which is still in circulation, of Billy in bandana and earrings. I guess Johnston was just making the most of the nickname.

It must have been something of a disappointment to Johnston when, after only seven successful fights in New York (one of them, against

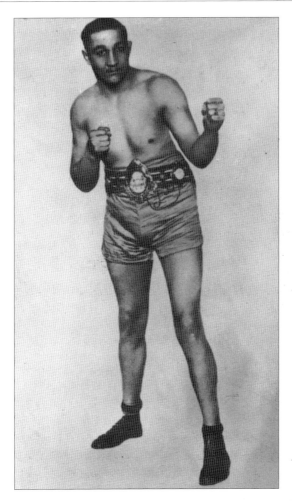

Billy 'Gypsy' Daniels in America (Brian Reading).

Charlie McKenna, was reported in some records as a loss and in others as a win), Billy decided to go home. The reasons for his decision are lost in the mists of time. I think Johnston must have been reluctant to let his promising protégé go—one of his impressive contests had been at Madison Square Gardens when he knocked out Fred Clarke in the fourth round. This was in February 1923.

Madison Square Gardens, the 'Home of Boxing' in New York, was then a magnificent building designed by Stanford White and completed in 1890. It stood on the site of the old Harlem and New York railroad station, bought in the 1870s by Barnum of circus fame, who had turned the old station into a hippodrome. Stanford White's Italianate-style edifice took up an entire block, that is with streets on all four of its facades. In this wonderful place all sorts of exciting events took place; circus and Wild West shows, and the first automobile show. Madame Adelina Patti, friend of King Edward VII, sang there long before she settled in Wales and commissioned the building of her stately home, Craig-y-Nos, in the Swansea valley.

It was probably the enormous potential real estate value of such a site in New York that resulted in the Stanford White building being demolished a mere two years after Gypsy Daniels fought there. However, it was to a different block, in a plain utilitarian building whose four sides contained shop fronts and offices, that the boxing venue was moved in 1925; the arena being housed in the middle. This was Madison Square Gardens until the end of the nineteen-sixties, when the familiar and distinctive rotunda with its accompanying office block was built on a yet another site, and became the boxing venue still known as Madison Square Gardens. There is a delightful story about the building that Gypsy Daniels knew:

> At its top, the statue of Diana, the work of Augustus St Gaudens, stood 346 feet above the street, a spectacular height at that time. The winds that raged around her soon tore off her metal veil with which the sculptor had draped her. When the old Garden was torn down to make way for the New York Life Insurance Company building, and Diana went to a museum in Pennsylvania, a surprising fact was revealed. The rivets that had failed to save her veil were nevertheless large enough to hold a battleship together.—John V. Grombach.

It was almost as though Diana, bored with being alone on her pedestal, had thrown caution to the winds!

Home again, but still ambiguous about his weight, Daniels 'took on middles, light-heavies and heavyweights as they came' according to Gilbert Odd, writing in *Boxing News*.

One contest at Stebonheath Park in his home town in July 1923, was against 'Shoeing Smith' Fred Davies of Newport which Billy won on points; it was almost exactly two years later, after taking on contests all over Britain, that he fought in Llanelli again. This time he scored a knockout in the third against the ex-British light-heavyweight champion Harry Reeve of Plaistow, at Stradey Park.

In the period between April 1923 and March 1927, he had some forty-four contests; he won thirty of them, three with a knockout. Some pundits at the time thought he should have developed that KO punch to greater effect—later on it proved to be an astounding asset—but no-one doubted his talent and he was one of the most popular performers in Britain. At this time he was travelling to venues the length and breadth of the country and occasionally hopping over to Stockholm, Paris or Berlin.

One opponent Billy had great trouble with was Phil Scott of Herne Bay who beat him on points the first time they met at Hoxton Baths, London on New Year's Eve, 1923. Their second fight at Liverpool Stadium in October, 1924, ended in a points win for Billy but it was a controversial decision, to say the least:

SCOTT WINS ALL THE WAY BUT LOSES FIGHT

Astounding Verdict for Gipsy Daniels

There was a sensation in store for the packed house at Liverpool Stadium on Monday night, when Mr Gamble dropped a bombshell in the shape of an astounding verdict in favour of Gipsy Daniels of Llanelli at the close of his fifteen 'three's' with Phil Scott of London. Scott, who showed much improvement upon his previous form here, boxed in a superior fashion and won all the way. By the tenth round he had established such a lead as to be in an impregnable position for Daniels never appeared likely to put over a sleeping draught—in fact he was mainly concerned with his own welfare. It was the running away tactics of the Welshman which caused the affair to drag in the last five sessions, Scott endeavouring to catch him all the way. If Scott did not win this, he will never win anything at all and yet the verdict went to Daniels. The crowd showed their disapproval . . .

Boxing, 1924

At their third and last meeting on 29th August 1925, it was Phil Scott's hand that was raised in final triumph. In a local newspaper article years later, Alfred Daniel remembered Billy's problem with Phil

Scott, and stated that Billy had 'had to jump' to hit Scott, who was six feet three inches tall. The following year Phil Scott won the British and British Empire heavyweight titles.

Welsh boxers were great favourites with fans at the big London venues; some appeared regularly at the National Sporting Club while others were often on the bill at Premierland. Billy's preferred venue was The Ring at Blackfriars where he fought thirty-three times during his career. In a glorious two-month period during the summer of 1926, he scored two knockouts at The Ring—one against Frenchman Paul Paillaux in the second round and the other in a second victory over Royal Marine Trinder in the sixth. In March 1927 Billy met American heavyweight Al Baker at the Ring and stopped him in the twelfth. And less than a month later on 11th April the same venue was the arena for the Welsh light-heavyweight title contest between Billy Gypsy Daniels and the great Frank Moody of Pontypridd. It was a twenty-round contest which went the distance, the decision going to Billy; the result was all the sweeter for Billy because Frank Moody had beaten him at Newport back in July 1923.

'The Old Guard', sports reporter for the *Daily Express*, said the fight 'as it went was the best possible argument for reducing twenty-round contests to the standard which obtains in America' as both fighters left the ring with all-too visible signs of their marathon battle. Gipsy had not done enough to win, in his opinion, and 'a section of those present evidently thought so too, since they booed heartily.'

Moody 'found in Daniels an exceedingly tough fellow who accepted his alleged fearsome right-hand blows and came back fighting. Not until the sixteenth round did we see Moody break loose, but though bleeding profusely from a deep cut in the lower lip, Daniels stuck to him like a leech. Daniels showed clever generalship in diving into close quarters whenever he was hurt, and I cannot understand why Moody, with all his experience, failed to keep him at a distance—as he could have done by using his feet. Gipsy Daniels fought pluckily up to the finish, though his face showed plentiful signs of the punishment he had taken. Moody did not escape scathless, and left the ring with an ear swollen to huge proportions, although his face, stabbed on numerous occasions by Daniels' left glove, carried few marks.'

Billy had done all the right things in the previous few months to advance his career and suddenly he was the talk of the town. Cashing in on the blaze of publicity, the respective managers and the National Sporting Club quickly arranged a match between Billy and Tom Berry, Custom House, for the British light-heavyweight title. Billy undertook his training for this event at Whetstone, North London. The contest took place at Holland Park Rink exactly a fortnight after Billy had won the Welsh title. In another 20-rounder, Billy's stamina held out and his points win was the cause of much rejoicing back in Llanelli where many a glass was raised to the new British cruiserweight champion. His opponent, the worthy Tom Berry was thirty-seven years old and must have needed phenomenal stamina to last the distance, but 'was able to leave the ring without any unhappy memories of what was probably his last important fight.'

The Times correspondent went on:

> In many respects too, it was Berry who made the contest an interesting study. Daniels physically looked the part of a shifty and punishing boxer and it really seemed when he began to let fly his right in the early rounds, that Berry would experience the knockout blow. Berry himself looked the complete veteran, rugged and battle worn of countenance, and apparently none too quick and steady on his legs.
>
> Daniels however, at heart is a cautious fighter, and Berry played upon this trait in his opponent's boxing character for the best part of an hour and a half. Daniels was much the faster man, both in the footwork and in the slinging of punches, and he met Berry with lefts to the face, right uppercuts to the body and occasional swings to the head. But none of these deterred Berry from his settled policy—that of bluffing his man into thinking, vulgarly speaking, that the old man was after him more or less all the time.
>
> Some of Berry's many well-wishers shouted out to him not to be in a hurry or to rush, but actually he was wondrous wise in meeting his defeat in the way he did. Daniels was kept moving about and ducking and clinching for quite two-thirds of every round, and Berry's clips to

the head—innocuous blows of themselves—were constant reminders of the fact that it was Berry who held the initiative.

It is fairly safe to say that if Berry had relaxed a whole round, his opponent's right would have quickly settled matters. Daniels never looked the complete champion but he staggered Berry several times and would have won much more decisively than he did if the wise old man in front of him had allowed him more time in which to think and more space in which to work his arms.

Boxing, like so many things in life, involves making some pretty drastic decisions as various opportunities present themselves and within a few months of his British triumph, young Billy, still only twenty-four, was on the horns of such a dilemma. He would have liked to defend his title, but whereas a short while ago the £250 purse would have been more than enough incentive for him, he found he was being courted by European promoters who proffered still more lucrative deals after seeing him in action at The Ring. NSC rules stated he could not hold his British title and take part in other non-NSC title promotions.

But the club's position was becoming untenable as it tried to retain a monopoly on British championships while not being able to offer large purses to the boxers. Billy had the potential to earn much more from the new breed of entrepreneurial promoters, but to accept a title bout from one of them would have consequences. The title bid could not be for the Lonsdale Belt and the NSC could strip him of 'their' title. The club actually took this action against some boxers who succumbed to the lure of other promoters, including bantamweight champion Johnny Brown of St Georges, who took a large purse to 'defend' his title against Teddy Baldock of Poplar. The NSC responded by matching Kid Pattenden with Kid Nicholson for the 'official' bantamweight title, leaving the sport with two champions and arguably undermining their own work to standardize British championships. Billy thought there was a better way to deal with his dilemma.

In a shock decision, Daniels gave up his British title, and the power of the NSC to control British boxers slipped still further as commercialism and eventually, the British Boxing Board of Control, took over.

After knocking out a couple more Frenchmen in November—Arthur Vermaut and Louis Morelle—Billy Gypsy Daniels set off for Germany to meet a youngster named Max Schmeling, 'who was being built up as possible world title contender'. He was at this time European light-heavyweight champion.

They met on Friday, 2nd December 1927, at the Sport Palace, Berlin. The following morning the *Daily Express* ran this short report:

BRITISH BOXER BEATEN—BERLIN, Friday Dec. 2

> In a ten-rounds boxing match at the Sport Palace here tonight the British boxer, Gipsy Daniels was beaten on points by the light-heavy-weight champion of Europe, Max Schmeling. The German was the attacker in most of the rounds, and frequently scored with heavy lefts to the body and face.

The Berlin press expressed surprise that Billy had stayed the distance:

> Yesterday's major boxing event in the Sportpalast provided good sport, exciting tough fights and a full house. During the main fight of the evening, the technically and tactically much superior Schmeling could only beat the tough Englishman [*sic*] Daniels on points. Daniels took enormous punishment but managed to survive the rounds.

Nonetheless, Billy had put up a performance which impressed the promoters and went down well with the crowd.

After his creditable effort, Billy returned home for the Christmas holidays. But maybe the holiday was a bit too long or his training dropped off a little because his first contest in 1928 resulted in a loss on points against Manchester's Len Johnson—another fine boxer and model sportsman, whose career was marred by the 'colour bar' that operated in sport at the time.

Some rigorous and hurried training and sparring was now called for because Billy had been asked back for a promotional return contest with Max Schmeling on 25th February—promoting Schmeling, that is, in a bid to advance his cause as a World title contender. Well, that was fine with Billy as he was being handsomely paid for his efforts, but he was obviously expected to put in another good performance.

This time the two met in Frankfurt. The bell sounded to start the first round and, 'eager to make a quick killing, young Max dashed into the attack, met a short straight right with the point of his chin and was knocked cold!'

There was something of a stunned silence in both corners, until the crowd broke into deserved applause for Gypsy Daniels' outstanding punch. He seemed a bit shocked himself by the unexpected outcome, but then he always had a habit of underestimating the power of his right. Billy's popularity as a fine contestant grew in Germany and, working even harder in training to develop that right knockout punch, he repeated his performance in Berlin in March, and Leipzig in April, disposing of Hans Breitenstraeter and Hein Domgoergen, both in the second round.

Two years later Max Schmeling was heavyweight champion of the world.

For some reason Gypsy Daniels had only one other recorded fight in 1928. He beat Jack Stanley of Deptford on points at Harringay. The hiatus seems strange, because at twenty-five and having had such outstanding success he appeared to be ascending the very peak of his career.

That this view was widely held is backed up by an article in the *Daily Mirror* in July 1929. Reporting that Max Schmeling had already had much success in New York at this time, the article stated that 'Tom O'Rourke, the veteran American promoter' had cabled Dan Sullivan, general manager of The Ring at Blackfriars, to ask what had happened to Gypsy Daniels. 'Why doesn't he come after Schmeling? is the text of the message.'

Daniels never fought for the European title—with his record and his win over champion Max Schmeling he must have been a contender in 1928—whether because of management problems, lack of support (seems unlikely), or for some other reason I cannot say.

There was certainly something amiss. If Billy had ever had his sights set on the European crown, he did nothing to further his cause in 1929.

In only five (some say seven) fights that year, he recorded five (seven) losses.

Gilbert Odd recorded that there was 'a real mystery' surrounding what some records show as his second contest of 1929; indeed, there is serious doubt about whether it ever took place.

After losing to American Jim Mendis at The Ring in January, Billy was supposed to have travelled to Milan to meet Italian contender Michele Bonaglia on 10th February, where some accounts say he got knocked out in the seventh. However, reliable European records show that on that date, Bonaglia fought Belgian Jack Etienne for the then vacant European title, and won.

Was Billy nominated for the title fight by the International Boxing Union (forerunner to the European Boxing Union) as some records show? Perhaps Jack Etienne was a substitute after Billy pulled out.

According to Gilbert Odd, Daniels' name does not appear among the five listed as contenders by the IBU at that time. Did he fail to respond to an invitation? Up till now he had certainly earned his chance.

There followed a series of four points losses reflecting what appeared to be a complete loss of form on Billy's part, against Franz Diener and Hein Mueller of Germany, Harry Crossley of Mexborough and France's Maurice Griselle.

Again there is a discrepancy in the records about a second meeting with Bonaglia in Rome on 13th October, showing Billy getting knocked out in the eighth round. European records indicate that Bonaglia did not have any fights in October 1929.

'What had happened to Billy at a time when he could have done himself a power of good?' lamented Gilbert Odd in 1979. Thirty years later there seems even less chance of unravelling the mystery but I bet there's a story there somewhere. Gypsy Daniels admitted that he loved the atmosphere of the ring and the acclaim of the crowd and 'that it had been too much of his life to think of anything else.' And so he carried on fighting.

Although 1930 started off badly for Billy when he was disqualified in the fourth against Belgian Louis Guillaume at The Ring in January, he seems to have recovered some of his fighting form in the shape of his knockout punch, which he used twice on Frank Berwick of Birmingham during the year. It also worked on Joe Mullings of Catford in the sixth round of a contest which took place at the West Bromwich Palais de Danse in October 1930. Billy fought Reggie Meen of Leicester twice that year, beating him on 25th March, when his corner threw in the towel after nine gruelling rounds, but losing to him when they met for the return contest in July.

For a long time, the Boxing Board of Control had waited patiently for Billy to defend his Welsh cruiserweight title, allowing him to hold it beyond a reasonable time. It could not be said that there were no worthy opponents.

So it was that Billy met his old adversary Frank Moody in Cardiff on 4th August 1930 in a title match.

The *Western Mail and South Wales News* reported that the attendance at the Welsh White City, Sloper Road, estimated at 15,000, was a record for Welsh boxing.

> . . . despite the fact that both had arrived at the veteran stage of their respective careers, the bout was the finest ever displayed by them.
>
> Daniels survived disaster in the opening round when with only a feeble guard for his jaw Moody crashed into him with his left and Daniels was lucky to hang on until the bell rang. From this they fought a ding-dong battle, Moody relentlessly forcing his way to close quarters and Daniels boxing cleverly on the retreat but always faced with the prospect of defeat. Daniels however won several rounds, notably the fourth, seventh, tenth and twelfth, but again in the fourteenth, when he made a desperate attempt to win by a knockout, he met with a fusillade of blows to the jaw that almost brought about the end. He gave a clever defensive display, but Moody proved to be in first-rate condition and hammered his way to victory by aggressive close-quarter tactics and surprising stamina.

The next two years were a bit of a roller-coaster ride for Billy whose fortunes were constantly changing at this time. He continued to be a popular figure in Germany and was always happy to take on some of their big names. In particular he had some notable battles with the young Walter Neusel who was later to tangle with Tommy Farr, and though Billy lost to him each time, he nevertheless gave the German hero a hard fight over the distance. Fellow Welshman Jack Petersen never managed to beat Neusel either.

In September 1931, Billy knocked out Louis Wusterad of Belgium, before taking a couple of losses. Two good points wins followed, against ex-Guardsman Arthur Gater of Dewsbury and down in Falmouth, against Australian Rene Morris.

In October 1932, Gypsy Daniels met Del Fontaine.

The contest as it happened was promoted and arranged by Johnny Vaughan acting on behalf of Ammanford Athletic Club, and took place in Llanelli Pavilion on 15th October.

The fight was over fifteen 'uninteresting' rounds, according to 'Southpaw' of the *Llanelly Guardian*:

> Daniels was attempting what was tantamount to a come-back, with a view to being matched with Jack Petersen, and to regaining the prestige he once held as (light-heavyweight) champion of Britain. He had done a considerable amount of training and before the fight was a popular favourite with one of the largest crowds ever attracted to a boxing match in Llanelly . . .
>
> Primarily he failed because he was not fully trained. He had done a lot of work in Llanelly and Ammanford in preparation for the fight, but it was not enough . . .
>
> When the men entered the ring it was seen that Daniels held an advantage in height, weight and reach. He opened the first round well. A right connected with Del Fontaine's body, and a second or so later, Daniels landed a beautiful straight left. Then Daniels went to the ropes and stayed there.
>
> Practically the same story can be told of all the rounds. Daniels would rush in, land one or two blows, and then go to the ropes. There is this to be said in his favour. While defending he was brilliant.
>
> Fontaine, a boxer with a knockout in both hands, tried all he knew to get home a decisive blow. But failed. Daniels' experience was invaluable to him. He kept out of danger by ring-craft and clever headwork.
>
> Del Fontaine was always a trier and thoroughly deserved the verdict.

BRITISH BOXING BOARD OF CONTROL (1929)

PROMOTER AND BOXER.

ARTICLES OF AGREEMENT.
(B.B.B. of C.   Form No. 35a.)

An Agreement entered into this   *29ᵗʰ* day of *September*   19 *32*, between

Johnny Vaughan on behalf of the Ammanford Athletic Club
of

(hereinafter called the Promoter) of the one part

And   *Billy ("Gipsy") Daniels*   of   *Llanelly*

(hereinafter called the Boxer) of the other part

WHEREBY IT IS AGREED AS FOLLOWS :—

I.   The Boxer agrees to appear at   *Llanelly Pavilion*
on the evening/~~afternoon~~ of   *October 15ᵗʰ*   19*32* , and box
Del Fontaine of   *Canada*   ...*15*...rounds
of   *2*   minutes each with an interval of one minute between each round at   stone   lbs.,
with *6* oz. gloves under National Sporting Club Boxing Rules (B.B.B.C. REG. 30). The Boxer
to weigh in at the   , at   on the day of the
contest. If over weight to forfeit the sum of £   . (One hour allowed to do the correct weight.)

2.   The Promoter to pay the Boxer the sum of £ *15⁻*   .   or   *25* per cent.
of the Gross receipts if he wins the said Contest : £ *15⁻*   or   *25⁻* per cent. of the Gross
receipts if he loses and £ *15⁻*   or   *25⁻* per cent. of the Gross receipts if the said
Contest is drawn.   (Gross receipts do not include Entertainment Tax.)

In the event of the Promoter breaking this contract he shall pay the Boxer £   damages.

In the event of the Boxer breaking this contract he shall pay the Promoter £   damages.

In the event of the Boxer's opponent breaking his contract, through unforeseen circumstances or
otherwise, The British Boxing Board of Control (1929) to settle any claim for compensation.

3.   If by mutual agreement the Purse money is to be deposited with The British Boxing Board of Control
(1929), same must be deposited on or before the

4.   The Boxer to deposit the sum of £   .   with the Promoter as a guarantee of his
appearance and his compliance with the conditions.   In the event of the Contest taking place, the sum deposited
shall be returned to the Boxer.

Johnny Vaughan promoted the contest between
Gypsy Daniels and Del Fontaine of Canada.

177

If Gypsy Daniels had slipped uncomfortably from his peak, to Del Fontaine getting past his best was a personal catastrophe. Indeed he had come to Britain in the first place to try and escape the fact that 'in Canada and the United States he was considered a washed-up fighter', as Gilbert Odd pointed out in *Boxing News* in 1986.

Nothing about Fontaine could be relied on to be completely genuine. Even his name, sounding to me like a 1950s rock'n'roll star, was made up. He was born Raymond Henry Bousquet in Winnipeg, Canada, in February 1904.

He was a born hard-as-nails fighter, with phenomenal punching power for a middleweight and he possessed the quality which it is said above all, makes a champion: the 'killer' instinct.

'There was no need for the referee to instruct the Canadian to "come out fighting",' said Gilbert Odd, 'he always came out fighting and what is more, he kept on fighting until either he or his opponent were incapable of fighting any longer.'

After a successful early career in Canada, Fontaine came over the border to take on the United States in 1928. For the next three years he met American middleweights, light-heavies and even heavyweights with the same ruthless, no-quarter-given-or-expected tactics which made him very popular with the more bloodthirsty of the American fans. One particularly memorable slugging bout was with light-heavyweight Lou Scozza, whose hand was raised after ten rounds of matching toe-to-toe staggering punches, at the end of which the crowd rose as one man to its feet and cheered the gladiators for a full ten minutes. The ring was covered in the brimmed straw hats worn in those days by New Yorkers in the summer, as the fans threw them in appreciation of a 'good fight'!

Fontaine made the serious mistake of thinking he was invincible.

Then a return match with Scozza had him taking an enforced five-month rest after he was beaten by the count in the seventh round. It wasn't long enough. Hurt pride taking priority over his physical condition led to another KO by Young Firpo in Seattle, followed by a couple of points losses. 'Whoever was managing his affairs,' as Gilbert Odd wrote with more than a hint of contempt, 'matched him with the redoubtable Mickey Walker, reigning middleweight champion of the world.' The champion disposed of Fontaine in four rounds. In 1931 it had become obvious that America had finished with him and Del Fontaine returned to Canada, a sadder but not necessarily wiser man. He tried to regain his lost form but somehow it wasn't working out.

One day he was stopped in the sixth round of a contest by an Englishman: Ted Moore from Plymouth. One of Moore's entourage half-jokingly suggested to Fontaine that he should try his luck in Britain, where he was pretty much unknown.

The idea grew in Fontaine's mind. If he chose his fights carefully, he might make enough money to give up this game which had let him down on his side of the Atlantic; maybe make enough to buy a farm on his return to Canada. He said 'goodbye' to his wife and family with this idea now more formed in his head. Characteristically unconventional, he signed on the *SS Valkyrie* as a cattleman; the ship was carrying a cargo of live steers, and arrived in Liverpool early in 1932.

He had a letter of introduction to British welterweight champion Jack Hood, who in turn, introduced Fontaine to his manager, Ted Broadribb, who was associated with Jeff Dickson in running a series of promotions at the Albert Hall.

Broadribb was impressed by Fontaine's file of newspaper cuttings showing he had met and beaten some very well-known American middle and light-heavyweights.

Naturally, Fontaine forgot to mention the name 'Mickey Walker' or that he had been knocked out three times in his last dozen fights.

It was decided to try the Canadian on the next Albert Hall programme. A change of scene, the sea air and above all, an enforced rest, had worked wonders for Fontaine. He disposed of his first couple of opponents with ease and rapidly gained a reputation as a colourful puncher.

He had regained his bravado and his mistaken notion that he could take anything and keep coming back for more. I'm not sure how the Boxing Board of Control's regulations restricting numbers of fights applied to foreigners in those early days. But, with the money rolling in, Del Fontaine took on far, far too many fights; twenty-three in 1932.

Over the next two years, he must have fought practically every middle and light-heavyweight boxer in Britain, in venues up and down the country, including several trips to Wales. Ammanford's Danny Evans beat him in 1934.

Archie Sexton certainly gave him a couple of boxing lessons. He took a 'fearful hiding' from 'Cast-Iron' Jack Casey in Newcastle, when a terrific uppercut in the fourth lifted Fontaine off his feet and sent him crashing to the boards.

Yet *six days later* he was back in Blackfriars Ring where astonishingly he managed to stop the notoriously awkward Harry Mason in thirteen rounds. A fortnight later, Fontaine went through another punishing defeat at the hands of Australian light-heavyweight Leo Banderas.

But perhaps the opponent who was finally one-too-many was Willie Unwin from South Africa. In two bouts within a period of six weeks, he and Fontaine pounded away at each other, covered in each other's blood. The first encounter resulted in a points win for Fontaine and was talked about by Blackfriars fans long afterwards for its savagery. The second, equally brutal, ended in a draw.

Managers finally called a halt and refused to get Fontaine any more fights. Friends urged him to give it up. If only he'd gone home to Canada. But the playboy side of Del Fontaine had other ideas. He liked to spend the money that he should have been saving for his Canadian farm—and he'd met a girl. Her name was Hilda Meek and she was a dancer from Bermondsey. He had always loved the adulation that came with success, and in her company, his money got spent as he forgot about his plans for his family. When he remembered though, he got desperate. He had to start saving; he needed to keep making money! He tried to get fights for himself, but doors were closing, his earning power had gone. The arguments between him and Hilda got worse as contests and purses dwindled. His mood darkened and after a fight, he would appear to be in a dream, as though unaware of his surroundings.

Where the gun came from was no doubt discussed later, but it was certainly in his hand on 10th July 1935, the day he found Hilda on the 'phone and jumped to the conclusion she was making a date with

Del Fontaine and Hilda Meek.

another man. Fontaine yelled at Hilda that he would kill her if she so much as looked at another man; Hilda ran terrified out of the house and onto the busy street. He ran after her, reached the street and started shooting. Three bullets struck the girl before she collapsed, dying, on the pavement. Passers-by began to scream and Hilda's mother, rushing out of the house to her daughter's side, was wounded by the last bullet from the revolver.

Fontaine was tried for the murder of Hilda Meek at the Old Bailey. His defence had argued that he was insane at the time of the shooting. A doctor who had been at the ringside after some of Fontaine's fights testified that after one of his defeats, Fontaine had complained of double vision, sleeplessness, unstable walk and depression.

Double vision meant that the base of the skull had been injured and, in view of this and the effect it would have had upon the brain, he was not surprised at the sudden attack on the girl. He considered that the boxer was suffering from melancholia and did not know the nature of his act when he shot Miss Meek.

Though a second doctor could find no evidence of insanity, he found it 'was not possible to rule out that the boxer had some brain injury which might account for his action.'

Despite the medical evidence, Del Fontaine was found guilty of murder. In those days, the sad consequence of his conviction was death by hanging. The sentence was carried out at Wandsworth prison, early in the morning of 29th October 1935.

Since his meeting with Del Fontaine, Gypsy Daniels had enjoyed a revival of some of his old form. A good points win at Swansea's Mannes-mann Hall over Bernard Cook of Finsbury Park in November 1932, was followed by what was to be his last trip to Germany. There he met again with Walter Neusel, forcing him to go the distance on two occasions, though losing to the clever German both times.

In the first week of the New Year he stopped Guardsman Arthur Gater in the fourteenth round at Hull and then had a fortnight to get himself fighting fit to meet the giant Italian Salvatore Ruggirello at Liverpool Stadium. But the difference in stature and style proved too much of a challenge for Billy and 'caused the referee to intervene in the eleventh round when the game Welshman was being freely battered around the ring.'

But the remainder of 1933 was a good year for Billy who chalked up eight wins, including a knockout against Frank Borrington of Derby at Llanelli Workingmen's Club. In the first of three contests with Jack London of West Hartlepool, Billy stopped his opponent in the sixth; he beat London over the distance the second time they met and held him to a draw on London's home ground on the third occasion at the end of July.

A chance to settle an old score with Harry Crossley of Mexborough, however, resulted in a defeat on points, the fourth time Crossley had got the better of Gypsy Daniels over the distance! The *Rotherham Advertiser*, however, described the bout as:

> One of the most stirring contests imaginable when the two contestants were ex-light-heavyweight champions of England. The referee was Joe Beckett, former heavyweight champion of England, and his decision of a points win for Crossley in a twelve-round bout, proved very popular . . . Twice (Crossley) might have stopped the fight had he stepped in quickly, but Daniels recovered each time, though he was very groggy in the final round.
>
> Daniels fought quite gamely, however, and though in the later rounds he was forced to retreat under a barrage of blows, he avoided many hefty punches by the skilful use of his arms and the ropes.

Towards the end of 1934 it was obvious that Billy was slowing down a lot; the contests were no longer coming his way. In December against Canada's Al Conquest, he was unable to repeat an earlier success against another Canadian, Teddy Phillips at Derby, whom he had beaten on points.

Strange really that these last two contests were against fellow country-men of Del Fontaine. 1935 was the year of his trial and execution.

Gypsy Daniels had no recorded fights during 1935. But it must have been some time during this year that he retreated to the relative sanctuary of a travelling boxing booth, staying with them for a number of years, mostly touring the West Country. Now he had plenty of time to look back over his long, interesting and sometimes glittering, career. It had given him opportunities to travel and meet with many different kinds of boxers, and had occasionally had unforgettable moments of glory. Now and again he was offered a contest still. He won both of his last recorded fights on points at Swansea in the spring of 1938; the first against fellow Welshman Dick Power, and the second against Manchester's Alf Robinson.

One day in 1939 the booth was set up in Bournemouth and the proprietor came over with a tousle-haired youngster in tow to introduce him to Billy.

'This is Freddie Mills, Billy. He's going to be joining us and I know you'll be happy to show him the ropes.' Billy agreed.

Above the music of the roundabouts, the voice of the barker invited one and all to step into the ring with the formidable veteran, Gypsy Daniels.

Freddie's first job for the booth owner was to position himself among the crowd front of house and set an example to the bashful by declaring 'I'll have a go with him!' To carnival folk the lad was known as a 'Gee'.

Billy was a quiet chap who kept himself to himself, but he got on well with young Freddie, and taught him all the tricks of the trade. There was one trick, however, that Freddie had to find out for himself.

The two were often called on to fight each other in the shows, when Freddie would do his utmost to land a big punch on his wily opponent, and they always got a good response from the crowd. After the fight they would go round collecting the 'nobbins' from the audience before going back to the caravan to rest and share out the bounty. After a while Freddie noticed that whereas he would always have a mixture of silver and copper coins in his dressing-gown pocket to put on the table, Gypsy's collection was mostly copper. One day he 'accidentally' picked up Gypsy's dressing-gown after the share-out and found that the left-hand pocket jingled. It contained sixpences, shillings and even half-crowns! Indignantly, Freddie confronted his mentor, to be met with Billy's disarming wide grin.

'Well it's like this, my young friend,' he said. 'I've never believed in letting my right hand know what my left hand is doing!' Freddie saw the funny side and the two remained the best of pals, but Freddie insisted that both pockets were emptied after that.

A few years later, Billy got a lot of satisfaction out of watching the successful career of his young protégé. Especially that never-to-be-forgotten night of 20th June 1942 in London when Freddie Mills beat the fine boxer Len Harvey, to lift the British, British Empire and 'World' light-heavyweight titles. The world title in this contest was the GB version and not recognised in Europe or America, but nothing

Gypsy Daniels with Alderman Mayor Harry Morris of Llanelli.

ventured, nothing gained: Freddie took the European title from Paul
Goffaux in September 1947, successfully defending it against Paco
Bueno the following February. As for the universally recognised World
title, Freddie took that too: from Gus Lesnevich, a Russian-American
from New Jersey at their second meeting in July, 1948. Some eighteen
months later, Freddie lost the World light-heavyweight title to Joey
Maxim. He retired undefeated as British, British Empire and European
Champion.

At some point during the war, Billy moved to Plymouth and was
employed at Devonport Dockyard. He had grown to love the Devon
coast and he decided to settle there after the war, though he made
frequent visits to his family in Llanelli. And it was on one such occasion

that he was delighted to find that a civic reception had been arranged for him, in recognition of his achievements in the boxing ring.

Sad news came in July 1965, when Billy heard that Freddie Mills, aged 46, had been found dead in his car, parked behind his Soho nightclub, with gunshot wounds to the head. Various theories were expounded about his death. The coroner's inquest recorded a verdict of suicide.

Billy Gypsy Daniels died at his home in Plymouth in June 1967.

Gilbert Odd paid this tribute:

> To stay as many years as he did in the profession when competition was particularly strong, says much for his skill in the ring and maintenance of physical condition. He was fearless and game.

Chapter 13

Amateur Boxing in the Amman Valley

If boxing booths represented the tough and uncompromising end of the boxing spectrum, the other extreme was amateur boxing with its emphasis on ring skills and self discipline.

In the early part of the twentieth century, just as it is today, the amateur discipline was probably the best start for a professional boxing career as well as being a very popular sport in its own right. In the difficult days of the 1920s many young boxers, frequently driven by the need to earn money and even by physical hunger, went straight into professional boxing by way of the booths or through one of the many gyms that appeared all over the country after the First World War.

But it should not be forgotten that alongside this phenomenon the fine tradition of amateur boxing was also carried on with great gusto at this period, and remarkably the Amman Valley was at the forefront of Welsh amateur success too.

For when Mervyn Meredyth Williams, amateur boxer from Taibach, near Port Talbot, came to Cwmamman and founded the Amman Valley Boxing Club in 1920, he could hardly have anticipated the decade of achievement that lay ahead.

Mervyn, who boxed as 'Boyo Meredyth', founded the club together with his brothers, Alun and Ellis, after he had started boxing in the army. Soon afterwards they elected a secretary, Arthur Jones. It was an exciting time to be in amateur boxing, that was for sure. For one thing, Mervyn Williams himself won the Welsh featherweight title that year, and for another, it was a time of renewal and change in amateur boxing following the end of the First World War.

'During 1915-19, in consequence of the War,' as the Welsh Amateur Boxing Association put it, the ABA championships were not held, and in the spirit of making a fresh start in 1920 the ABA decided to introduce three new divisions to the pre-war five. Championships were now to be offered at flyweight, bantamweight, featherweight, lightweight, welterweight, middleweight, light-heavy and heavyweight.

As news spread that Cwmaman sported a Welsh amateur champion, many aspiring boxers turned up at the Amman Hotel where training was being held on three nights a week under the watchful eye of Bill Thomas who had been appointed trainer. The interests of the club were guided by Cardiff schoolteacher Tom Morris who was a member of the Welsh ABA Council. I have often thought about the spirit of enthusiasm and sportsmanship that must have existed in that gym then, and how that spirit produced consistent success for the little club.

Mervyn Meredyth Williams
(Featherweight Amateur Champion of Wales, 1920).

Over the next nine years, boxers from the Amman Valley club won a total of seventeen Welsh titles; the club also produced a European champion, none other than Archie Rule, and the great Tom Evans, who was the first Welsh heavyweight to win the British amateur title, in 1922. As well as being one of the best boxers of the 1920s, Tom Evans also captained Neath Rugby Club and his photograph can still be found in the Gnoll clubhouse along with those of all the other Neath captains.

At the end of the 1921 season, the club was already able to look back on a very good year. Mervyn Williams had successfully defended his Welsh featherweight title, and he was joined by one of the club's new youngsters, Ike Lloyd, who took the Welsh lightweight title. The following year brought more acclaim when Tom Evans won the British heavyweight title and Mervyn Jones added to the tally of Welsh titles, at bantamweight. Mervyn Williams and Ike Lloyd both retained their titles.

The new regime incorporating eight weight divisions was proving very popular and standards in amateur boxing rose sharply as more youngsters, inspired by the example of the British Army role models like Jim Driscoll, Johnny Basham and Bombardier Billy Wells took up boxing as a sport.

Among the Amman Valley's most promising newcomers was Tommy Stamp, who became the new Welsh flyweight champion in 1923. The club built on its achievement once more as Tom Evans again won the Welsh heavyweight final and Mervyn Williams held the featherweight title for the fourth successive year.

Young Tommy Stamp's boxing days were cut tragically short when, in July 1925, he was killed in a mining accident. His brother Gil once told me how their mother made a cushion cover out of Tommy's red championship vest after his death and that it was put on the sofa, proudly proclaiming her son's boxing prowess to all visitors to the house.

In 1924, the name Archie Rule was added to the club's roll of honour, when he became Welsh ABA bantamweight champion, was runner-up in the British finals and was somehow overlooked for the British boxing team in the Olympics of that year. Ike Lloyd recaptured the Welsh lightweight title.

Archie Rule with trophies.

I have no doubt that it was the tremendous encouragement and help he received from the Amman Valley club that spurred Archie Rule to even greater efforts when he was sorely disappointed over being left out of the Olympic team. After successfully defending his Welsh title in 1925, he was selected to box in the European Amateur Boxing Championships at Stockholm, and he came home with a gold medal at last. In the same year, Mervyn Williams regained the Welsh featherweight title for the second time and PC Jack Rees won the Welsh welterweight title. Archie retained his Welsh title in 1926.

Tom Evans's young brother Danny, was the next to win glory for the club when he became Welsh welterweight champion in 1927, before turning professional. Archie, along with another Welshman, flyweight Cuthbert Taylor, were successful at European level in amateur competitions held in Germany.

Although 1928 was a year barren of titles for the Amman valley, the club completed a glittering decade in 1929 when Ike Williams had his hand raised as Welsh lightweight champion for the fourth time. Archie Rule finished boxing around 1929.

In 1934, Amman Valley Boxing Club sent no less than eight boxers to the Welsh ABA finals competition. They were flyweight Iori Morris; bantamweight Gwyn Davies; featherweight Don Chiswell; lightweight Etto Cresci; middleweight David Jones (Dai 'Farmer'); light-heavyweight Meidrim Thomas and heavyweight Rhys Davies. There was particular

The Amman Valley Boxing Club, taken midway through their 'Golden Decade'.
Standing, left to right: Dick Evans, Joe Jones, Willie Haydn Evans, Gwyn Peregrine,
Dai Jones, Wil Sampster, Cliff Sampster, Charles Lloyd.
Centre: Crad Rule, Dai Richards, Myrddin Jones, Tom Evans, Dai Evans,
Ike Lloyd, Theo Davies. Front: Archie Rule and Mervyn Williams.

interest in the amateur boxing world that year: 1934 was the year that the British Empire Games (later the Commonwealth Games) was held in London. It was only the second British Empire Games ever held—the first was in Canada in 1930. Finalists in the ABA competition stood a good chance of being picked for the games, so the Welsh lads were hoping to make it through to the British finals. The standard was understandably high that year and there were a record ninety-two entries in the Welsh competition. Although some of the Ammanford boys were clever boxers (Iorrie Morris, Don Chiswell, Meidrim Thomas and Dai 'Farmer' Jones went on to box professionally for Johnny Vaughan), none of them got through to the finals of the British competition. However, Rhys Davies got what I think was a bronze trialist's medal for the British Empire Games.

Rhys was the father of John Rhys Davies, who starred with Harrison Ford in the Indiana Jones blockbuster films.

British team for European Amateur Boxing Championships.

Ironically, after all their success, it would be another twenty years before another Amman Valley boxer got a Welsh ABA title—Ken James was welterweight champion in 1954, followed by Rufus Price of Llandybie who won the middleweight title in 1955, and Martin Edwards won at lightweight in the same year.

Four Welshmen are listed as having won boxing medals in the British Empire Games of 1934; one of them was Alf Barnes of Cardiff who was the British ABA bantamweight champion that year and who subsequently got the silver medal at the games. Another was the 1934 Welsh ABA flyweight champion, Jackie Potttinger, who went on to get a bronze medal.

The Amman Valley club appears to have been inactive during the latter part of the 1930s. Four of their best boxers had joined Johnny Vaughan's gym as professionals, and Dai Farmer Jones in particular was pursuing a successful boxing career at this period. Then in September 1939 the war intervened, with its inevitable disruption to sporting activities. Dai Jones cut short his boxing career to become a policeman in the Carmarthenshire Constabulary.

When at last the war was over, peace and a new prosperity had come to the Amman Valley. Several factories had been opened in New Road, Ammanford, employing lots of local people and the miners were working flat out, trying to keep pace with the enormous demand for coal. The biggest of the factories was Pullman's, operated by the Pullman Spring-Filled Company Ltd., which also had branches in London, Walsall and Brussels, with offices in Mayfair. The brand new Ammanford factory boasting up-to-the-minute canteen and sick-bay facilities, manufactured mostly car seats, and was a congenial place to work. Sports and other leisure time activities were actively encouraged by the management, keen to keep their modern work force healthy and enthusiastic.

Thus in 1946, the Pullman Amateur Boxing Club was provided with facilities in part of the canteen area, where training, sparring and workouts carried on for nine years. During this time Danny Evans and Archie Rule were working for Pullman's and were featured on the 'Personality' page of the company's in-house magazine, *Pullman Post*, during 1947. The article featuring Archie '(Chargehand, Car Seat Section)', after listing his achievements as an amateur boxer, concludes with a quote from 'a sporting journal':

Archie Rule of Ammanford, who won a European championship, is generally recognised as the best Welsh amateur boxer who never won a British title.

In the ABA 1924 competition, Rule disposed of the now famous British professional champion, Nel Tarleton of Liverpool in the first series, but was beaten in the final by L. M. Tarrant. This boxer not being available for the European Championships, Rule got his great chance, which he literally ringed with both hands, to gain a great triumph.

In 1955, management reluctantly decided they could no longer find space for the boxing club as an increase in staff meant more space was needed for the canteen. But there was still much demand for the club to keep going; indeed it was enjoying renewed vigour as it produced two new Welsh ABA champions, Ken James and Rufus Price. It was at this time that John Jones, landlord of the New Inn, stepped in and provided them, free of charge, with a room above the old stable at the rear of the inn in Quay Street. A decade earlier, these premises had housed Edwin Evans's gym, before it was moved to the Cooper's Inn at Betws.

The name of the club changed too. After discussion it was agreed that the old name Amman Valley Boxing Club be adopted, and it was remarked at the meeting that it meant the club 'had a great deal to live up to'. Club president at this time was D. J. Herbert and members of the committee were Cliff and Gwyn Peregrine, Bertie Davies and Sered Thomas.

Sered had no less than five sons—Clive, Terry, Jimmy, Mike and Peter, who were all enthusiastic boxers for the club, along with brothers Ken and Gerallt James, and Martin 'Punch' and Keith Edwards. Clive Thomas, on becoming British ABA Schoolboy Champion was presented with his prize at the Albert Hall by Field Marshall Montgomery.

In 1956, Rufus Price was the only boxer at the Welsh Senior championships to defend his title, at Cardiff on 3rd March. He outpointed T. Southall of Newbridge to remain 'the middleweight king-pin' as *Boxing News* reported it. But he was joined that year by fellow Amman Valley boxer Olgan Bowen, at light-heavyweight, who knocked out Ken Stallard of Fernhill, to win the championship. Unfortunately, an error was made in recording the winners that year and Olgan's name was

Amman Valley Boxing Club, 1956.
Back row, left to right: Ron Davies, Olgan Bowen, Rufus Price, Johnny Smith,
Sered Thomas. Front: Danny Caulfield, Cliff Peregrine, Haydn Evans.
Seated: Roy Lewis.

omitted from the official record, although it was added to the Wilf Humphries Memorial Shield. Rufus Price's son, Adam Price, became the Plaid Cymru M.P. for Carmarthenshire East constituency in 2001.

Trainer Cliff Peregrine, who had already been picked to train the Welsh ABA team a number of times, was chosen in 1958 to be an official for the British Empire (Commonwealth) Games, which were held in Cardiff that year.

Amman Valley Boxing Club, c.1957.
Back row, left to right: Gwyn Morris, John Salisbury, Wyn Leonard, Mike Thomas,
Sered Thomas, Ken Davies, Peter Thomas, David Morris, Cliff Peregrine.
Middle row, left to right: Raymond Leonard, Ronnie Morris, Tony (Wilbert) Williams,
Michael Stamp, Nigel Williams. Front: the Danter twins, Don and Ron.

Ammanford Urban District Council, of a long-gone genre of local government which, together with its other duties, concerned itself with the sporting and charitable activities of its little town, presented Amman Valley Boxing Club in 1960, with a plaque bearing the town's coat of arms and an inscription: 'In Recognition of Valuable Service Rendered by the Club in Fostering Amateur Boxing in the Amman Valley'.

The club had been the first in Wales to act as hosts to a club from another European country: Kolscheid ABC visited Ammanford in 1953, prompting much interest, and Amman Valley club returned the visit to Kolscheid in due course. In 1962 another German club, Aachen, were guests in Ammanford and were happy to return the honours when the Amman Valley club visited them.

In 1965, the National Coal Board provided the club with two large sheds and these were converted into the gymnasium which stood on the recreation ground in Ammanford. The gym was officially opened on 1st November 1965, by Councillor T. C. Bevan.

The following year, Amman Valley Boxing Club was delighted to offer its gym facilities to professional boxer, Brian Curvis, when he was preparing to fight for the vacant European welterweight title against Jean Josselin in Paris.

Brian, who already held the British and Commonwealth titles, is best remembered for his epic World title battle with Emile Griffith, which he lost on points in 1964.

Of the gym, Curvis remarked that although it was not palatial, 'it constituted a real and lasting tribute to a few men whose love was box-

Billy Quinlen, Archie Rule, Tommy Davies, Mrs Davies, Maud Vaughan and Ginger Jones, attended an Amman Valley Boxing Club show at the Regal Ballroom, Ammanford, c.1965.

ing, and only boxing'. To say 'thanks', Brian Curvis presented the club with a punchbag.

When he was 66, Archie Rule, then living at the Uplands Post Office, Swansea, recalled his happy days as a member of the Amman Valley Boxing Club during the golden decade of the 1920s, for E. Noel Lewis, sports editor of the *South Wales Guardian*:

> They were the best friends I ever had and were true champions at various weights. They worked hard—when work was available—trained hard and fought hard.
>
> They brought undying fame and honour to the district and maintained the very best traditions of the sport—traditions which I am proud to see the present club doing so much to carry on.

By the early 1970s, Cliff Peregrine's sons, Malcolm and Keith, had become the youngest amateur boxing referees in the country, but over the following years, the fortunes of the once-proud Amman Valley Boxing Club declined as the number of boys coming forward dwindled. Rival clubs had grown up, sometimes successfully; in particular, the Towy Boxing Club still offers youngsters of the district the opportunity to train in the art of boxing.

Brian Curvis's words about the gym on the recreation ground being 'a lasting tribute' came back to haunt the former members of the club rather dramatically in 1984, when the building which had been disused for some time, was gutted by fire. 'A sporting link with the past went up in smoke', as the *South Wales Guardian* put it.

In all, the Amman Valley Boxing Club had organised around 300 tournaments and many charity shows, including a successful enterprise which raised over £1,000 to re-hang the church bells in a Monmouth church. It had been widely and justifiably praised over the years for its achievements, hard work and above all, its promotion of amateur boxing as a sport.

I'm happy to say that the tradition of amateur boxing in the Amman Valley is carried on still. Arising rather like a phoenix, Towy Boxing

Club moved its gym from Llandeilo to new premises on Ammanford recreation ground close to where the old gym had burned down. The club's trainer is still, and has been for forty-three years, Hywel Davies, known throughout amateur boxing circles as 'Cass'.

The 1970s-80s was a particularly successful period for the Towy Club. Two of the boxers, Paul England and Stanley Jones, won Welsh schoolboy titles five times each; Paul England went on to gain a British schoolboy title on two occasions. At Senior level during the same period, Welsh titles were won by Neil Saunders, Steve and Martin Toms, Stanley Jones and Penybanc's Phil Dicks.

Towy Amateur Boxing Club Committee, 1983.
Left to right: Aeron Jones, Brian George, Tony Lee,
Neville Meade (British Heavyweight Champion), Gwynfor Thomas,
Hywel 'Cass' Davies, Peter Percival, Alan Roberts.

Chapter 14

Archie Rule

'A good trainer is one who knows what a smack on the nose feels like!'
– Archie Rule

When I was a kid in the nineteen-fifties Archie Rule was one of the best known trainers in Britain. He was also among the most knowledgeable, having had an all-round boxing career beginning around the time of the First World War.

Boxers who trained under Archie would sometimes complain about the strict regime of road work he insisted on. Archie was dismissive. The complaining boxer would be told the story of how, as a boy, hardly more than a toddler, Archie and his brother and sisters walked with their mother (baby Crad in her arms) from Cwmaman near Aberdare to Penybanc above Ammanford, when the family moved house. As this was a walk of round about thirty miles it's not surprising that Archie never forgot it. His father, George Rule, led the horse who pulled all the family possessions in a gambo (large hay wagon) over the mountainous roads. 'That was the longest walk of my life,' Archie would finish up with, looking serious, 'and that's saying something!'

The family settled into their new home in what is now Trefrhiw Terrace, Penybanc, and continued to grow. Eventually, there were twelve children in the Rule household: boys Archie, Crad, Viv and Vic and girls Maggie, Annie, Nettie, Phyllis, Addie, Olga, Lavinia and Mona.

Archie, born in February 1902 and christened Archibald Leonard, being one of the older ones, was expected to start earning money as soon as reasonably possible. In fact, though small and 'puny', he looked forward to following his father and neighbour William Vaughan, Johnny's father, down the Wernos pit. He was fourteen when he started work, having finished his schooling at Tycroes National School and taken exams at Ammanford school. He was so short in stature that the miner's lamp he carried would bump along the ground as he walked.

Work wasn't the only thing Archie was enthusiastic about. He had watched his father training and sparring with Johnny Vaughan in their home and in the shed at the back of the house; these sessions were often under the supervision of Jack Scarrott, fair and boxing booth proprietor who took an interest in the young Vaughan. Johnny had gone on to train and box at Porth and was something of a hero to Archie. During his school years Archie had been accustomed to getting beaten by bigger boys. 'Mind you,' he once confessed to Dave Phillips of the *South Wales Echo*, 'I wasn't a very good fighter as a kid. As a matter of fact people still come up to me and say: "I licked you once as a kid, Archie", and I'm not surprised. Everybody used to beat me when I was at school.'

It wasn't that Archie didn't try. It had long been a favourite game for Archie and his friends to pretend to be the boxing heroes on the cigarette cards they all collected, using cloth caps wound round their hands, they would gather in any place they could find to hold their impromptu fights. It was more a question of physical strength or rather, lack of it, in his case.

The time had come to get in some serious training and Archie set to. One frosty February morning, Archie was concentrating on a sparring session in the garden with brother Crad, when the landlord called round. He complained to the boys: 'If it's exercise you want then dig the garden! I didn't rent this house to your parents to be used as a boxing booth!' Recounting this incident later, Archie exclaimed: 'Exercise indeed! I'd been working all night underground before that sparring session!'

It did illustrate though that anti-boxing sentiment was still quite common in the valleys, as it had been since the time of the Nonconformist Revival in 1904. However, it coincided with a surge of popular interest in boxing in South Wales that has never been equalled.

In Archie's street the landlord was in a minority of one. The neighbours all encouraged Archie's endeavours. In particular he remembered

Mrs Merriman and Mrs Goodrich who would bring him fresh eggs in the mornings; his Mam, not to be outdone, saved up and bought a bottle of sherry. Two 'well-known Ammanford characters' as Archie called them, Will Wilson and Stan Lake, offered to buy him a pair of 'sand slippers' to box in, at the price of 1s.11d, but it was Mam once more, who somehow found the money to purchase them.

The beginning of Archie's career as a boxer is not well documented and Archie himself did not talk much about these early contests in interviews. We do know that he boxed in Ammanford on 25th September 1920 when he beat Tommy Davies of Ystalyfera on points over six rounds.

Among the records that do exist is a report of a tournament at Ystalyfera in 1921, when Archie was nineteen years old. A. G. Hales's famous 'John Bull Boxers' gave a series of exhibition bouts of three rounds each, with Chris Langdon and Luther Thomas as the chief attraction. The report mentions that Archie Rule was held to a draw by Young Elwyn Williams of Ystradgynlais.

During the same year he appeared on a bill at Pontardulais where entrepreneur Bert W. Price staged a boxing tournament at the gym. Top of the bill was a return contest between Archie and Elwyn Williams, Ystradgynlais, and the 15-rounder again ended in a draw. However, the matter was finally resolved when Elwyn Williams beat Archie in a closely fought six-round contest at Ystalyfera.

In a tournament described as an 'Assault-at-Arms'—which was often a fund-raising event for hospitals or war veterans, perhaps—Archie boxed an exhibition bout with Curly Wilson to close the evening's entertainment. On the same bill there was an exhibition bout between two Ammanford boys: Young Phillips and Tommy Stamp.

Tommy Stamp went on to win the Welsh amateur flyweight title in 1923, but sadly, he was killed in a mining accident in July 1925.

There seem to be two good reasons why there is not much evidence of Archie's early contests: the first is that it is likely that many of his fights were in boxing booths where no records were kept and which were not all reported in the local press; the second is that Archie himself had no interest in recalling them because of an unusual decision he made in 1923, and the events that followed.

We know Archie and his brother Crad grew up immersed in boxing, through their father George. A frequent visitor to the house was Jack Scarrott who owned a boxing booth and who was always on the look-out for likely young boxers. Clearly Archie had been training hard for some reason: sometimes he was out training at 5.30 in the morning, and returning to the house would ask his mother to soak him with a bucket of cold water before setting off to work!

It is inevitable that he would have gravitated towards the booths which accompanied the travelling fairs at Ammanford, Pontardulais, Ystayfera and Ystradgynlais and other small towns; ending the season in the grand fair at Neath where many travelling families would combine their attractions for one last concerted attempt to part the public from their money before the winter set in. Although much diminished and obviously minus its boxing booths, Neath Fair is still an important date on the calendar in South Wales to this day.

Certainly there were enough booths to keep many boxers in employment albeit on a very casual, part-time basis: Scarrotts, Joe Gess, Taylors and Bassets, were among the best-known of the booths operating in the Swansea, Neath and Amman valleys. In those days, fairground families kept very few records and by their very nature, where 'all-comers' may or may not have given their real names, and where 'results' of fights would often have been difficult to define, booths went pretty much unheeded as far as records and regulations were concerned. It wasn't until as late as 1951 that the Boxing Board of Control drew up regulations which affected the booths—historically it spelled the beginning of the end for most of them.

'Peerless' Jim Driscoll, writing about his early career at the turn of the twentieth century, said:

> . . . it would seem that our boys today have, as a rule, engaged in from twice to three times as many contests as the most combative of the old-timers, but then the record books are far from being reliable sources of

information in this respect, at least so far as the old-timers were concerned. In the first place there were no record books at all in their days; and in the second, the majority of the old-timers' fights were of the kind that did not get recorded.

It was much the same in my early days. I started as a booth boxer, and went up and down Wales and the West of England, meeting all comers at all weights and under all sorts of conditions. We never used to trouble about asking an opponent to tell us his name, and even if we heard it by accident or knew him more or less casually, we would promptly forget all about it. We weren't dreaming of championships in those days, or if we were, we certainly never gave a thought to the possibility of record books, or that there would ever arise a public which would demand a full and complete history of our lives, triumphs and sorrows.

So it seems certain that Archie supplemented his miner's wages to help feed the family throughout these early years with earnings from the booths. And why not? Another great Welsh boxer, Johnny Basham, had this to say:

> . . . and at last I was persuaded to enter a boys' competition in the boxing booth of that well-known showman, Jack Scarrott, who has had, I should think, every champion of Wales in his booth at one time or another.

Even so, Archie made very little reference to this part of his life at all. Sports editor, Noel Lewis, writing in the *South Wales Guardian* in the 1960s, refers to a trophy that Archie won at Llandovery in 1921 'during the strike'. I think this was the Harry Watkins Cup but I do not know whether the competition was amateur or professional. Anyway, Archie won it very convincingly by beating Danny Rees, Brynamman, in the first bout, Tommy Trotman, Cwmgors, in the semi-finals and Reg Marley of Garnswllt in the final. All of these were points wins. Reg Marley was the uncle of Billy and Reg Quinlen.

And so we come to 1923 and a likely reason for Archie's reticence. At the beginning of that year he decided to apply for re-instatement as an amateur boxer. The events that followed, I suspect, did not go entirely as planned.

The significant factor about boxing in the booths was that the boxers were 'paid' and therefore 'professional'. At that time, other than the National Sporting Club rules, professional booth boxing was largely unregulated until the formation of the British Boxing Board of Control in 1929. On the other hand, amateur boxing had been subject to strict rules since at least 1881, when the first ABA championships were held. One of these rules was that you could not box in amateur competitions if you had been fighting for money. We know that in January 1923 the Welsh Amateur Boxing Association held a meeting and wrote to Archie Rule confirming his re-instatement to amateur status. It seems that the amateur discipline had become or had always been, attractive to Archie. I believe the reason he applied for re-instatement at this time may well have been that Archie thought he had a good chance of making the British team for the 1924 Olympics in Paris.

He would have been encouraged in this hope by the trainers at the Amman Valley Boxing Club where he and Crad were active participants. In 1923, he was runner-up in the Welsh ABA Championships at bantamweight, beaten in the final by G. Thompson. In 1924 he got the Welsh title and travelled to London with high hopes for the British title. One of his opponents there was Nel Tarleton who later turned pro and held the British featherweight title between 1934 and 1936. During this semi-final bout something strange and rather ominous occurred after some organisational glitch caused the semi-finals to be held in an annexe with a makeshift ring. Writing in the *South Wales Echo*, Dave Phillips took up the story:

> Right from the start, young Rule, knowing all about 'Nella's' fabulous jarring left, decided to take the fight to his man and he forced the pace from the opening gong. Rule (Wales) was giving Tarleton (England) a right clobbering when it happened . . . the ring collapsed!
>
> Quick repairs allowed the semi-final to go on . . . and Rule again tore into his man with a vengeance. Then when things were really warming

up, the ring collapsed again and the unhappy Tarleton, anchored down by sagging ropes and ring posts, was a sitting duck for the fusillade of left hooks and right swings from the Welshman.

Tarleton, the man who was later to make English ring history, was belted with everything in the Rule book . . .!

Having resoundingly won the semi-final, Archie was pipped at the post in the final by L. M. Tarrant of the Armstrong-Siddeley club, Coventry. At this point, however, Archie was not too downhearted; there was a buzz of excitement among all the finalists who knew their names may be among those picked for the British Olympic team.

We can only imagine how devastated he must have been when he discovered that 'A. Rule' was reportedly the only name left off the team list out of all the winners and runners-up in that year's championships.

Was it possible that the Olympic committee or the hierarchy of the Amateur Boxing Association thought that Archie's past was too murky to include him in the team? Did someone disagree with the Welsh ABA's decision to re-instate him?

In the end Archie got to go to the Paris Olympics—as a spectator. One thing he was never short of was friends, and among those who sympathised with his disappointment was trawler owner Wilf Neale of Neale and West Ltd., who took Archie over to see the games. Dave Phillips wrote:

> The Olympic bantamweight title went to Willie Smith (South Africa) who beat an American in the final—'I think I could have beaten Smith six days a week and twice on Sundays . . . Even if he did go on to win the world professional title by beating the cockney Teddy Baldock,' says Archie.

When Archie got some much better news in a letter informing him that he'd been selected to represent Great Britain in the European Amateur Boxing Championships in Stockholm in 1925, it was Wilf Neale again who suggested that he go to Cardiff to do his training. Here he met up with Jackie Davies who held the Welsh amateur welterweight title from 1921 to 1923. Jackie loaned Archie a pair of boxing boots and told him he could keep them if he came home with the title. Archie got stuck into his training at the Central Club under a trainer who impressed him very much, Jack Imperato, and did some pretty intensive sparring with well-known boxers such as Minty Rose, Kid Anthony and Frank Singer as well as Jackie Davies. Consequently, when Archie sailed for Stockholm he was sporting two black eyes.

But his conviction that he could have won gold at the Olympics made him determined to win in Stockholm. He'd show 'em!

And he did it. Beating some formidable opposition in the shape of Axel Norman of Norway and in the final bout, Franz Deubbers of Germany. How sweet the victory tasted to Archie!

The following year was 1926; the year of the general strike. Archie was among many of his contemporaries from Welsh mining areas to take a cheap passage to the United States. But it wasn't to one of America's coal mines that Archie went. He thought he'd have a look at some of this vast country first, paying his way through his boxing skills. He hitch-hiked his way to Pittsburgh, Philadelphia, Cleveland and across to Niagara and Toronto, picking up money by sparring with both professional and amateur boxers as he went. It was in Philadelphia in September that he saw the first Jack Dempsey v. Gene Tunney fight. In fact Archie turned sports reporter for the night, sending his first-hand account of the contest to the *South Wales Echo*.

In 1958, recalling this tremendous fight, Archie told Dave Phillips: 'Jack Dempsey was the best big 'un I've ever seen. Tunney beat him, but my faith in Dempsey still remains. The greatest heavyweight champion of them all.'

Nonetheless, a year later Tunney retained the World title by beating Jack Dempsey for the second time in the 'Battle of the Long Count':

> The fight was held in Soldier field in Chicago. Jimmy Barry, once a great bantamweight champion of the world, was the referee. More than 100,000 people were on hand—most of them hoping to see an old precedent broken and Dempsey win his old title back. For the first

seven rounds, it was almost a replica of their first Philadelphia fight. Then suddenly in the seventh round, it happened. An old-time flurry of punches by Dempsey, and Tunney, battered and glassy-eyed, lay on the floor in a corner of the ring. The timekeeper began his count, but Dempsey stood in the corner about a yard away. Referee Barry motioned to Dempsey to go to a neutral corner but the latter hesitated. Finally Barry led him to a neutral corner and, returning to the side of the prostrate Tunney, began his count over again. At 'six' Tunney got to his knee and at 'nine', Tunney arose and began to back-pedal around the ring with quick sliding steps. Dempsey pursued him, but . . . Tunney weathered the seventh, and from then on, fighting cautiously, he proceeded to outbox the former champion. Dempsey had failed as all had failed before him, to regain the heavyweight title.

John V. Grombach, The Saga of the Fist

As history records, both Jack Dempsey and Gene Tunney went on to have distinguished records in the Second World War.

Archie decided his future lay in Great Britain after all and was home by Christmas.

In 1927 Archie was runner-up to Fred Perry for the Welsh ABA bantamweight title and the same year he was selected as a one of a team of Welsh boxers to fight in amateur contests in Germany. He and Cuthbert Taylor recorded wins in Hamburg, and Archie had a particularly good contest.

Back home in the Rule household, George read out the newspaper reports to the rest of the family, seated at breakfast in the kitchen. One headline proclaimed: 'Rule Brings the House Down!' Little Lavinia looked up in astonishment. 'Will Archie have to pay for it?' she asked her mother anxiously.

Archie's career as a boxer came to an end in 1929 when he moved to London. But he continued to take an active role in boxing over the years, sometimes working as an instructor in the amateur discipline, training students, army cadets and schoolboys at various schools and clubs. He was also on hand as a professional trainer and second whenever any of the Welsh boys came up to fight at Blackfriars, Holborn or the other London venues.

Archie Rule with his portrait, painted by his father.
The portrait now hangs in the clubhouse at Penybanc RFC.

On one such occasion he was in the corner for Ginger Jones, when Ginger met tall Kid Berry of Bethnal Green on 8th April 1929, in the National Sporting Club.

Ginger never forgot this fight because he knocked the experienced London boxer clean out. He explained that he 'had a tendency to hit rather high on the jaw of opponents of my own height, but as this man was so much taller, he suited my style'. In the second round: 'Berry strides towards me with very purposeful ideas. He led at me with a left hand, which I slipped and at once crossed with my right, catching him right on the point of the jaw, due to his being so much taller than I. He crashed to the floor with his eyes wide open and was unconscious for nearly ten minutes. I was really frightened, but Archie spoke to me in Welsh, and reassured me that things were alright.'

The newly-formed British Boxing Board of Control began to issue licences for professional trainers.

It was after the war that Archie's training skills came to be widely recognised. By this time he was living in Wales again and still very much involved in boxing.

He presented a series of boxing tournaments at the Tirydail Stadium, later the Regal Ballroom, in Ammanford. On one of these bills, on 22nd November 1948, there was a final eliminator contest for the Welsh lightweight title, between Reg Quinlen and Bryn Davies of Skewen. Quinlen won on points over twelve three-minute rounds. On the same bill Dudley Lewis of Brecon beat Gareth Bevan of Gorseinon. Bevan later became trainer to Colin Jones, British, Commonwealth and European welterweight champion.

Among his first successes as a trainer was Tommy Davies of Cwmgors who was middleweight champion of Wales from 1943 until he retired from boxing in February 1951. He was managed by Johnny Vaughan who had called on Archie's services as a trainer and corner man.

Then there was featherweight Len 'Davo' Davies, from Swansea. He delighted Archie by beating the great Nel Tarleton, some nineteen years after Archie had beaten him as an amateur in 1924.

Len Davies, whose real name was Glyn—his brother was named Len—did all his early training in the 1930s with Dai Nancurvis, father of the famous Swansea boxers, Cliff and Brian Curvis. He turned pro in 1937, and joined up with the Royal Welsh Fusiliers during the war. As Ron Olver writing in *Boxing News*, stated: 'he must have been stationed in Britain for according to the records he had 32 bouts during the war years, losing only ten.' One of these was a convincing win over Jim Brady, reigning Empire bantamweight champion, in 1943, quickly followed up by his defeat of Nel Tarleton at the Birmingham Queensberry All-Services Club. *Boxing News* reported the fight:

> Davies fully deserved his win. Tarleton, although he showed flashes of form, appeared to be generally puzzled by the speed and cleverness of his rival. Davies bustled into his man, and when Tarleton landed solidly to the body, Len speeded up and Tarleton was hard pressed. Davies continued his fast scoring in the last round to be returned a very popular winner.

Although his manager, Joe Carr of Newport, issued a challenge to Tarleton for the British title on behalf of Len, and although he outpointed World flyweight champion Jackie Paterson in September 1943, Len Davies never got the British title. In August 1944 he was disqualified in a final eliminator against Al Phillips—a man who had beaten him three times already. He joined the ranks of first-class Welsh boxers who were good enough to win a British title but never did.

It was Archie's firm but kindly regime that guided the career of Joe Erskine from 1954 to 1964 and helped him towards the British heavyweight title in 1956. Archie shared with many others a very high opinion of Joe Erskine's skill: 'If you can tell me of a better boxing brain among British heavyweights at any time in history then I will listen to you,' he once said.

In 1959, Erskine met American Willie Pastrano, who became light-heavyweight champion of the world in 1963 when he beat Harold Johnson. Pastrano and Erskine met in Wembley and Erskine outpointed him.

Joe Erskine, British Heavyweight Champion, with trainer Archie Rule.
Gent with towels is Joe Erskine's father.

A biographer of Willie Pastrano said of the contest: 'Erskine, the former British champion from Cardiff, was perhaps the only man in Pastrano's entire career who out-boxed him. Erskine was brilliant and for once, Pastrano was made to look ordinary.'

Among Erskine's other opponents were Ingemar Johansson who beat Joe in a bid for the European title in Gothenburg on a technical knock-out, and German southpaw, Karl Mildenburger, who outpointed Joe in October 1963.

Joe had a total of fifty-four fights of which he won forty-five.

Archie also trained Phil Edwards, of Cardiff, of whom he said: 'Phil is a deliberate-thinking fighter, but he has genuine box-office appeal.' He was always obsessed with how neat his hair looked. He got the Welsh middleweight title in August, 1957 by beating Freddie Cross over twelve rounds on points, successfully defending it in a return with Cross. He fought Terry Downes for the vacant British title in Septem-

212

ber 1958, but lost when the referee stopped the contest in the thirteenth round. He tried again against Terry Downes in 1960, but was stopped in the twelfth.

But above all I guess Archie Rule is remembered in Wales for his World champion, the late Howard Winstone of Merthyr, whose courage in chasing a World featherweight championship was boosted by Archie's training and encouragement.

Howard Winstone had already proved himself as one of the worthiest of British and European champions. He originally took the British featherweight title from Terry Spinks in May 1961, when he stopped Spinks in the tenth round. The European title came his way in July 1963 when he beat Alberto Serti in Cardiff. His opponent retired in the fourteenth round. He successfully defended his British title three times, his European title four times and the combined British and European titles three times.

Archie Rule and Howard Winstone, who had just won gold in the Empire Games featherweight division. Archie had won at the European ABA Championships in 1925 at bantamweight. Howard was the first Welsh boxer to win a gold medal since 1938.

Howard's first attempt at the World title was at Earls Court on 7th September 1965 against NBA champion Vincente Saldivar of Mexico:

> Many thought Winstone would try to out-box the champion but instead he elected to fight. This proved his undoing when he tired in the latter stages. Saldivar, who had pressured throughout, got on top to take the decision after a blistering battle.
>
> *British Boxing Yearbook*

It was at Ninian Park in Cardiff that Winstone met Saldivar for a second attempt at the World title on 15th June 1967:

> The Welshman carried the fight to Saldivar right up to the halfway stage. Still boxing superbly, Winstone began to tire and the bull-like Mexican began to power forward, downing him in the fourteenth. Fighting like a tornado Saldivar just about finished in front after a wonderfully close contest.
>
> *British Boxing Yearbook*

The referee on this occasion was Wally Thom, who had taken the British and British Empire (Commonwealth) welterweight title from Howard Winstone's manager, Eddie Thomas, in 1951.

Howard's performance was easily considered good enough for another defence of the World title to be arranged between the two boxers for October of the same year, this time in Mexico City. Howard held off his opponent for eleven rounds with some 'effective jabbing', but was put down in the twelfth for a long count. The *British Boxing Yearbook* recounts that: 'He was then battered from pillar to post, receiving damage to both eyes before the towel was thrown in.'

Finally, he got yet another chance to become Featherweight Champion of the World. On 23rd January 1968 he met Japan's Mitsunori Seki at the Albert Hall to decide the vacant WBC championship:

> . . . Winstone began to get into gear with his better boxing when the bout was suddenly halted on Seki sustaining a cut eye.
>
> *British Boxing Yearbook*

It was in the ninth round that the referee stopped the contest and raised Winstone's hand. At last his determination and Archie's hours of road training paid off! Howard came home to a rapturous welcome in the valleys.

Six months later the hard-won title was lost to Cuba's Jose Legra at Coney Beach Arena, Porthcawl, when the referee again stopped the contest, this time to save Howard from further punishment.

However, Howard Winstone retired undefeated as both British and European featherweight champion.

When Ken Buchanan of Scotland was making his bid his bid for the World lightweight title he was managed by Eddie Thomas. Archie, by now in his late sixties and still respected for his knowledge and wisdom, found time to be involved in the Scotsman's training.

Buchanan had beaten Maurice Cullen for the British lightweight title at the Anglo-American Club, London on 19th February 1968; after putting has opponent down five times, Buchanan won on a knockout.

Buchanan soon set his sights on a bigger goal and gradually worked his way up the world rankings, beating Leonard Tavarez and Angel Garcia. An attempt at the European lightweight title came unstuck when he was beaten by the World junior welterweight champion Miguel Velazquez over fifteen rounds in January 1970.

But after a successful defence of his British title, when he knocked out Brian Hudson in the fifth, and beating three more contenders, Buchanan got his chance at the WBA title against Ismael Laguna in a swelteringly hot ring in San Juan, Puerto Rico, in September 1970. Somehow, the man from Scotland got through fifteen rounds to get the decision and the World title, which he successfully defended twice before losing it to Roberto Duran in June 1972 on a dubious decision.

Archie never got to see that. Having lived in Swansea during the later years of his life, where he worked as a commissionaire for the BBC at their Swansea studios during the late 1950s, Archie died in May 1971.

His ashes were scattered by his family over Betws mountain, overlooking Ammanford, where he had done many, many hours of roadwork.

Chapter 15

Joe Gess and Tommy Farr

'Many boxing booth families are neglected due to lack of historical material . . . Scarrett . . . Jack Gage and the Gess family among others. They and many of their contemporaries are the unsung heroes of boxing history.'
—Vanessa Toulmin, *A Fair Fight.*

Joe Gess must have been an unassuming man. He doesn't seem to have left much of a record of his life behind. He probably wasn't much of a book reader or even a bookkeeper—in common with others like him, the records of his boxers' fights were sketchy or non-existent. Joe lived the only life he knew. He was a travelling boxing booth proprietor, around South and West Wales.

And yet without him, it is *probable* that Tommy Farr would never have stepped into the ring with Joe Louis in New York on that night in August 1937.

For a couple of years of Farr's young life Joe Gess was part-trainer and employer, part-mentor, part-father figure to the moody, mixed-up kid from Tonypandy. Above all he was totally convinced of Farr's exceptional ability as a boxer, predicting over two years before the Louis fight that Farr could one day be a contender for the world crown.

Joe Gess was born into a travelling family around 1880, but it could have been some years earlier. He followed his brother Frank into the boxing booth. Frank had been a fighter in the early years of the twentieth century and a claimant to the British title at 9 stone 10lbs. Joe clearly admired his brother and soaked up his boxing knowledge voraciously.

'In a sense, my brother Frank linked up the atmosphere of the mountain air and the sawdust with the more modern arc lights and resined canvas,' Joe once said.

'Very little of the boiled shirt and diamond studs did Frank ever see, and I very rarely have had that experience myself, but boiled shirts do not necessarily make good boxing brains!'

In those early days, when Frank was in charge of the boxing pavilion and Joe a young teenager, he began tentatively standing up 'front of house' and taking on all-comers. Standing on the dais with him, the brightly painted depictions of boxers on the wooden front of the booth behind them, were such great fighters as Joe White, Bobby Dobbs, and Owen Moran. Moran was a hero to Joe who described him as the finest fighter the world has ever seen. Other early comrades were Spike Robson who worked for the booth for seven years, the lanky George Phelan who surely must have been one of the tallest featherweights; he was over 6ft. 1in., and Fred Delaney.

Although Joe talked about these times as the 'bad old days' he was probably referring to the lack of financial reward for hard work and perhaps, the violence that followed the cult of the mountain fighters into the booths in those early days. The best part was that he rubbed shoulders with giants. He remembered Peerless Jim Driscoll: 'The Jewel of Cardiff,' who sometimes boxed for Jack Scarrott as well as for Gess, earning:

> . . . as much as twelve shillings in one day, but this meant six fights at two bob a time.
>
> Of course, they could not earn this every day because in wet weather the fighting men of the valleys could not be persuaded to come to the booth at all.
>
> Our boxers at that time used to be graded. Boyo Driscoll, who was the fastest fighter over three rounds I ever saw, used to get 1s.6d. a fight, (Jim) Driscoll 2s., and Tom Thomas, middleweight champion of England, would work for 2s.6d. a fight.

In an interview for the *South Wales Echo and Express* in 1937, Joe recalled the big annual fairs where many travellers, including several

Joe Gess, son, and dog.

boxing booths, would all meet up for what was hoped to be one of the most lucrative weeks of the year for them. For these events, the Gess family would travel much further than usual.

> On one occasion at Birmingham Fair, Spike Robson knocked out twenty-three opponents in the same day. The total for all the lads on the booth was 45 knock-outs—the biggest number I can remember during my 50 years active work on booth and fairground.

The earliest fight I could find recorded as taking place in Joe Gess's boxing booth actually took place in Ammanford, between Jack Leyshon —who became a well-known referee, one of the first licensed by the Board of Control—and Tom Davies of Pontamman, in 1914. The *Carmarthen Journal* gave a magnificent report:

The contest was held in Mr Guess's Boxing Booth in the Fair Ground and was witnessed by a large crowd who, with the exception of a slight disturbance caused by one or two funny individuals—who had the honour of being shown out by the police—gave perfect fair play and quietness.

In Leyshon's corner was Tom Phillips, Ben Christmas and Taylor, and in Davies's was Ivor Day, Alec Weaver and Frank Davies. Mr Jack Brooks refereed.

Round 1: Both men sparred for an opening, Davies opening pre-liminaries with a right to the body . . . On the breakaway Leyshon landed a heavy right jab to the body and Davies countered with a series of heavy body punches.

Round 2: Both men rushed in to clinch and the referee had to force them apart. On the breakaway, Leyshon landed a stinging left to the body. Davies tried to counter with the right which Leyshon cleverly blocked, and clinched from here to the end of the round.

The report continued in much the same way in what was clearly an evenly matched contest, for the full ten rounds, and finished with the verdict: 'The referee declared the contest a draw, which met with un-animous approval.'

Joe was a proud man but circumspect about his place in the world:

In the show business, we are expected to be more upright in our dealings with the public than the ordinary private promoter. For years we have felt a prejudice against our people because, I suppose, we are always roving. We don't stop long enough in one place for people to realise that we are as honest and as good as they are. The public are always ready to give us the worst end of the stick.

But neither was he a pushover. Joe had literally learned how to stand up for himself, and a booth proprietor needed his wits about him in those hard days.

Many of the 'huskies' who came forward to have a go at the booth boxers were suspicious that they would not be given their £1 prize-money if they won, and for the sake of credibility Joe was sometimes obliged to pay up before the fight. The rule was: get beaten within three rounds and you leave with nothing.

If the brave contender subsequently got floored within three rounds, the boxer would bring his opponent round once he hit the boards while Joe's job was to get the pound back. Sometimes the opponent's friend, his butty, would be called upon to hold the money and so the other booth boxers would stand along with Joe on either side of him until the pound was returned. The subdued opponent and his butty would leave a little wiser perhaps, but no richer.

'They never left my booth better off by £1 if they did not earn my money but I never failed them if they did,' said Joe.

Rain or shine, Joe Gess's boxing pavilion was the venue of a boxing show every week in some town or village in South or West Wales. Sometimes he'd stay in a place for a few weeks; no doubt taking advantage of higher takings there.

During the heyday of its popularity as a centre of boxing, Ammanford was one such place. Although Johnny Vaughan was the promoter at the forefront of the town's boxing successes, there's no doubt the two men collaborated to put on some wonderful shows using Gess's facilities. Johnny recorded in his diary on 6th September 1929, that he'd received a wire from Joe Gess to arrange for shows to be held in Ammanford on the tenth, thirteenth and fourteenth of September. After a trip up the valley to Brynamman for a show on 5th October, Gess's booth was back in Ammanford for 12th October and the locals were treated to boxing every week until the end of November, when Gess decided to stay put until after Christmas!

Tommy Farr himself records that he was 'rising sixteen' when he went to Joe Gess and offered to fight for him. It was not, however, his first appearance on Gess's boxing pavilion. It is generally thought that his first fight for Gess was against one of the Moody brothers, Jackie, in 1927, which he lost over six rounds.

Young Farr's first recorded fight took place a few days before Christmas 1926 at Tonypandy when he beat Jack Jones on points over six rounds and he had a similar victory on Boxing Day against Young Snowball.

This particular 'Young Snowball' was from Clydach Vale but there were a number of boxers who used the name. Strange to tell, Ted Broadribb who was Tommy Farr's manager when he met Joe Louis, had also boxed under the name Young Snowball. He had stopped boxing in 1911 because of problems with his eyes.

They were both gruelling battles in which Tommy, though little more than a child, gave his opponents a real battering. The money he won probably helped to put Christmas dinner on the table. His birth certificate shows that he was born on 12th March 1913, so he was thirteen years old at the time of these victories, but for some reason Tommy apparently claimed that he was twelve. So when he met Joe Louis the Brown Bomber on 30th August 1937, he was twenty-four. But even the 'boxing bible', Nat Fleischer's *Ring* record book, erroneously records that this fight took place when Farr was twenty-three.

Confusion over his age was the least of his problems. Today, it is difficult to imagine a childhood as hard as Tommy's was. He was one of eight children; his father, George Farr, was a coal miner originally from Cork, who supplemented the family income as so many did, with some mountain fighting. He was a tough giant of a man.

Life at home was already far from easy when Tommy's mother died, aged 39. His sister Phyllis remembered their mother as being from fighting stock herself, and that their grandfather was involved in Gypsy Daniels' early career. Tommy was nine years old when she died. According to Phyllis, as their mother held Tommy for the last time she said, 'There's a fighter for you.'

Less than a year later, struggling to be both breadwinner and home-maker, his broken-hearted father was struck down with some kind of paralysis from which he never fully recovered. George was a hard-living, no doubt hard-drinking man, and his battered body gave up. One of the jobs he had been tackling in the evenings after finishing work, was the family's washing; getting the girls to hang it on the line the following morning so the neighbours wouldn't know he was doing the household chores. In George Farr's world it was demeaning for a man to do housework.

Somehow, miraculously, the family stayed together, but now the children, under the leadership of eldest sister, Phyllis, had to put food on the table as well as look after Dad, who needed constant care until he died some years later.

During this terrible time, while kindly neighbours and chapel goers prayed 'loud and long' as Tommy described it, he 'refused to believe it has to be . . . I remained a rebel, dry-eyed and consumed with bitterness.' The children would go from door to door selling anything they were able to, from reels of cotton to home-brewed herb beer and Tommy built his own handcart, extending his endeavours to deliveries for local grocer's shops. Fighting was instinctive to Tommy and he was always drawn to fairgrounds and boxing venues. He boxed from a very young age although what records remain of his early fights shows he had courage but not much success.

After one contest, sister Phyllis remembered, 'Tommy asked the promoter for his money as he was leaving. "You'll have to wait until tomorrow when we can change the gate money into notes," said the promoter. Tommy wasn't having any—he came home that night with his blood stained towel simply bursting with his winnings, all in two-shilling pieces. But every shilling he won he brought home to the family. The money was a godsend. We had many mouths to feed.'

Two important events in his young life combined to build his physical strength and his self confidence. At the age of fourteen he inevitably began work in the colliery where a particularly brutal form of fighting known as 'in the holes' was a common recreation for the men. They would bet on fighters who would each stand in a hole dug in the ground to the depth of their waists and a couple of feet apart from each other. The fight would end when one or other was unconscious. Young Farr got so good at this barbaric pastime that his fellow pugilists refused to fight him and the idea grew in his head that boxing was a better way to make money than working underground (he had already suffered a colliery accident which scarred his face for the rest of his life). In the end he worked underground for two years before an argument with a foreman who lashed out at Tommy with a shovel, proved to be the straw that broke the camel's back. 'I sacked myself on the spot, cashed in my pay ticket to become a Jack-of-all-trades,' said Tommy, adding that in periods of unemployment he was poorly clad and ill-fed and 'gave rein to a temper quick to rise.'

But the other event that shaped his destiny was his meeting with his 'guiding star', Job Churchill, 'who, having had a leg torn away while working in the pits, had set himself up as a saddler.' Churchill, understandably not a fan of coalmining as a living, actively encouraged young Tommy to go for his goals once he saw how determined he was. Churchill had an extensive knowledge of boxing himself as well as being a good listener and he was absolutely the right person to guide Tommy at that time. Recognising that this troubled young man would benefit from a change of scene, he sent him to work for the summer in an hotel in Ilfracombe. There he breathed the seaside air, got big regular meals and learned that if you didn't scowl but were pleasant to the customers, you got bigger tips!

It was 'with Joby's blessing' that Tommy approached Joe Gess at Tylorstown and asked if he could fight for him. Apparently, Joe wasn't overly impressed with the idea because Young Farr who was already well-known to Joe, had been pretty inconsistent as a boxer and besides, at that stage he was still on the puny side. Undeterred, Tommy persisted:

> If you will take me on I will guarantee that you won't be sorry. I know that you understand the game from A to Z. I don't seem to have anyone willing to coach me, and I know that all I require is advice and guidance. I don't mind how hard I have to work, and if strength can do it, I will take on any job, but I do want you to let me have plenty of fights.

Eventually, Gess agreed to take him on at £1 a week plus his keep 'but he would have to earn it'. This meant doing anything required of him: putting up and dismantling the booth and general handyman duties. Tommy was thrilled and ran home to collect his clothes; he started work in the booth that very day.

The truth was that Joe Gess had learned a great deal over the years about boxers, and his discerning eye, cast over Tommy as he shuffled and tried to explain his reasons for wanting this job, had spotted the potential in him.

'In his own mind of course, he was already a champion and I think it was this imagination that really carried him through because he had to put up with all sorts of teasing and criticism. Promoters laughed at the very idea of his being a champion and he has been turned down so much that only a lad of great courage would have stuck to his guns.

'I had a good look at him, and I thought to myself, "You look like a fighter and big enough." I noticed he had long arms, had plenty of room to fill out and with a bit of coaching, he might be handy for the booth.'

Joe was recounting these memories in March 1937 when Tommy Farr had just become British and Empire heavyweight champion, beating Ben Foord on points over 15 rounds at Harringay.

> Little did I know at the time that he would blossom forth into a British heavyweight champion. I thought he would grow into a middleweight and no more, but what I liked about him was that he was very fast, even for a lightweight.
> It occurred to me that if he became only a moderate boxer his speed might carry him through. In those days he had no punch to speak of, but plenty of buck.

This observation may be judged with hindsight: of his total of one hundred and ninety-seven recorded fights Tommy won only twelve by a knockout.

In due course, a jubilant Tommy was promoted to doing the 'housework', which was Joe Gess's word for standing up in front to take on anyone from the crowd who fancied their chances against one of the boxers. He had proved to Joe that he could handle himself well after serving his time as a bouncer, keeping gatecrashers out of the canvas-walled booth.

'I warned him,' said Joe, 'there would be no messing. He would not only have to fight but beat all the fellers—and husky devils there were, I tell you—or he would be on no dough. Was he scared? Not a bit of it.'

During his first week, standing alongside the other boxers with his customary scowl and arms folded, he noticed he was being eyed up by a 'great navvy' from Swansea Docks who was clearly itching to have a go at him. Joe was a little anxious, noticing Tommy's pale face, but he need not have worried. Some judicious work to the big man's body followed by a well-aimed right to the chin earned Tommy his wages in the first round, and Joe breathed a satisfied sigh of relief.

Dozens of fights followed against colliers, farmers and many 'other classes of people'. Tommy grew in confidence as well as in stature (to the concern of Joe Gess, because the bigger the boxer the less likely someone from the crowd will challenge him!) and gained friends and fans wherever he went. He was given a dressing gown by the local boys in Pontardulais and a cigarette case from fans in Garnant. He continued to please his employer who almost never had to pay out £1 to Tommy's challengers.

Once, however, there was a notable exception to this case. One night in Pontycymer a dandyish fellow in fancy clothes and with a cut-glass accent stepped up to challenge Tommy Farr. He proceeded to astonish Joe by thoroughly beating his boxer over the three rounds, knocking him down sixteen times and taking everything Tommy could land on him. In a state of shock, Tommy watched this unlikely contender get dressed, refuse his prizemoney and disappear through the bemused crowd. No-one had asked his name and he hadn't volunteered it. They never saw him again. Some time later, still shaking his head in wonderment, Tommy remarked: 'All I know is that somewhere out there, the champion of the world is walking around at large!'

While Farr was with him, Joe took on two particularly significant roles in the youngster's life. Stepping temporarily into Job Churchill's shoes, Joe Gess was always around if Tommy needed to talk. In the evenings 'after a hard day's graft' he and Tommy would sometimes sit in a cosy corner of Joe's caravan while Tommy confided in him about his family, his childhood, of his short violent time in the colliery and his disappointment that his boxing ambitions were not materialising. But Tommy was also very aware of Joe's vast knowledge and experience in boxing and would pick his brains at every opportunity.

'Tommy was a curious sort of chap. He had a tremendous belief in his future . . . He had made up his mind he was going to stick to the road until the time came to launch out in the big lights. There were plenty of corners to be knocked off and he admitted it.'

'Come on, Joe bach,' Tommy would say coaxingly, 'Tell me what's wrong with my left hand,' or 'Do I use my feet properly?' Joe would stop what he was doing to give an impromptu training session, though not always with good grace.

'Frequently', he complained 'I would be in the middle of attending to the booth—putting a stay right here or patching up a bit of canvas there. But he would persist in having his questions answered.

'I have talked to him in such a way that if I had spoken in a similar way to others I would expect a punch on the whiskers. More than once I felt like kicking him in the pants all the way back to his darned Rhondda but he always had his way. Behind that pugnaciousness of his I could see something else. He was consumed with the idea of becoming a champion and so I tolerated his why's and wherefore's'.

Up to a point. Though Tommy Farr was known for his charm and was very popular ('He could make friends as easily as he could knock them over,' said Joe), he could also be moody and sulky. But then, so could Joe Gess. Sometimes the booth had to travel 30 miles in a day, and there may be up to a dozen shows to stage some weeks, so it was always a case of all hands on deck to get everything ready. After a particularly bad morning at Pontardulais, when the pair of them had argued about a bucket of water, the whole entourage was travelling to Pontardawe when the lorry 'conked out'. Joe called to Tommy to use the starting handle but, try as he might, he could not get it to work. In a temper Joe jumped down and 'called him something you cannot print. He buttoned up to me.' Joe rounded on him furiously and told him to get his cards and clear off home, but having tried the handle himself, Joe discovered that he hadn't engaged the starter switch. 'But I was still in a temper and refused to give in.'

With three other boxers, Joe opened the booth that night. Out of the corner of his eye he could see Tommy was still hanging about and told him again to clear off. Finally, the evening over, the two of them shook hands. It was all part of the travelling life and Tommy understood this.

But they both sensed that Tommy had learned pretty much all he could doing the 'housework' for Gess's boxing booth and Tommy's ambitions made him restless for change. In the comforting and familiar corner of Joe's caravan, he and Joe had a final 'heart-to-heart' chat before he left for home. Shaking hands and expressing his confidence in his ability, Joe's parting words were: 'Tommy, you've improved a ton since you've been with me and I'm sure that before long you will be winning a title.'

But that was not quite the end of their association.

Young Tommy Farr, impetuous, penniless and optimistic, set off, whistling, from Tonypandy one morning with some bread and cheese in his jacket pocket and walked to London. It took him several days. Getting as far as Slough, he decided to look around the town and the first thing he noticed was a branch of Lloyd's Bank. The familiar Welsh name struck a chord with him and Tommy recalled in a radio interview years later, that he thought this might be a nice place to come back to. At the back of his mind he had an idea that he had heard of Welsh people coming to live in Slough.

When he eventually got to London he found not one boxing gymnasium that was prepared to take on a scruffy unknown boxer from Wales, and so he continued sleeping rough, getting what work he could and finding it as hard to get in London as it was in Wales. Ironically, he ended up shovelling coal to stoke up the furnace on a Thames rubbish barge, and sharing his sleeping quarters with the cunning Thames rats. After three months he could stick it no more and finding his way to Paddington, had a rare stroke of luck. He met a fellow Welshman who listened sympathetically to his story and gave Tommy his own return ticket! Gratefully, Tommy went home to Tonypandy, to his brothers and sisters and to Job Churchill. After a good square meal and a philosophical talk with Job, who told him to put his escapade down to experience, Tommy knew his ambition to box was undiminished.

But what was his next step to be? He decided to issue challenges to local boxers of his weight through the press while Job Churchill saw to it that Tommy embarked on and stuck to a proper training regime. Churchill also enrolled him in evening classes to learn more about catering and the hotel trade because Tommy agreed that the summer he had spent working in a hotel had been one of the happier parts of his life and it would be sensible to have a trade when the boxing was out of his system. He also took on the task of improving Tommy's skills in reading and writing. But still Tommy was restless. Progress was slow and he was desperate to prove himself as a boxer.

And so it was Job that came up with the solution once more. Why not, he suggested, approach Joe Gess again, but this time to ask Joe to arrange decision fights for Tommy in pre-advertised shows? Joe's heart lifted when he saw his protégé approaching him across the field with a cheery wave. The crowds had thinned out a bit lately and he partly put this down to Tommy's departure from the booth. He jumped at the chance to arrange matches for Tommy because the staged bouts were the more lucrative part of his business and he reckoned that with the popular Young Farr topping the bill they would both be on a winner.

It was 2nd August 1932 when Young Farr stepped into Joe Gess's ring in Tredegar to meet Ashton Jones, an experienced boxer from Trealaw. He hadn't had a contest since May 1931, but his head was held high and he was raring to go. They went the full ten scheduled rounds and the fight was declared a draw. But Tommy's lively performance had delighted the audience, and there was a bigger crowd for his next fight, with Bunny Edgington at Pontycymer. This too, ended in a draw.

Tommy was used to short sharp fights of three or six rounds though he had boxed some ten-rounders too. Now Joe matched him in a twelve-round contest against Albert Donovan at Tredegar which went the distance. But it was Donovan's hand that was raised at the end.

Tommy learned and adapted to this different game. The booth was full to capacity on the following Saturday, 27th August, for Young Farr's contest with Bob Jarrett of Cardiff at Aberavon. Tommy loved that. Always popular with his audiences, he was building a loyal fan base which would stand him in good stead for things to come.

And that day, at last, the decision went to Farr. Amazingly, though still in his teens, he had had over eighty recorded contests by this time, winning only thirty of them, while seventeen were drawn and twelve resulted in no decision.

These no decision results seem a bit strange to us today. In America during this period, no decision results were frequently used by referees because of complex rules about points decisions. In Britain, however, no-decisions were not in general use—except in Wales. There may have been a number of reasons for this. Some may have been the conclusion of exhibition bouts. Perhaps some no-decisions were for bouts that took place in boxing booths. It is known that the burgeoning British Boxing Board of Control was concerned about the standard of refereeing in Wales during the thirties and it may have been a way of 'playing safe' at a time when licences were being issued by the Board for all functions in boxing, including refereeing.

They were, nonetheless, recorded fights, and so added to Tommy's already long record. Of course this list does not take into account the countless three rounders he did for Joe Gess, which he almost always won, or the barbaric bouts he had at the colliery for the vicarious pleasure of the betting men. And Tommy Farr had hardly started on his illustrious boxing career.

Now, the discipline gained in Joe Gess's boxing booth, Joby's insistence on a training regime and Tommy's ambition began to show. Tommy had grown in stature and confidence and was still willing to do his share of the work. One day he walked five miles to get petrol when the lorry ran out in some remote spot.

Unfortunately, this was the very day, 15th September 1932, that Joe Gess had arranged for Tommy to fight Hopkin Harry at Clydach. This was an important fight for him because Gess, knowing that Tommy would soon be moving on to a higher level of professional boxing, had also arranged for him to meet the classy and experienced Young ('Tiger') Ellis a few days later.

According to Gess, Harry was a big boxer with a punch like the kick of a mule. Tommy, unfazed, held his own until the fifth round, but a cut above his left eye was bleeding badly and the decision was made to pull him out. Inevitably, it put him at a big disadvantage when he met former Welsh champion Ellis on his home ground at Ystradgynlais and though he tried to box long range, his wily opponent soon worsened the injury and the referee stopped the fight in the fifth.

There was no alternative for Tommy but to give his inflamed and badly cut eye a chance to heal properly and Gess had to cancel a couple of contests. Finally, towards the end of November, it was deemed good enough to stand up to a ten-round contest against Bert Mallin at Pontardulais. Boxing cautiously to protect his eye, Tommy went the distance and won easily enough. A poster for the same day, 25th November 1932, shows Tommy top-lining in another ten-rounder with Dick Smith of Neath, at Joe's pavilion. Clearly, Joe thought Tommy's lay-off had been long enough and he didn't want to cancel any more bouts!

It was in December that Tommy's fortunes turned around and he began to get the attention he had so definitely earned.

As it turned out, it would be his last fight for Joe Gess.

Between them they had come up with a good one this time. Farr had been invited to have a 'try-out' with Jim Wilde whom he was later to fight for the Welsh heavyweight title and who even then was 'a big fellow, about 13 stone I should say,' said Joe. Wilde was preparing for a competition at the time. Considering Tommy had only recently fought Tiger Ellis in a welterweight contest he would have been giving away a fair amount of weight but, after the try-out, he came to Joe and said he thought he would like to take Wilde on over ten rounds. Joe agreed and the contest was arranged, but over twelve rounds.

The try-out had given Tommy the measure of his man and so he was able to overcome the weight handicap, and he beat Wilde on points. It was something Joe had come to recognise in Farr: his caution until he had weighed up his opponent and worked out his strategy.

BOXING!

GESS PAVILION
FAIRGROUND, Pontardulais

FRIDAY, NOV. 25th, 1932

TEN ROUND CONTEST

TOMMY KID FARR, Tonypandy

Who put up such a splendid fight against Hopkin Harry a few weeks ago and has a win over Bunny Eddington, Pontycymmer,

v.

DICK SMITH, Neath

the Glamorgan Middleweight Champion and runner-up in the Territorial Championships, 1932; since turning professional he has won all his contests with a knock-out, including Bob Jarratt, Aberavon; Ben Mellin, Neath; Jim Henderson, London, and several others

SIX ROUNDS CONTEST

JIM SMITH v. KID MORRIS
GLYNNEATH   BRITON FERRY

TEN ROUNDS CONTEST

BRYN EDWARDS, Garnant

Without doubt one of the best in West Wales at his weight, who has defeated some of the best featherweights in England and Wales.

v.

BILLY EVANS, Ystrad,

Ex-Featherweight Champion of Wales, who last Wednesday defeated Danny Carry, Featherweight Champion at Manchester.

SIX ROUNDS CONTEST

Young Brace, Treorchy v. Ed. Evans, Pontypridd

SIX ROUNDS

BERTIE DAVIES, Garnant
v.
KID JONES, Ammanford

Referee - Mr. PARRY, Porth.

Admission, 1/- (including Tax). : Doors open 7.30, first contest 8 prompt

Read the "Western Mail" for all Boxing Results

"South Wales Voice," Ystalyfera

231

Tommy Farr being interviewed.
Welsh Heavyweight Champion, 1936.

'Now, it was strange about Farr that whilst he always expressed belief in himself, when he entered the ring some of his confidence was shed until he had been able to find out just how good his opponent was. Once he got settled down, Farr quickly found his best form.'

There was no time for goodbyes or cosy caravan chats when Joe and Tommy parted company again. One afternoon, Tommy's brother turned up and said he had persuaded a local matchmaker, Rees Henry, to try Tommy out. News of his performance against Big Jim Wilde had spread through the valleys, well—like wildfire. Suddenly, he was a contender.

In 1935 he fought Eddie Phillips for the British light-heavywight title, losing on points. Disappointed and restless, Tommy decided he was 'tired and weary of being classed as a small town fighter' and that he needed to live nearer London. He thought of the town that had impressed him so much some years earlier; he bought a house in Slough.

The rest of Tommy Farr's well-documented career is, as they say, history. He went on to a total of around 197 recorded bouts, losing only forty-three. He fought the best in the world, beating both Max Baer and Ribbentrop's protégé, Walter Neusel, both in the same year, 1937, as his historic meeting with Joe Louis. It was also the year he won the British heavyweight crown.

Ribbentrop, who was the Nazi ambassador in London, came to the Farr-Neusel fight with other officials from Hitler's embassy and Neusel gave the 'heil Hitler' salute from the ring.

Tommy kept up pressure on the German throughout the fight, and though Neusel was a tough fighter, the sustained attack seemed to confound and frustrate him and he crumbled within three rounds, when he sank to his knees, unable to continue. Ribbentrop stormed out of the hall to show his disgust with Neusel. After the fight's performance, two years before the outbreak of war, Farr became a hero. He achieved legendary status when he fought Joe Louis.

As for Joe Gess, in total contrast, we know very little. After 1934, he is no longer mentioned in Johnny Vaughan's diaries and it seems likely that he stopped bringing his booth to the Amman Valley around then, perhaps concentrating on what may have been the more lucrative areas of the Rhondda and Swansea valleys. What with the increasing vigilance of the Boxing Board of Control over booth fighting and the approaching World War, things got tougher and tougher for the Gess family. Joe's wife—always respectfully known as Mrs Gess—was a stalwart help to him through the hard times. Her main job on the booth was to collect the money and pay the boxers, which she did alongside running their caravan home. As she used to remark: 'I was born in the boxing booth show business. So I know the ways of it.'

She looked back on their time with Tommy Farr quite matter-of-factly:

> He was a little bit of a fellow when he came to us, and as cocky as they make 'em.
> Joe used to have to cuff him over the head now and then to keep him quiet. But Tommy was a bright boy and he came along wonderfully. I used to see that he got a good plate of food, and how that boy could

eat! We looked after him the way we look after all our boys. Treat them right and they treat you right.

While Joe and Mrs Gess were still bringing their booth to Ammanford, they often depended on the local boxers to get a show together or to stand up front and take on challengers. One particularly loyal pair were brothers Cliff and Gwyn Peregrine. On one occasion, Gwyn had taken his girlfriend to the Palace cinema at the top of Ammanford's arcade. Aware of a disturbance during the interval, he saw Mrs Gess clambering along the row of seats towards him. 'Can you come and help out, Gwyn?' she whispered. 'We've got a big crowd out front this fine evening and not enough boxers!'

Gwyn went, to his credit, and at least he earned a few bob for his trouble, though I don't know what his girlfriend had to say to him. Later on, as she paid him out, Mrs Gess told Gwyn: 'Sometimes I think we'd have to close up if it wasn't for you boys.'

There is plenty of evidence that Joe Gess's booth was active up until the latter part of the 1930s, mostly in the Rhondda Valley and East Wales to the borders. The excellent Brecon boxer Dudley Lewis, who gained the Welsh flyweight title when he stopped Dickie Lewis of Stanleytown at Mountain Ash in April 1938, had a number of contests in Gess's booth during 1937, after Joe had taken him under his wing and agreed to train him for twelve months. Dudley had a terrific right, and he was popular with the crowds. In some reports he was called Douglas Lewis—I have no idea why.

On one occasion, he met up with Harry Morris of Aberdare when the Gess Pavilion was at Pontypool:

> Lewis set the terrific pace, and reaped the reward for his whirlwind tactics. Morris had been building up a reputation as a determined fighter, and recently gained a smart victory over Jerry O'Neill (Merthyr), the ex-flyweight champion of Wales.
>
> But the lad from Brecon, who seems to wear a perpetual smile even when the battle is fiercest, launched his barrage of blows from the first gong and Morris was overwhelmed. He tried to stem the torrent of

punches, but his hardest blows only had the effect of momentarily checking the advances of the antagonist.

Lewis was the non-stop fighter, and he was very quick in getting in blows to the head on the break-away. One right swing caught Morris flush on the jaw as he was retreating in the first round and he dropped to the floor for a count of nine.

Morris lasted until the fourth when he went down again and was counted out.

On 27th August 1937, Dudley Lewis knocked out Billy Griffiths of Abertridwr, again in Gess's booth, at Tongwynlais.

One of Joe Gess's last big shows was for Pontypool Hospital when Dudley Lewis fought Johnny Mason, of Pentre and Birmingham. To Joe's satisfaction, Dudley stopped his opponent in the ninth round. Tommy Farr, it was advertised in the local press, was to make an appearance there in support of his old mentor, one of a number of times he was able to help Joe out following his success.

Dudley, or Douglas, Lewis later joined the Swansea camp run by Dai James, who was Ronnie James's father, and was managed by him on a four-year contract when he continued to be a successful boxer.

One of the largely unremarked effects of the war was the devastating impact it had on fairground folk. The blackout meant they were unable to show any lights and so could not trade in the evenings after dusk. Boxing booths in particular, were obviously also hit by the fact that their young male customers, the 'all-comers' as well as the audience, not to mention the boxers, had gone off to fight in a different kind of conflict —for the second time in 25 years.

The booths were already slowly declining in popularity and never recovered after the long years of war; many of the proprietors were elderly by then and it was too hard a life for them to encourage their sons to take it up. Gess's Pavilion, whose canvas walls had witnessed so many hugely entertaining evenings, was at some point, dismantled for the last time. I am sorry to say that I do not know what happened to Joe Gess, though I do know his son served in the Second World War.

Chapter 16

A Policeman's Lot—
Dai 'Farmer' Jones and Iori Morris

If you ever go to Laugharne in the West of Carmarthenshire, you may marvel at its tranquil air of belonging to another time. Most people of course, associate the sleepy little estuary town with Dylan Thomas, and go to visit The Boathouse which was his home and where much of his writing was done, in a little shed out at the back. The strong outer walls of the castle still stand looking out over the water, and on a quiet evening stroll along the shingle, you may hear little else but curlews calling.

Hard to believe then, that at the end of the 1940s, when Dylan Thomas went to live there with his wife Caitlin, it was regarded by some as a bit of a 'frontier' town, where drunkenness and brawling were a persistent problem for the Carmarthenshire Police Force, especially at the weekends. What were they to do about it?—that was the question.

Then someone came up with a possible answer: why not send in the fighting farmer from Ammanford—Constable David Samuel Jones?

Before the war, he was better known as Dai 'Farmer' Jones. He had a different career then, too. He was a professional boxer.

Although Dai did not grow up to be a farmer, he was born on a farm: Llwyn Celyn in Betws, Ammanford, in March 1914, where his parents farmed. As he grew, always an 'outdoors' sort of boy, he developed an interest in sport of all kinds. Inspired by the success of the amateur boxers at the Amman Valley Boxing Club, he began to run and work out to strengthen his muscles, fitting his self-imposed training regime around his farming chores.

But his toughest task was to persuade his parents that it was a good idea for him to join the gym. They finally gave their blessing when Dai enlisted the help of his friend and neighbour, young Meidrim Thomas, who was also eager to join.

Together with friends, Don Chiswell and Iori Morris, they were soon in training for the forthcoming Welsh ABA finals of 1934.

Although nine really promising young boxers, including Dai and his three friends, were sent to the finals from the Amman Valley that year, such was the fierceness of the competition that not one of them was successful. But all four of them had decided at some point during the competition that they wanted to take the extra step and turn professional.

After some further cajoling, Dai's parents agreed that he could contact Johnny Vaughan and see what he had to say about the matter.

In fact his parents turned out to be staunch supporters as Dai's career progressed and they were very proud of his achievements.

Johnny Vaughan was quite impressed with the youngster who presented himself for training. All four lads were keen and willing to learn; Dai was the biggest and had clearly worked hard to build his strength. Beside him, young Iori at bantamweight, looked tiny. But the pair of them were to do Johnny Vaughan proud over the years leading up to the war.

Iorwerth Milton Morris, or Iori to his friends, was born on 26th July 1915. He had done well as an amateur boxer. In the 1934 finals, he lost on points to the amateur flyweight champion J. Pottinger, who held the title until 1937.

Johnny Vaughan put Iori and Dai on the same bill in Neath on 21st April, when Iori outpointed Ginger Williams and Dai held Ambrose Jones to a draw. Dai and Iori were to appear on the same bill many times through their respective boxing careers.

On the same night, but on one of Johnny's own bills in the Ammanford pavilion, Meidrim Thomas drew with Hopkin Jones.

Dai's next opponent was Bertie Bevan of Swansea, and he found him a tough nut to crack, losing twice to him over the summer of 1934. It

Johnny Vaughan with Edwin Evans, Martin Fury,
Meidrim Thomas and Dai Farmer Jones.

wasn't until November that Dai got his first win, on points over ten
rounds against Jack Horton at Ystradgynlais.

Iori, in the meantime, having lost in May to Syd Williams of Pontardawe, went on to beat him in July, over six rounds at Swansea.

Dai had found a training regime with Johnny that suited him well
and he finished up the year with two wins: outpointing Griff Lewis at
the Mannesmann Hall in Swansea on 26th November and stopping
Eddie Evans of Abercrave in round three, at the same venue, on 17th
December. A couple of weeks earlier, Iori had a good points win over
Bert 'Boyo' Rees, of Swansea (not to be confused with Boyo Rees, Abercwmboi, lightweight champion of Wales).

1935 was an excellent year for both Iori Morris and Dai Jones, who
carried on bringing prestige to the Ammanford camp. After a points
loss against Caryl Taylor of Swansea in January, Iori appeared with Dai

on the same bill in Merthyr on 19th January, when Dai outpointed Jack Whiting and Iori beat Douglas (Dudley) Lewis from Brecon:

> This contest introduced us to a newcomer in Douglas Lewis, a charming lad from Brecon, who fought a hard fight with a smile on his face throughout, which earned for him an ovation at the finish. He had already earned a good reputation which he fully justified by the confident and clever fight he put up against Iorrie Morris, one of the cleverest boxers in South Wales at his weight. And he needed all his skilful boxing to deal with Douglas Lewis who made him go all the way. Lewis is undoubtedly smart and can hit with power. In that respect he was superior to Morris and he was equally as fast, which is saying something, but Morris has had more experience and is a very brainy fighter.
>
> At the finish he was awarded the verdict on points after an even and exciting contest fought at a very fast pace. When these two meet again I hope to be there.—*Carmarthen Journal.*

Douglas, who was just as often known as Dudley, Lewis, was the same Brecon boxer who was trained during part of his career by Joe Gess.

Iori went on to score seven more victories up to June, including a knockout in the second round at Ammanford against Dai Harries from Maesteg. He also had two draws over this period—the first in a contest with Dick Lewis of Tylorstown, in February, when he was again on the same bill as Dai Farmer Jones, who beat Bunny Edgington. Iori outpointed Dick Lewis in their return bout a month later. He also drew with Eddie Davies of Cwmparc, on 8th June, after beating him in April.

Iori had a bit of a rest after this, resuming his training in time to meet Les Hall of Clydach on 21st September, at the Vetch Field, but he was outpointed by Hall over six rounds.

Dai had certainly enjoyed a successful year, chalking up a total of thirteen wins up to September, with only one loss, against Les Ward at Trealaw in April. Five of the wins were inside the distance, against Jack Whiting, Jack Morgan, Eddie Manning, Hopkin Harry and Dai

Beynon. He and Johnny had worked hard to develop that right hook, and it was beginning to pay off.

Dai also drew twice with Bertie Bevan, but as he had lost twice to him the previous year, he felt he was getting somewhere. He was right. Having had the time to get used to Bevan's style and learning all the while, Dai was much more confident against him when they met for an eliminator for the Welsh middleweight title on 21st November 1935, at the Mannesmann Hall, Swansea. This time there was no doubt; Dai kayoed Bevan in the ninth.

On the same night, Iori outpointed Douglas (Dudley) Lewis, though it was a close thing. When he met him again the following April, he again got the decision by a narrow margin:

> Morris is also very clever in defence, and he needed it. At one time he tired slightly and looked serious, but he just held the whip handle throughout, to get the decision against a very plucky and clever loser.

On Boxing Day 1935, Dai outpointed Les Ward in Llanelli and Iori shared a bill at the Drill Hall, Carmarthen, with another Ammanford boxer, Martin Fury. Iori beat Matt Powell of Penygraig over ten rounds and Martin Fury knocked out Edgar Evans of Porth in the second round.

Dai Farmer Jones faced his biggest challenge so far in February 1936. A fortnight earlier, he had met, and lost on points, to a really tough opponent, South African Eddie McGuire up in Leicester, but the loss had not discouraged him. On 24th February, he stepped into the ring at the Mannesmann Hall to face the middleweight champion of Wales, Billy Thomas of Bargoed, with the Welsh title at stake. The *Carmarthen Journal* reported:

> Dai Jones (Ammanford) provided a sensation in a 15 round contest for the middleweight championship of Wales at Plasmarl, Swansea, on Monday night, when he knocked out Billy Thomas (Bargoed), the holder, in the third round with a terrific right to the chin.
>
> Benny Price (Ammanford), making his first appearance in public, knocked out Wyndham Lewis (Abercrave), in the last of a six-round

contest, after Lewis had been down for two counts of nine in the fourth round.

The new Welsh middleweight champion waved triumphantly to his supporters and returned home to the warm congratulations of his parents.

Yet another young boxer making his mark from Ammanford, Benny Price, added two more knockouts to this dazzling start, during 1936. He continued to do quite well under Johnny's guidance up to the start of the war but afterwards, though still boxing until 1948, he wasn't able to capitalise on his early promise. In an attempt at the Welsh welterweight title in January 1945, he lost to Gwyn Williams of Pontycymer, retiring in the tenth round of a fifteen round contest at Oxford Town Hall. His last win, in contrast, was a knockout against Cliff's and Brian's less well-known brother Ken Curvis, at Pontardawe, on 3rd March 1948.

After beating Ginger Dawkins over the distance at Neath on 10th March 1936, Dai was knocked out in the first round of a contest in Rushden against Bob Simpkins on 23rd March. It shook him badly. He rested for a month before resuming training, but his confidence had also taken a knock, and he was outpointed for the second time by Eddie McGuire, on 11th May, this time in Swansea.

A run of three points wins followed though as he got back in his stride, including a win over twelve rounds against Glen Moody, which particularly pleased Dai and Johnny.

On 1st June 1936, Dai was matched against Tommy Smith of Cardiff at Carmarthen.

> Smith began the attacking and Jones replied with right jabs to the chin. Jones caught Smith with a right hook in the first round, but missed badly with another two.
>
> It was easily distinguishable at the beginning of the second round that Jones was a tough fighter and was as strong as a lion. He caught Smith with a nicely-timed right to the face early in the second session and with another heavy right after some in-fighting. These must have been stunning punches as Smith, who was able to take hard punish-

ment, was not the same after he had received a few of Jones's rights. He slipped to his knees, but got up before the count started.

In round three, Smith was checked with nicely timed rights which caused injury to his eye. The short left and right jabs which he took from Jones were obviously having their effect, and Smith failed to land any powerful punches to Jones, owing to the latter's clever defence. Early in the fourth round Jones, although not quite as steady on his feet as at the end of the last round, landed a terrific right hook to Smith's body which sent him out of the ring, and so ended the last fight of the evening with a knockout'.

It proved to be a very successful night for the Ammanford friends. Meidrim Thomas beat Norman Gardener from Milford Haven on points. The *Carmarthen Journal* said:

Thomas was by far the best-built boxer and he took advantage of this throughout the fight . . . doing all the attacking in the early stages, but Gardener replied to almost every punch. Gardener was liable to drop his guard too often, and every opportunity of landing a punch was taken by Thomas. However, Gardener, a cool boxer who took no risks, managed to deliver two nasty uppercuts to his opponent's jaw in the second round. Of the punches that were exchanged in the third and fourth rounds, Thomas's were by far the heavier and Gardener showed signs of weakness. During the fifth and sixth rounds, Thomas was all out for a k.o. and caught Gardener with a few nicely-timed rights, but he was cautioned by the referee for low punching.

On the same bill, Iori Morris outpointed Dave Williams of Blaenau, over ten two-minute rounds.

This fight was full of thrills, and the spectators showed their appreciation on a few occasions. Morris was the aggressor in the opening rounds but Williams delivered some well-timed uppercuts and left jabs to his opponent's face. The terrific pace which they took up at the beginning lasted the whole fight, without any signs of exhaustion. Morris's punches were aimed at Williams's body, but Williams seldom missed a reply with an uppercut.

In the fifth round, Morris missed badly with his right, but Williams, who had by now got used to his opponent's tactics, landed many right uppercuts which were a menace to Morris's defence throughout the fight.

They remained pretty even until the end of the bout when: 'The verdict was given in favour of Morris, but only by a small margin of points.'

A mere two days later, Dai was beaten by Ocky Davies of Milford Haven, and had to wait until December for a return with Ocky, when he turned the tables.

Following the defeat, Johnny recorded in his diary that the next day Dai had to have his hand put in plaster, and this kept him out of action until the end of July.

Iori met Vic Davies twice in the first week of June, beating him once and then holding him to a draw, before outpointing Evan Phillips at Llanelli on 27th June.

A further win and a draw, against Jim O'Connor and Wyndham Lewis respectively, finished up the year for Iori, who then took a five-month break from boxing.

Dai, having beaten Cock Moffat at Wrexham over twelve rounds in July, was outpointed by Cheo Morejon in Swansea at the beginning of August. It would be almost a year and a half before he got even with Morejon, by outpointing him over twelve rounds in Bristol in December 1937. It says a great deal about Dai Farmer Jones's defensive tactics that he went the distance twice with the Cuban. Cheo Morejon had a very high rate of knockouts, though these were mostly in Europe and Cuba. His five or six UK contests all went the distance.

Meanwhile, in August 1936, Dai had a pleasant trip down to Plymouth, where he met Tommy Martin twice and outpointed him once. Their second contest ended in a draw. This certainly did Dai some good, as Martin was considered a potential contender for the British middleweight title and Johnny was obviously thinking along those lines for Dai.

On 12th September, Dai scored a knockout in nine rounds over Ginger Dawkins at Bargoed. *Boxing* reported the bout:

Dawkins offered stubborn resistance for several rounds, fighting back strongly with both hands. In the fourth round the Gelligaer man had the bad luck to come up against a particularly heavy right which landed on the jaw. He never really recovered from this punch, though continuing to fight pluckily. Jones got home a number of terrific blows both to the head and body, which gradually weakened Dawkins, but he retaliated gamely up to the eighth round. At the end of this session however, the towel came in from his corner, Jones being declared the winner. It had been a gruelling affair, but there was no question of Jones being the better man. He timed his punches with more precision and also put more power into his blows. At the same time Dawkins deserves praise for his grit.

Exactly one month later he employed similar tactics to knock out Jacky McLeod down at the Mannesmann Hall in Plasmarl, this time in the second round.

This was Dai's biggest test to date because it was an eliminator contest for the British title, and he passed it with flying colours. The old spark was rekindled in Johnny's heart. Was it possible this time he might have a British champion in training? He'd come so close with Danny Evans, Ginger Jones and Billy Quinlen. Now he reckoned, he had another chance with Dai Farmer Jones.

Dai had at this time rarely ventured up to London, but his next contest took place in Holborn Stadium against Ben Valentine, a boxer originally from Fiji. He was a successful boxer with a good punch, but Dai could punch too, and he took Valentine the distance, losing narrowly on points. After another couple of points wins—one against Roy Mills at Nottingham and the other over Ocky Davies—Dai met another boxer with a knockout punch, Canadian Paul Schaeffer, in Cardiff. It was a hard fight that went the full twelve rounds, with Dai the loser in his last fight of the year. It was time for a well-earned rest.

Two months later, Schaeffer lost to the brilliant Liverpool boxer, Ernie Roderick.

Towards the end of 1936, Johnny asked Dai to consider how serious he was about going for the British title. He was going to have to step up the training even more if he meant to be a contender—OK, he'd gone the distance with Valentine and Schaeffer, but he'd lost on points. He was going to have to meet tougher opponents than them; was he prepared to give it a go? Dai assured him that he was, and Johnny then had no hesitation in finalising the arrangements already in hand, for Dai to meet the experienced boxer, Jack Hyams, in a final eliminator for the British and British Empire (Commonwealth) Middleweight title.

Jack Hyams, from Stepney, London, had beaten Bill Hardy in a British title eliminator in 1936 when the referee stopped the fight in the eleventh round.

Hyams and Dai Jones met at Earls Court Arena, London, on 22nd February 1937, three weeks after Dai had outpointed Bob Simpkins in the Mannesmann Hall.

Again Dai forced his opponent to go the distance, but he lost to Hyams over fifteen rounds. The following October, therefore, it was Hyams and not Dai Farmer Jones who met the tough fighter from Rochdale, Jock McAvoy, who was defending his British and British Empire middleweight titles.

Despite a recent injury to his neck, caused by a horse-riding accident, McAvoy battled his way to retaining his title against Hyams, and the referee had to step in in the eleventh round to stop further damage to Hyams's eye.

Jack Hyams continued boxing during the war, finishing around 1943, with an excellent record of over 160 recorded fights, of which at least 100 were wins.

On the same night that Dai Jones was battling Hyams at Earls Court, Iori Morris outpointed Dai Davies of Neath at the Mannesman Hall, Plasmarl.

A week later the two friends appeared on the same bill once more, this time in Maesteg. Dai outpointed Tim Sheehan over twelve rounds while Iori beat Syd Worgan over six rounds.

Young Syd Worgan from Llanharan, though he was one of six brothers, had no history of boxing in his family, developing his interest after being given his first pair of boxing gloves by his only sister,

Elizabeth. He turned pro at the age of eighteen and had just turned twenty when he met Iori in February 1937. He always combined his boxing with his work in Llanharan colliery and among the opponents he defeated during his career were Gus Foran, Dave Crowley, Dudley Lewis and Kid Tanner. He boxed throughout the war, and in 1944, won the Welsh featherweight title by outpointing Tommy Davies of Nantyglo at Newport. He was undefeated when he hung up his boxing gloves in 1947. He remained actively interested in boxing though, particularly with the Welsh Ex-boxers Association in his later years.

Worgan and Iori met again in June 1937, by which time Syd had improved his boxing sufficiently to turn the tables on Iori, beating him on points at the Mannesmann Hall. Iori had hit a losing streak, unfortunately. Having already lost to Dai Davies in May, he went on to be outpointed by Douglas (Dudley) Lewis, Brecon—these too were boxers he had beaten on previous occasions.

Then, in October, he was knocked out in the third round of a 15-round contest at Cardiff, by Mog Mason from Gilfach Goch. This contest was for the Welsh bantamweight title; Iori's only title fight. Having been a clever and successful boxer, he seemed to have just lost heart, so that coming up against the experienced and wily Mason, who had first won the Welsh title in 1934, Iori was completely outclassed. Iori had three more wins out of five contests before retiring.

Dai Farmer Jones ploughed on steadily through 1937, proving both his tremendous punching power and his superb defence against top liners and champions alike; he gave them all a run for their money. In April and again in June, he beat Seaman Jim Lawlor—a tough southpaw from the Suffolk coast, who clocked up well over a hundred fights between 1933 and 1939, at which time he was recalled to active service.

Dai's first meeting with Lawlor ended with a controversial foul delivery by Lawlor in round twelve, but there was no doubting Dai's fair-and-square points win at their second meeting on 28th June, when Johnny's diary records Dai's weight as eleven stone eight and a half pounds. Also on the bill that night was the match between Iori Morris and Syd Worgan, which Worgan won on points; Don Chiswell was outpointed by Dai James of Clydach.

Iori Morris.   *Dai Farmer Jones.*

In between the two victories over Lawlor, Dai Jones met the current British and British Empire middleweight champion Jock McAvoy, in a non-title fight at Bristol.

McAvoy was not his real name, nor was he a Scotsman, but he was a brilliant champion who held the British middleweight title for twelve years, from 1933 to 1945 and the British Empire middleweight title from 1933 to 1939, eventually retiring undefeated in both championships. He also had championship contests for European and World light-heavyweight titles and even fought Jack Petersen for the British and British Empire heavyweight title, which he lost on points, his hands badly damaged in a previous fight.

Jock McAvoy was born Joseph Bamford in Burnley, but the family moved to Rochdale when he was small, where his father operated a horse-drawn wagon in the haulage business. After a couple of years of working at jobs he did not enjoy, he got friendly with local boxing brothers Charlie and Stanley Hall, who had converted the cellar at their home into a gym, and there he did some sparring and found it suited him just fine. But, mostly because of his mother's opposition to professional boxing, he was nearly twenty years old when he finally turned up at the Royton Club and asked for a try-out with one of promoter Joe Tolley's lads.

He got a fight that same afternoon and kayoed a lad called Billy Longworth in two rounds. He always said that he ended up with his fighting name by mistake at the very start of his boxing career. An admirer of Kid McCoy, Jock had asked the promoter to announce him as Jock McCoy, because he didn't want his mother to find out he was boxing. It was down to bad handwriting, he said, that he was actually announced as Jock McAvoy, and he was stuck with it then.

In spite of Joe Tolley's management and the fact he had read Jack Dempsey's *How to Box* book from cover to cover, Jock was a bit naive about training methods to begin with. Matched with Billy Chew over ten rounds in 1928, he decided to go on a six-mile hike across the moors on the afternoon of the fight, reckoning that it would be an excellent preparation. When the fight was due to begin his legs were aching and worse still, so were his arms. He retired at the start of the eighth round, the first of only fourteen losses over his long career of 147 contests.

A year and a half before his meeting with Dai Farmer Jones, McAvoy had travelled to America with an ambition to fight John Henry Lewis for the World light-heavyweight title. But it was against 'Babe' Risko that he had what was arguably the best bout any British boxer ever had in America. The fight took place five days before Christmas 1935. A blizzard was raging in New York, which unfortunately affected the attendance at Madison Square Garden. McAvoy had injured his thumb five days earlier and had not trained since so that he came in at two pounds over the stipulated weight, but it would not have made any difference to the outcome. The American magazine *The Ring* reported the occasion:

McAvoy rushed out of his corner, crashed a right to the jaw, and down went Risko with a thud. Six times the American champion hit the canvas before he was counted out.

That was it. It took two minutes, 48 seconds.

When Risko's camp wanted a return, Jock's manager, Dave Lumiansky agreed, but on condition that Risko's New York/NBA title came with it. He never had a reply.

When Jock McAvoy realised his ambition and met John Henry Lewis for the World light-heavyweight crown some three months later, it was something of an anti-climax—he lost to Lewis on points over fifteen rounds.

Unfortunately, it was Dai's turn to be outpointed by the champion McAvoy, when they met at Bristol's Colston Hall in May 1937:

PLUCKY DAI JONES

Fresh from his victory over Eddie Phillips, which gained him a second title, Jock McAvoy was on view . . . on Monday night, his opponent in a ten-rounds bout being Dai Jones, the Welsh middleweight champion.

One would have excused the Manchester man had he asked the promoter to postpone this contest seeing that it came so soon after his title fight, but Jock was in excellent shape and when he stepped into the ring no one would have guessed that less than a week previously he had been through a hectic fourteen rounds.

Jones was soon to find that McAvoy was in tip-top form, for he was subjected to a double-handed attack. The Welshman stood up well to this rough treatment and gave a game display, although he was forced to hold considerably in order to avoid punishment.

The champion was always on top, and scored almost as he liked, but Jones got him a good many times with a straight left, and occasionally tried a right, but with little effect. In the sixth and seventh the Welshman took a great deal of punishment and only his gameness prevented McAvoy from scoring a decisive victory.

Jones came back somewhat in the next, and pulled McAvoy up with a fine right to the jaw, but the man from Manchester was unhurt and coming on, gave his rival a severe buffeting. Jock tried hard to finish matters in the final round, and opening with a characteristic whirlwind attack, had Jones going with a powerful left to the jaw. How the Welshman kept his feet is a mystery, yet he did so in spite of the way his energetic rival charged in, and hit out lustily with either hand.

Swings and uppercuts had Jones in distress and the final bell must have come as a welcome sound to his ears. McAvoy took every round except the eighth, which was even, but the Welshman came in for an ovation on account of his plucky showing.

Johnny Vaughan's spark of hope had dimmed once again.

His man was, nonetheless, up there with the best of them, and he was already arranging for another first-class opponent for Dai: South African Eddie Peirce.

There was no time to reflect on what might have been.

First of all, they took a little trip up to Llanybyther where Dai stopped Ginger Dawkins again, this time in the sixth round.

Dai Jones and Eddie Peirce, the South African middleweight titleholder, were second-liners on the bill at St Helen's, Swansea, on Monday, 19th July 1937. Top of the bill was a contest between Swansea's Big Jim Wilde and Jack London of West Hartlepool.

Peirce had recently returned to Britain from a successful trip to America where, according to G. G. Lowry of the *South Wales Evening Post*, he had 'clearly defeated all his thirteen opponents.' Before he went to the States, Peirce had beaten both Jack Hyams and Archie Sexton. On his way back, he stopped off at Dublin and beat Bill Hardy of Leicester. Peirce was a formidable opponent indeed, and Dai's training was watched with special interest by Swansea and Ammanford fans alike. A report of the fight appeared in the *South Wales Evening Post* the following day:

> The contest between Dai 'Farmer' Jones . . . and Eddie Peirce, the South African champion, ended in a points verdict for the latter, a decision which he fully deserved.
>
> Jones fought a good fight but Peirce, although he was a little disappointing, knew too many tricks for the Welshman.

Dai in the ring with Big Jim Wilde.

In the early rounds Jones tried to force matters, but he missed a great deal with his right swings and hooks, while inside Peirce was far too clever for him. Peirce did not seem unduly worried by the punches and he usually made up for them a moment or so later.

It was an interesting fight and while Jones was beaten by a better all-round exponent of the game, he was by no means disgraced.

Jack London beat Jim Wilde on the night, by a knockout. Seven years later, London took the British and British Empire heavyweight titles from Freddie Mills. He was of course, the father of Brian London, the 'Blackpool Bomber', and was his son's staunchest supporter. Jack was in Brian's corner on the night of 29th August 1960, when the famous 'Brawl in Porthcawl' took place. But he never expected that he would be the one ending up on the canvas.

251

Brian London was a sincere admirer of the skill of Welsh boxer Joe Erskine; it had not been easy taking the British heavyweight title from Joe and he may not have done it had it not been for Joe's cut eye. It was a proud moment for father and son, when the Lonsdale Belt was put round Brian's waist in June 1958. The following January, he lost it to Henry Cooper.

The Welshman who faced him at the Coney Beach Arena on that warm August night was an altogether more rugged fighter of less even temperament than Erskine. Dick Richardson from Newport had held Joe Bygraves to 'a creditable draw' in his first attempt at a title: a contest for the British Empire crown in Cardiff some three years earlier. However, in March 1960 Richardson travelled to Dortmund where he took the European heavyweight title from Hans Kalbfell. The *Boxing Yearbook* described the fight:

> In a bruising battle Richardson suffered a bad eye injury before coming through in sensational fashion. Kalbfell was floored for eight in the thirteenth round, but upon rising was immediately flattened, with his corner claiming that no 'box on' instructions had been given.

The contest with Brian London was Richardson's first defence of his European title. Richardson, by virtue of his strength and ruggedness, was tipped to beat the Northerner, but once the fight began, London thought he could win it. He began to relax into the fight, and the Welsh crowd seemed to be with him, cheering what was seen as his clear superiority over Richardson. Richardson got more and more frustrated, and he tended to throw his head forward as he lunged in trying to land his punches, and had to be warned several times about the use of his head. London complained about it in the fifth, sixth and seventh rounds. He sustained a cut in the sixth round, severe enough for trainer, Jackie Bates, to want to retire him. Brian refused and rushed out from his corner at the start of the seventh, intending to stop his opponent there and then. But, big as an ox, Dick Richardson stayed resolutely upright right to the bell.

At once, Brian London's corner retired their man—and all hell broke loose.

In his entertaining biography of Brian London, Andrew Sumner described the events that followed:

> Brian's version of what happened is interesting but not necessarily accurate:
>
>> 'I went across to Richardson's corner to shake his hand but I saw somebody coming at me and I let him have one! I've never been involved in anything like that before.'
>
> A more objective version of events had London stalking across to Richardson's corner, at which point Dick's trainer Johnny Lewis, moved towards him. There was a skirmish during which Lewis was floored. In the melee that followed Richardson's handlers, officials and London's father Jack, were all involved in a wild scuffle, during which London senior hit the deck. One man was knocked clean through the ropes, another was felled by a punch, a third man toppled over the temporarily prone form of Jack London.
>
> Chairs and bottles were thrown as the crowd erupted and a police cordon was quickly set up around the ring. London needed an escort to reach the safety of the dressing room as the crowd vented its anger, booing and jeering.
>
> There was a certain irony in London's pre-fight comment to the press:
>
>> 'Anything can happen in boxing, such as a cut eye, or one silly fatal mistake.'

Brian London's cut eye needed seven stitches thanks to the head butting from Richardson, but after he had calmed down, his sense of humour returned: 'I'm training for my next fight with Richardson,' he announced, 'by getting a billy goat as a sparring partner!'

The British Boxing Board of Control, stung by the press descriptions of 'scenes reminiscent of a Western saloon bar brawl' duly deliberated, and fined Brian London £1,000, which they took from his purse money. He was also given a serious reprimand for doing 'great harm to the sport'. No doubt to the enormous relief of the Board though, the potentially explosive return bout never took place.

It was also a hot August evening, in 1937, when Dai Farmer Jones found himself in the Market Hall, Carmarthen, 'in an atmosphere that reminded one of a greenhouse' as the *Carmarthen Journal* put it.

He was defending a title too—his Welsh middleweight title—against Tim Sheehan from Merthyr. At the weigh-in, Dai was 11 stone 4lbs and Sheehan was 11 stone.

> From the start it was obvious that Jones was the stronger boxer, with most of his weight in chest and shoulders. In the opening stages Sheehan managed to keep his opponent away with some good straight lefts (which spoke well of his boxing technique), but Jones in time was able to smother these, and in the third round went in with such fury that Sheehan tottered like a tree in a hurricane and then crumpled under some vicious right swings and a lightning uppercut.
>
> Sheehan went down for a count of eight but came up for more, and got it. Jones, using his right with deadly effect, measured his man and, in delivering a left hook, nearly overbalanced.
>
> He drove Sheehan to the ropes and kept plugging away at him as though he were a punchbag, a comparison not beyond belief, for Sheehan by this time was practically out on his feet. He pluckily continued and after being sent to the ropes, went down once more for a count of eight. Jones was now all out for the 'hors de combat' and got in some thudding rights to Sheehan's heart and plexus. The contender was on the canvas for eight and then for nine, and as the gong went for the end of the (third) round, the referee raised Jones's hand and declared that he was the winner on a technical knockout.
>
> Loud applause greeted the decision, not so much because Jones had won, but because Sheehan had stuck gamely to the end, long after his seconds would have been justified in throwing in the towel.

Dai had a three-month lay-off after this fight, and it was at the end of November that he travelled up to Blackburn to meet 'Battling' Charlie Parkin of Mansfield. Again he stopped his opponent, this time in the seventh round. Dai's last fight of 1937 was the return with the

Cuban, Cheo Morejon, who had beaten him in 1936. In an exciting contest that went the distance, Dai Farmer Jones came out the winner; a good way to end the year.

Charlie Parkin's backers had lost no time in arranging a return bout for their man against Dai Jones. A convenient venue was Hereford on 4th January 1938, but the local press reported that it didn't go according to the Ammanford camp's plan.

> Dai 'Farmer' Jones, Ammanford, the Welsh middleweight champion, disappointed badly at Hereford on Tuesday night, when he could only get a share of the decision with 'Battling' Charlie Parkin, Mansfield. Jones had every chance to win a clear-cut victory, but not only was his punching out of range, but ill-timed, and many of the punches went behind his opponent's back.
>
> The surprise of the evening was the fine victory of Benny Price, Ammanford, over Bob Barlow, Nottingham. Price put his opponent down no fewer than nine times and then was only able to win on points.

Johnny Vaughan took advantage of an opportunity for Dai to go to Germany to fight on the undercard of a contest in Hamburg on 30th January, between Max Schmeling and South Africa's Ben Foord. Johnny sent the signed contracts back to Germany on 11th January, and was obliged to sort out a passport for Dai who had never been overseas before. The tickets for the sea passage to Germany arrived on 25th January and the following day, Dai travelled to Southampton to board his ship. Dai was to meet Jupp Besselmann, the German middleweight champion. According to the *Carmarthen Journal*, it proved to be 'probably the most interesting fight in the whole programme'.

Dai made a very gallant fight indeed:

> Until the eighth round, Jones looked a winner but he had apparently shot his bolt, and took heavy punishment in the last few rounds, and was distinctly groggy at the finish.

Besselmann had won on points; Max Schmeling outpointed Ben Foord.

After previous attempts, Jupp or Josef, Besselmann eventually gained the EBU European title in May1942 when he beat Mario Casadei in Stuttgart.

Dai must have been pretty tired after his encounter with Besselmann, followed by a hasty trip back to Wales via Southampton, but it was less than a week later when he got into the ring with Dave McCleave from Battersea. McCleave had been British welterweight champion for a couple of months in 1936, when he beat Chuck Parker but was knocked out by Jake Kilrain in the eighth round of their contest.

He had moved up a weight by 1938, and Dai travelled to Hackney for the fight. The *Carmarthen Journal* reported:

> After a gruelling ten-round contest, Dave McCleave (London), former British welterweight champion, beat Dai Jones (Ammanford), the Welsh champion, on points at the Devonshire Club, London.
>
> McCleave was the more forceful but he had to struggle for his points.
>
> Jones put up a stout defence and it was not until the sixth round that McCleave began to score with heavy punches. Jones weakened towards the finish, and in a hectic battle McCleave just won through by a narrow margin.

There was still no time to rest for Dai—ten days later he took on another Londoner, Albert O'Brien from Hoxton. This time though the venue was a little nearer home: Haverfordwest. And at least Dai didn't have to go the scheduled ten rounds, because O'Brien was disqualified in the second round.

On the same bill, Don Chiswell went ten rounds with Willie Piper of Swansea, but lost, and Dai Bowen of Penybanc lost on points to Jim Lewis.

In his fifth fight in less than a month, on 21st February, Dai Jones beat Ginger Dawkins when the referee stopped the fight in the fourth.

So perhaps it was not surprising that he hit a bit of a bad patch in March when he suffered three points defeats in as many weeks. The first was by George Davis of Notting Hill at Holborn Stadium Club:

Dai Jones put up a very hard fight before being beaten on points by George Davis, Notting Hill, in a ten-round contest at the Stadium Club on Monday night.

Jones put in some clever defensive work, foiling the Londoner's efforts to get home with hooks to the body. Davis appeared to be the stronger puncher, but was shaken in the fifth round, when Jones connected with a short left to the jaw.

Both got home with good rights to the jaw during the seventh round, but Davis punched powerfully with both hands, and although his greater aggression just gained him the verdict, there could have been very little in it.

Dai's second defeat on 28th March was by 'Battling' Charlie Parkin of Mansfield at their third meeting in five months. Charlie Parkin finally got even with Dai:

Dai 'Farmer' Jones (Ammanford), the Welsh middleweight champion, was narrowly outpointed by 'Battling' Charles Parkin (Mansfield), the North of England champion, in a ten-round middleweight contest at Sutton-in-Ashfield, Nottingham on Monday night.

The fighting by both men was extremely clever for the first three rounds, Jones using a good left to the face and Parkin countering smartly with a two-handed attack to the body. But the fight deteriorated in the next three rounds through frequent clinching.

Parkin attacked well in the eighth and ninth rounds, but Jones still used his left in grand style, especially in the last round, so the verdict met with a mixed reception, Jones fully deserving to draw.

Three days later, he suffered his third defeat, against the Fijian Ben Valentine; his second meeting with Valentine, and a second points loss.

And still there was little rest for the Ammanford man. Four days later, on 4th April, he stopped Norman Rees of Abercwmboi at the Moutain Ash Pavilion, and before the month was out he held Ginger Sadd to a draw on Sadd's home ground in Norwich.

A fourth meeting with Charlie Parkin took place some three weeks later, this time down at the Bandstand in Paignton, which was no doubt as nice a place as any to meet an old adversary, as spring ripened into summer. The bout was over twelve rounds and was reported by the *Carmarthen Journal* as a draw: 'Jones piled up points in the early rounds but Parkin rallied in the last two rounds and just about deserved to share the honours.'

The even matching of these two boxers provided excellent entertainment for their audience, to the satisfaction of their respective managers.

Over the following month Dai took on three more of the best middleweights in Britain: Ernie Butcher Gascoigne of Rotherham, beating him on points, Ernie Roderick and, for the second time, Dave McCleave. Interestingly, both Dave McCleave and Butcher Gascoigne outpointed Freddie Mills, in 1938 and 1939 respectively.

It was perhaps no disgrace when Dai lost to Ernie Roderick over ten rounds on Roderick's home ground, Liverpool. Roderick already had an almost impeccable record by June 1938, and over the next ten years went on to win British welterweight and British middleweight titles, and was European welterweight champion from 1946 to 1947. *Boxing* reported the fight:

> The Welsh champion proved an exceedingly tough opponent and he absorbed Roderick's punches unflinchingly. Roderick had no easy trip, for on several occasions terrific head punches rocked the local badly, but Roderick proved his cleverness. In the sixth, he had the Welshman staggering from a terrific jaw punch. Jones used his extra weight well and Roderick had difficulty in getting clear of the ropes. There was some tremendous hitting in the closing stages which excited the crowd. Roderick proved a worthy winner.

But Dai was disappointed to be outpointed for a second time by Dave McCleave, this time over eight rounds, on 28th June.

Johnny Vaughan had been organising a special boxing show to be held on Thursday, 7th July, with all proceeds to go towards the Amman Valley Cottage Hospital. He had persuaded Danny Evans out of retirement to fight Dai Jones as the main attraction, along with supporting bouts.

Gentle Danny proved no match for the 'Fighting Farmer', but took him to nine rounds, to the general approval of the large audience, when the referee stopped the fight on a technical knockout. Don Chiswell beat Wally Hitchings; Dai Bowen (Penybanc) beat Arthur Paris; Tommy Davies lost on points to Crad Rule and Meidrim Thomas beat Ivor Davies on points. The *Amman Valley Chronicle* recorded that 'Gentleman' Jack Petersen had 'travelled down specially to help the event', together with Mr D. R. Llewellyn, the amateur heavyweight champion of Wales in 1938, 'who is a son of Captain M. H. Llewellyn of Wernoleu, Ammanford. They were given a rousing reception when introduced from the ring, as also was Jim Wilde, the ex-heavyweight champion of Wales.'

Johnny agreed that a short and well-deserved rest was what Dai needed next, but after a couple of weeks, he was back in training to defend his Welsh title, against Elfryn Morris of West Bromwich.

The contest took place at the Market Hall, Carmarthen, which, according to *Boxing* was 'regarded by an important London syndicate as one of the finest in Wales for boxing contests.' The hall was packed for the contest, which was promoted by The Carmarthen Sports and Attractions Association.

HOW JONES KEPT TITLE

'The contestants were to have fought fifteen three-minute rounds, but in the fourth round Jones was awarded the verdict on a knockout.

ROUND ONE.
A cautious opening, and then came the fireworks. Both men attacked to the body, and 'Farmer' Jones, leading with his left, followed up with several powerful right-arm jabs. Both men were boxing on similar lines, and at the bell were on even terms. 'Farmer' Jones who had scaled 11st.3lbs.12ozs had a one and three-quarter pound advantage in weight and was a few inches taller than Morris.

ROUND TWO.
More in-fighting and Morris ran into a right hook and was down for a

259

count of 'three', but despite swift following up by Jones he was able to recover, and at the bell was still fighting strongly.

ROUND THREE.

Morris came in and peppered the champion's body. In no way perturbed, the 'Farmer' weathered the storm and a right hook jolted the contender's head back. Then a left to the solar plexus sent the West Bromwich man to the boards for a count of 'six'. Obviously in pain, he rose and met the ensuing attack cautiously but quite competently.

ROUND FOUR.

The contender, encouraged by the crowd, attacked fiercely, raining blows on the champion's body. A whirlwind counter by Jones, however, had Morris floundering and, seizing the opportunity, the champion threw over his favourite punch—a right to the pit of the stomach. Morris dropped like a log and rolled over, groaning on the canvas. A superhuman effort by the contender brought him with a jump to his feet at the count of 'nine' but then it was too late, and the referee, Mr C. B. Thomas of Porthcawl, sent him back to his corner, ruling that he was not in a position to defend himself at the count of 'nine'. Mutely, Morris appealed to be allowed to continue, but in vain. Then, overcome with pain, he sagged against the ropes but with an effort controlled himself and, without a word to his seconds, stumbled towards his dressing room. It was some time before the crowd realised the fight was over. There was the usual hubbub, and querying of the validity of the punch which had put paid to Morris's aspirations.

In the supporting bouts Ginger Dawkins of Bargoed (deputising for Granville Davies of West Bromwich) beat Arthur James (Porth) on points; Ned Jones (Treorchy) secured a points win over Don Chiswell of Ammanford; Ike Leonard (Cwmparc) defeated Johnny Mason (Treherbert) on points; Meidrim Thomas (Ammanford) and Dai Price (Cross Hands), deputising for Ivor Davies, fought a draw over six rounds.

Two wins at the Mannesmann Hall, Plasmarl, took Dai up to the end of October 1938. On 26th September he got the measure of South African, Eddie McGuire, who had outpointed him way back at the beginning of 1936. Dai beat him over twelve rounds.

On 24th October, he stopped Reg Gregory of Liverpool in the fourth round, and a week later, he and Johnny travelled up to London:

DAI JONES WINS AGAIN

Finishing the fight with his face smothered in blood at the National Sporting Club's ring in Earls Court, London, on Monday night, Dai Farmer Jones, the Welsh middleweight champion, outpointed Mohamed Fahmy of Egypt over eight rounds. Jones won comfortably but in the last round, a left hook by Fahmy during a bout of close-quarter work, opened a cut over Jones's right eye.

The Welshman was the superior boxer.

The crowning victory for Dai, finishing up a prolific year of twenty contests—even the losses were mostly by a small points margin—was a points win over another boxer who had previously beaten him: Paul Schaeffer of Canada, at Plasmarl, over twelve rounds at the beginning of December.

In the New Year of 1939, Dai and Johnny had a chat about Dai's weight. It had become obvious during 1938 that despite the phenomenal work rate, with very little time off from training, Dai had been having to work much harder to make middleweight. Johnny thought that, come the spring, he might put Dai in for the Welsh light-heavyweight title. He had already met some bigger boxers and Dai certainly had some heavyweight punches!

At the beginning of February, Dai was back in Earls Court, where he fought the Jamaican, Stafford Barton, beating him on points. A week later, Eddie McGuire, smarting from his defeat at Dai's hands the previous September, had a return with the Ammanford man in Norwich. It was the South African's turn to win, over ten rounds.

March duly arrived and Dai's training regime did not have to include so much of the usual concentration on weight loss, because his next contest, with Glen Moody, was for the vacant Welsh light-heavyweight title, over fifteen rounds, on 27th March.

Glen was the middle one of the famous Moody boxing trio and was one of thirteen children in all. Big brother Frank, adopted as the first

Dai Farmer Jones and Eddie Bach Thomas.

official Welsh light-heavyweight champion in 1928, was the inspiration for Glen and Jackie: 'We were very close,' he once said, 'Frank helped me and my brothers all he could.'

Three of the other four brothers also boxed, but Frank, Glen and Jackie had remarkable success and were household names. Jackie, having survived the war, was killed in a mining accident in 1945. 'He could have been the best boxer of the lot,' Glen said.

Glen's own career over the late twenties and the thirties had been pretty impressive. In twelve months from August 1930, he had fourteen successive wins; in March 1931, he beat Jerry Daley at a second attempt, to win the Welsh middleweight title. Daley tried to get it back a year later in Ammanford, but failed and Glen held the title until 1933.

By 1939, Glen Moody had also gone up a weight, and jumped at the chance to follow in brother Frank's footsteps when the Welsh light-heavyweight title fell vacant.

The contest between Glen and Dai took place in Haverfordwest and resulted in a points win for Glen, thus completing a unique family double. Frank had held the Welsh middleweight title (back in 1923), as well as the light-heavyweight title and now Glen had done the same. Neither boxer lost either title in the ring.

Glen Moody rated Dai as a very good boxer, 'and he was a proper gent,' he once told me at an ex-boxers meeting.

During a three-month lay-off Dai was thinking about his future. The British Prime Minister, Neville Chamberlain, had abandoned his appeasement strategy and the newspapers were full of the inevitability of war breaking out. There was not going to be much money to be made in professional boxing for the duration, Dai reasoned. He was not in a reserved occupation, as the miners were. Should he just wait to be called up, or what?

It was probably an admirer of Dai 'Farmer' Jones's boxing prowess, J. W. Picton Phillips, who came up with an answer which would enable Dai to have a good wage, as well as doing his duty towards the war effort. Mr Picton Phillips just happened to be the chief constable of the Carmarthenshire Police Force and, having been an active supporter of

Welsh boxing for many years, was well-acquainted with the Ammanford boxer.

Dai was a useful man and he could do very well in the police force.

On 28th June 1939, Dai had his final battle with 'Battling' Charlie Parkin, stopping him in the fifth round, and in August—it was the last recorded fight of his exceptional career in boxing—he travelled to Liverpool to meet an Australian, Fred Henneberry. Dai came out on top when his opponent was disqualified in the third round.

In September, the Prime Minister announced that, as the necessary undertaking had not been received from Germany, Britain was now at war. In October, Dai joined the Carmarthenshire police and his life changed for ever.

Johnny Vaughan was really sorry to lose him. 'You could keep in training, Dai,' he urged—he knew Dai would keep himself fit—'and I can still try and get you some fights. You're at your peak now. Who knows? You might be in for a chance at a British title again.'

Dai shook his head ruefully: 'I thank you for everything you've done for me,' he said, 'but I can't do justice to both boxing and the police.'

The respect and loyalty he had given to Johnny Vaughan, he now felt he owed to his Chief Constable, the man he had known for some years, Mr Picton-Phillips.

While Dai was settling to his new duties, Glen Moody joined the Royal Engineers and was posted to France a fortnight later, where he was caught up in the horrors of Dunkirk in May 1940. Among the rescues he helped to carry out in the mass evacuation of British and allied troops from the beaches, was, astonishingly, that of Ronnie James, who was to become British lightweight champion in 1944.

Glen found Ronnie stranded without boots, stumbling along with his feet badly cut and carried him on his back until they came across an Army lorry. Unable to procure any boots for him, Glen was finally given a pair of carpet slippers which he presented to Ronnie, having sought him out on the beach. A man named Joe Morgan was still many miles off Dunkirk when Glen met up with him, and by that time he was helpless, with many pieces of shrapnel in his body. Glen carried him to a hospital train and stayed with him until they got to medical facilities at Dunkirk.

In 1941, back in Britain, Glen was in a bomb disposal squad, working in London and Clydeside. For his heroic efforts in this field, he was awarded the B.E.M.

Glen did some boxing in the war, thanks to the scheme which sometimes gave servicemen leave to do this. Once he boxed at the Queensberry All-Services Club. *Boxing News* reported: 'Moody, now well into his thirties, gave Pat O'Connor a lesson and a half in the art of boxing. The veteran was never really troubled.'

In 1962, Glen Moody was amazed when Eamonn Andrews walked up to him with his famous red book to say: 'Glen Moody—This Is Your Life!'

Ernie Roderick also did some boxing during the war, including a couple of defences of his British title, so he was usually in training. One day there was an air raid over Liverpool. Ernie was about to follow the crowd down the steps to Liverpool Central Underground Station, when he noticed a girl hesitating on the street. He asked if he could help, and she told him of her need to get home immediately; she lived about a mile away. Roderick seized her hand and literally ran her off her feet all the way to her door. She just about managed to mouth a breathless 'thank you!' before closing the door and sinking exhausted on to the floor. But her super-fit young rescuer was already well on his way back to the underground station, completely oblivious to her plight!

While the country gradually returned to a semblance of normality after the war Dai Jones, who had served during the war in Llanelli, was eventually posted to Laugharne in 1949.

J. W. Picton Phillips had retired by then, but may well have been the person who suggested Dai for the posting. In those days it was considered useful for a policeman to know how to defuse a potentially dangerous situation by means of, let us say, a little bit of physical force.

Dai was getting used to his little 'outpost' and the twelve-mile cycle ride that constituted his beat, and kept him fit. He knew a lot of the locals and had got the measure of those likely to start some trouble. One weekend evening there was a real hullabaloo going on outside Brown's

Hotel, which was Dylan Thomas's favourite watering hole. By the time Dai got down there it had developed into a full-scale drunken brawl.

Dai stepped out of the shadows unhurriedly and told the brawlers to break it up and go home to sober up. The ringleader, already well-known to Dai, defiantly started to make his way into the hotel.

Dai quickly barred his way: 'You can go home the easy way or the hard way,' he explained, but the troublemaker was having none of it, until a swiftly-timed right to the jaw laid him out on the pavement. The others stood around uncertainly. 'Now,' said Dai, 'who else wants to go in for a drink?' There was some shuffling and muttering about 'having to get home', and the crowd dispersed into the darkness.

This was the usual sort of incident Dai had to deal with, and apart from breaking the news of accidental death to families, drunken and loutish behaviour was about as bad as it got.

So when in 1953, not one, but *two* murders occurred in Carmarthenshire—both as it happened in areas where Dai had been posted—they were a cause of much astonishment and consternation.

The first happened in a family that Dai knew quite well: John Harries, aged 63, and his wife Phoebe, who was 54, had disappeared from their home at Derlwyn Farm, Llangynin, near Whitland. Dai was involved in the initial search, along with my uncle, William Price Davies, who had recently retired as a police sergeant with the Carmarthenshire force, and his son, my cousin Eric. They joined many other members of the local community who scoured woodland, wells, rivers, ponds and disused mines. No bodies were found.

'Missing' posters were put up, but produced no sightings or leads of any kind. But an examination of Derlwyn farmhouse revealed untidiness which suggested a disturbance. Milk had been left on the table to go sour and an uncooked joint of meat was found in the cooker, indicating they had left in a hurry.

Police were keen to question Ronnie Harries whose father was a second cousin to John Harries. It was well known locally that he had been spending a lot of time at Derlwyn Farm. Enquiries revealed that

Ronnie was in serious debt. Detective Superintendent John Capstick of Scotland Yard was called in to assist the Carmarthenshire force.

Harries's story was not consistent. He said he thought 'Aunt and Uncle had gone to London,' after he had dropped them off at the railway station, but another time said that before they left, they had been staying in his parents' home, Cadno Farm.

This set off another line of enquiry and a thorough search was made of land around Cadno Farm. Finally, a gruesome discovery was made in a field of kale. The bodies of John and Phoebe Harries were buried there. They had been beaten to death.

Harries was brought to trial for the murder of John and Phoebe Harries at Carmarthen Court, and remanded in Swansea Prison.

A search for the murder weapon had produced a hammer, found in a nearby hedgerow. It had been badly corroded but when it was shown in evidence in court, a pathologist stated that severe injuries to their skulls were consistent with blows that would be caused by such a weapon.

It is probable that Ronnie Harries transported them to the field in their own Austin car, which he was seen driving often after their disappearance. He must have made up some story to lure them, one at a time, across the field—and to their deaths.

Evidence showed that he had borrowed the hammer from a neighbour, but Harries never once admitted to the crime.

Part of Dai's duties while Harries's case was being heard was to help control the crowd of many hundreds that gathered outside the court. It was larger than ever on the day the verdict was due to be given. Ronnie Harries was found guilty of murder and sentenced to be hanged. The execution was carried out in Swansea Prison on 28th April 1954.

The second murder in 1953 took place near Llandeilo, which was Dai Jones's first posting at the beginning of the war, though I do not think that Dai was involved in the investigation this time. A Polish ex-Army officer, Michael Onufrejczyk, who had been wounded twice in the First World War and received medals for gallantry in the Second World War, had bought a farm, Cefn Hendre. He had bought it with the help of The Polish Resettlement Corps. (South Wales). He was a

Crowd control at trial of Ronnie Harries (1953).
Centre policeman is Dai Farmer Jones.

solitary man who apparently made little effort to integrate with the local community, living in any case in an isolated place. He soon found he could not make the farm pay, so in April 1953, he took on a partner, Stanislaw Sykut, because he had about £600 to invest. But almost immediately the two fell out and Sykut took steps to have the partnership dissolved. A short while later, he had disappeared. Onufrejczyk claimed that he had gone back to Poland, but blood found on walls and floors, which proved to be human, could not be explained away as the blood of rabbits that he'd killed.

Despite extensive searching Sykut's body was never found. Onufrejczyk however was brought to trial; the first time in Wales that a suspect was charged with murder when no body was found. A guilty verdict was brought in and Onufrejczyk was sentenced to death, but this was commuted to life imprisonment (the case has been quoted as a precedent in other cases where no body is found). He was released in 1965 and killed in a road accident a year later. Although speculation abounded that the body had been cut up and fed to the pigs on the farm, several of the policemen that I spoke to about the case pointed out that there was a large open chimney in the farmhouse, wide enough for a body to have been hung in. Did the body 'cook' sufficiently for the pigs to have consumed everything, bones as well? Or was it burnt to a cinder?

J. W. Picton Phillips died in November 1955. Dai would have attended the funeral both as a member of Carmarthenshire Police Force, and as a friend.

In February 1960, Dai was transferred to Pontyberem and was promoted to sergeant in September of that year. In January 1962 he was awarded the Police long service medal and a good conduct medal. He retired from the force in May 1969 and, sadly, died in December of that year.

Iori Morris, Dai's close friend and 'stablemate', died at the age of 29, in July 1944.

His death certificate showed that the cause of death was peritonitis.

During the making of the cinema film 'Pandora and the Flying Dutchman',
on Pendine Sands, one ex-Welsh champion, PC Dai Jones, found time to chat
to one ex-British heavyweight champion, Bombardier Billy Wells.

Chapter 17

Tommy Davies and Ronnie James

If you travel east along the Amman Valley from Ammanford you will
come to a railway crossing at Gwaun-Cae-Gurwen; a little further on
along the road is the village of Cwmgors, which was Tommy Davies's
home. After that, the road goes south towards Neath, but before you get
there you reach Alltwen on the other side of Pontardawe, where Ronnie
James lived.

Tommy grew up in Cwmgors—he was born there on 7th May 1920
to Edith and John Davies, and named Thomas Glanville. He was one
of twelve children. As a child and young man he would have remembered the greengrocer in a flat cap who came round the streets of the
villages selling fruit and vegetables from a cart pulled by a gentle horse.

The greengrocer was Johnnie Owens, formerly of Aberaman, the
named Champion of Wales at nine stone 6lbs. in 1907. It was actually
Tommy who many years ago, first drew my attention to the old champion by showing me the belt Owens won, which was kept in a glass
display cabinet in Cwmgors Workingmen's Club, together with his
boxing record.

Sadly, the club was pulled down a few years ago and I do not know
what happened to the belt, but Johnnie had been a fair boxer in his day.
He had beaten Larry Cronin and George Phalin, of Birmingham; both
had fought Jim Driscoll, and he had once held Harry Mansfield to a
draw. Mansfield beat Driscoll in August 1904 over ten rounds. Owens
himself met Driscoll at Barry Docks in February 1904, but lost on points
over twenty rounds. He also fought the Welsh Wizard, Freddie Welsh,
who knocked Johnnie out in the seventh round on 20th May 1907.

Johnnie Owens, Aberdare, once fought Jim Driscoll,
and became a greengrocer in Cwmgors.

Whether Johnnie was part of the reason why young Tommy decided to take up boxing professionally I'm not sure, but there was no history of boxing in Tommy's family. He first put the gloves on at the age of sixteen, spurned the idea of doing any amateur boxing, and had his first decision fight when he had just turned eighteen, in Carmarthen.

His opponent was Martin Fury of Ammanford, and Tommy out-pointed him over six rounds on 6th June 1938.

Like many local boxers before him, Tommy went to work in the nearby colliery on leaving school, and stayed there until his retirement 45 years later. During the time of his employment in the mine, he enjoyed greater security of employment as well as much improved safety and working conditions after the war, than had our hungry fighters of the 1920s and early 1930s. Tommy boxed because he wanted to. He was lucky enough to have one of the best trainers and cornermen in the business, Archie Rule, and his one and only manager was Johnny Vaughan.

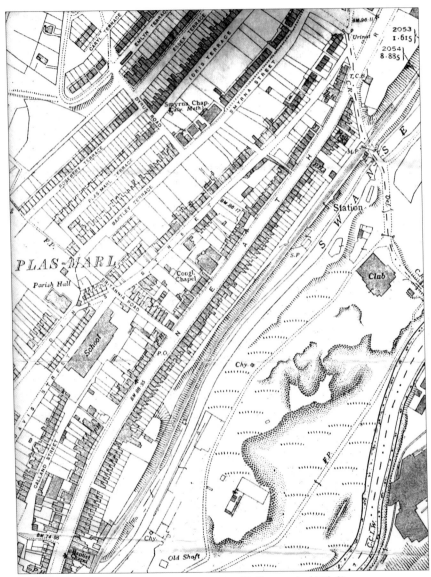

Map showing Mannesmann Hall – marked 'Club'.

A month after his first fight, Tommy was beaten by Archie's brother Crad Rule in Ammanford, over six rounds, but during the late summer and autumn of 1938 he had four outstanding wins, all at the Mannesmann Hall in Plasmarl.

You will perhaps have noticed that the Mannesmann was a favourite venue for the Ammanford boxers during the 1930s, and the hall saw many terrific nights of boxing. There were boxing shows held virtually every week at the Mannesmann throughout most of the 1930s. So what and where was this important venue?

The building itself was described by Don Finn, who lived close to it and used to attend the fights held there, as 'really a very large garden shed, maybe 70ft by 50ft in size. It was of wood, steel and corrugated sheeting with a sloping flat felt roof. It was 100 per cent a fire hazard.'

It is shown on a large-scale map, for which I am indebted to Ken Fifield, as being situated on land between the Swansea Canal and the River Tawe, where it is described as 'Club'. Across the river is the massive area of the Landore Steel Works, on which was also situated the Mannesmann and Baldwin works. The hall itself was presumably under the auspices of a club associated with the works.

To the north lies the residential area of Plasmarl, and access to the hall was from that side, off the Neath road, and across the canal. The building was in a kind of brutal industrial wasteland with a massive slag heap 'dumped long ago' to the front and smaller slag heaps to the back of it and on the river side.

It held perhaps 500-600 people, many of whom were in a standing area for which they had paid a cheap entrance fee as local unemployed.

But what contests they witnessed there!

In their book *Wales and its Boxers*, Peter Stead and Gareth Williams describe Ronnie James making his debut at the Mannesmann as a fifteen-year-old in 1933, at a time 'when the boxing press was packed with weekly reports from small hall promotions.'

Boxing recorded that 'Ronnie James emphasised a useful left and proved too strong for Sid Williams (Pontardawe) and won in the second round.'

273

Apart from the Ammanford boxers and their many opponents, among others for whom this unlikely place played such an important role in their careers, were Swansea's own Len Beynon and Big Jim Wilde.

Ronnie James was born on 8th October 1917, and inherited his love of the fight game from his father, who boxed as an amateur.

Following his big night at the Mannesmann Hall, young Ronnie ran up a total of thirty fights without defeat. Still under nineteen years old, Ronnie had fought fifty-three times when he met Dave Crowley in 1936, and tasted his first defeat inside the distance, unfortunately on a disqualification. Crowley, from Clerkenwell, challenged Mike Belloise for the World featherweight title in New York a few months later in September 1936, but was counted out in the ninth round. Two years after that he became British lightweight champion when he beat Jimmy Walsh in Liverpool.

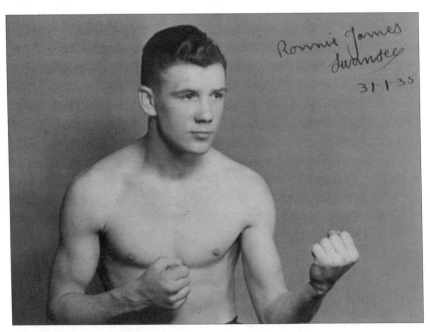

Ronnie James, British lightweight champion.

A couple of weeks before meeting Crowley, Ronnie had outpointed the brilliant American featherweight, Jackie Wilson, over ten rounds. Wilson won the NBA World featherweight title in 1941.

In 1938 Ronnie James was given a chance to fight the former World featherweight champion, Freddie Miller, who had recently beaten Len Beynon. Miller was an American southpaw from Ohio, and had the reputation of being able to put an opponent down from any angle with either fist.

The fight took place on 27th June. Although the American came straight into the attack, trying to set his opponent up with his powerful right-hand lead, Ronnie, who had probably studied Miller's style, retaliated by smashing his own right hand under Miller's heart. In the eighth round, another right from Ronnie into Miller's ribs, brought the ex-champion down with no hope of beating the count. To his astonishment though, Ronnie was disqualified by the referee for a low blow.

The Board of Control sanctioned a final eliminator between Ronnie James and Dave Crowley for the British lightweight title on 17th April 1939. Crowley was making an attempt to regain the British title which he had recently lost. The contest took place on Swansea's Vetch Field and thousands of Welsh fight fans flocked to witness the event. Unbelievably, in what must have been one of the unluckiest hat-tricks in sporting history, Ronnie was disqualified once again on a foul! In a total of almost 135 bouts in his 14-year career, of which he won 113, only five of Ronnie's fights were lost on a disqualification.

It just happened that the first three were in such significant bouts.

Tommy Davies and Ronnie appeared on the same bill at the Mannesmann Hall at least once, in November 1938.

It was 14th September 1938 that young Tommy had a fight there for the first time, against Tommy Jones and he beat him on points over six rounds. Twelve days later he was back to stop Bryn Davies in the second round; a performance Tommy repeated, again at the Mannesmann, on 10th October against Jerry Walsh. His next opponent, Billy Rees, lasted until the third round before Tommy stopped him.

In December he met his namesake Tommy Davies (what a nightmare that fight would have been for a commentator, had there been one!),

SOCIAL CLUB AND INSTITUTE GROUNDS, AMMANFORD

Monday, June 24th, 1940

TWO TOP LINERS
12 Rounds Contest

TOMMY DAVIES v. IVOR PICKENS
CWMGORSE   CAERAU

12 Rounds Contest

DON CHISWELL v. MOG GWILLIAM
AMMANFORD   PENCOED

Also Other Contests

Doors open at 6-15; First Contest at 7 p.m. prompt

and beat him on points over six rounds. He finished up the year with a trip to Abertillery on 17th December where his opponent Albert Williams was disqualified in the fourth.

In 1939 Tommy had six contests, losing only one of them. He scored a knockout at Swansea against Ned Jones in April, and outpointed notable boxers, Trevor Burt and Mog Gwilliam in July and August respectively. When the war began in September of that year, it did not cause as much disruption to Tommy's life as it did to many other young men, because he was in a reserved occupation. That meant that along with his work as a miner, he was able to continue boxing whenever he was able to get a contest. During the first couple of years though, contests were hard to come by, and in 1940 and 1941 he only managed to get seven fights, losing two of them—the first against Dick Turpin on 3rd June 1940. *Boxing News* reported:

> There might have been a surprise if Davies, who substituted for Dai Farmer Jones (*Dai had given up boxing by then*), had begun his challenge earlier than the eighth of his ten-rounds fight with Dick Turpin, challenger for the Empire middleweight title.

Turpin was a comfortable winner, but Davies's fine display brings another promising figure into the already crowded lists of the middle-weight division.

The other five contests all ended in victory inside the distance, over Billy Davies, Ivor Pickens of Caerau, Sid Williams, Tommy Harlow of Lancaster and Sergeant Jackie Clarke, once again at the Mannesmann Hall.

The fight with Ivor Pickens, on 24th June 1940, was reported in the *Carmarthen Journal*:

> In the main bout of an interesting charity boxing show held at Amman-ford in the grounds of the Social Club on Monday evening. Tommy Davies (Cwmgors) the Welsh welterweight contender, without exerting himself unduly, scored a decisive success over Ivor Pickens, Caerau, ex-welterweight champion.
>
> It was only his ringcraft and experience that carried Pickens to the seventh round, when he was almost 'out' on his feet and the towel was thrown in from his corner.
>
> Billy Davies, the veteran lightweight, who deputised for Mog Gwilliam, Pencoed, who has been stricken with illness, made a tireless fight of it against Don Chiswell, Ammanford, but the contest going the full distance, Chiswell was declared the winner on points.
>
> Dave Williams, Blaenau, won narrowly on points over Iori Morris, Ammanford, over eight rounds and had the satisfaction of avenging a defeat in the previous hospital show.
>
> . . . There was a large attendance to witness the show, which again was put on by Mr Johnny Vaughan in aid of the Amman Valley Hospital and he had the support of officials of the hospital's entertainments committee.

Ronnie James had joined up shortly after the outbreak of war, and among his wartime experiences was his encounter with Glen Moody on and around the beaches at Dunkirk in 1940, when Glen was able to lend a helping hand. But Ronnie was sometimes able to get leave to do some boxing during the long years of conflict.

Between May 1939 and May 1942 he didn't lose a single contest—he had fifteen—and nine of them were wins inside the distance. Then he lost on a disqualification against Eric Dolby. But that particular disqualification seemed to break a jinx because his very next contest was against old adversary Dave Crowley and this time Ronnie knocked him out in the third round! He would have been both looking forward to, and at the same time been apprehensive about the encounter, and the result must have been a relief. In fact Ronnie had become one of only five boxers to beat Dave Crowley inside the distance throughout his career. Although Crowley held the British lightweight title for only six months—he lost it to Eric Boon in December 1938—he was a formidable opponent who totalled 128 wins before retiring around 1945.

Tommy Davies began 1942 with a loss on points to Billy Jones of Cwmparc, which was the second time Jones had outpointed Tommy. But he was soon back to winning form, having no less than six wins inside the distance in 1942, against Billy (Kid) Andrews of Dundee, Trevor Burt of Ogmore Vale, Jimmy Moore, Birkenhead, George Gale of Whittlesey, Jackie Moody and Jock Gibbons of Manchester.

On 11th September 1942, Tommy outpointed Ireland's Paddy Roche at the Pontypool Palais de Danse, and on 24th October, he held Harry Watson of Aldgate to a draw at Cardiff.

He suffered two losses during the year, against Dave McCleave, the former British welterweight champion, who had beaten Dai Jones twice a few years earlier, and Frank Duffy from Bootle, who got the decision over Tommy on the last day of the year, at Liverpool Stadium. This was Tommy's second appearance at the famous Liverpool Stadium —he had won on a disqualification against Jimmy Moore of Birkenhead back in July.

Following on from his victory over Dave Crowley, Ronnie knocked out three more opponents to finish up 1942 with a flourish: Tommy Smith, Jimmy Watson and Freddie Simpson. In November he got a points decision over Jimmy Molloy.

A Jamaican boxer who went by the name of Lefty Satan Flynn had come over to Britain a few years before the war, and had had some

278

notable success in British rings. In 1942 he outpointed the Scottish champion Jake Kilrain, who had held the British welterweight title from 1936 until 1939, when he lost it to Ernie Roderick. What's more, the following year the Jamaican beat Ernie Roderick himself. Roderick was then the current holder of the British welterweight title and went on to become European welterweight champion, as well as gaining the British middleweight title.

Lefty Flynn, real name Selvin Campbell, was already thirty years old by then, having been born in British Honduras in March 1913. He went to school in Kingston, Jamaica, and started boxing around 1928, eventually achieving the welterweight championship of Jamaica. During the war, he served in the Merchant Navy, but was able to carry on boxing, and it was in 1943 that he had several battles with both Ronnie James and Tommy Davies.

Ronnie met him first, on 3rd February, and managed to knock him out in the sixth round despite the Jamaican's weight advantage. However, succeeding bouts between the two in May and July both resulted in points losses for Ronnie.

Tommy had not had a fight in 1943 until May, when he was offered a contest at the Queensberry Club against Ireland's Pat O'Connor. He lost over eight rounds; it was his first appearance at the club, which was set up in Soho, London, for boxing in wartime. Following a second win against Trevor Burt in Cardiff, Tommy travelled to Willenhall to meet Lefty Flynn on 19th June. He calmly beat him on points over ten rounds.

Tommy was getting into a different league now. The following month he found himself in the ring at Nottingham with Ernie Roderick, putting up a creditable performance although outpointed by the champion.

Johnny Vaughan and Archie pulled out all the stops—there had been a Welsh title fight for Tommy scheduled for some time. So before July was out Tommy Davies and Tommy Smith from Merthyr were slogging it out for the Welsh middleweight title at St Helen's, Swansea, in front of an audience of eight thousand for the scheduled fifteen round contest. The end, however, came in the sixth round when the referee stopped the fight to save Smith from further punishment. The *Western Mail and South Wales News* reported:

Tommy Davies had little difficulty in winning the Welsh middleweight title, the referee stopping his fight with Tommy Smith in the sixth round. Smith took seven counts in the fifth round and was saved by the bell after falling out of the ring. He took eight counts in the sixth round before the referee called a halt.

On the same bill on 31st July, Ronnie James was outpointed for the second time by Lefty Flynn, but as the *Western Mail* stated: 'There was little separating the two boxers at the end and the decision of referee C. B. Thomas was well received.'

On the under card, another of Johnny Vaughan's boxers, Bobby Hunt from Garnant, beat Don Cooper of Pyle.

Tommy Davies, the new Welsh champion, travelled to Dudley Sports Centre a little over a week later to take on George Odwell from Cam-

Tommy Davies, Welsh middleweight champion.

den Town, and outpointed him over eight rounds. He didn't fight again until October, trying to get in all the training he could in the meantime while working long shifts at the colliery, where wartime production was in full swing.

Tommy settled a couple of old scores in October and November, against Pat O'Connor and Frank Duffy, both of whom had beaten him in previous contests.

In December and again in January 1944, up popped Lefty Satan Flynn for another go. But he presented little trouble to Tommy who got the decision over eight rounds at the Albert Hall, and then stopped Flynn again, in the sixth of eight rounds at the Queensberry Club.

An up-and-coming young boxer from Eastleigh, Hampshire, Vince Hawkins, had ambitions for a crack at the British middleweight title and was steadily working his way through the middleweight list.

It was Vince Hawkins' father that encouraged him to box, after some bullying in school and, as Vince told Ron Olver in 1988, his first boxing shorts were a pair of his mother's knickers which she had altered to fit him. He joined the boxing section of sports training in his school.

In 1940, Vince won the ABA junior title at 9st. 7lbs. His father had already taken him to see professional boxing manager, John Simpson at Basingstoke, where Vince was soon doing regular Saturday morning sparring sessions. He made his professional debut in 1940 at Southampton Sportsdrome, and among the opponents he had beaten before he met Tommy Davies were Spike Robson, Battling Charlie Parkin, Paddy Roche, Frank Duffy, Ginger Sadd and Trevor Burt.

Tommy and Vince Hawkins had their first contest at Birmingham in March 1944:

> The principal contest of ten three-minute rounds between Tommy Davies, Middleweight champion of Wales, and Vince Hawkins (Eastleigh) was one of the best bouts between middleweights that we have seen for years. The decision of a draw did not meet with universal approval, many being of the opinion that it flattered Davies. In the first round Hawkins got in with solid punches to the body and Davies was

made to miss with his right and was countered with a left hook to the jaw, followed by a rapid tattoo to the body. Hawkins was consistently forceful while Davies boxed in cool fashion under pressure and countered with a good right to the jaw at the end of the second round. There were many punch for punch passages in the third. Davies used his left well, though Hawkins was the more aggressive and scored with a good left hook to the jaw.

Davies improved, used his left with judgement and caused Hawkins to break ground in a spell of free punching in the fourth, which was contested at a terrific pace. The Welshman continued to use his left but Hawkins punched away to the body and ribs. Near the end of the fifth Hawkins' left ear was injured by a heavy right counter. This however, did not deter him. He generally managed to secure the inside position at close quarters and often beat Davies to the punch. Quick fire punches to the body rattled Davies in the seventh round, but he got in with a series of head blows while having to take heavy punishment. The eighth round was Davies' best; he used his left well and often put Hawkins out of distance through this medium. Davies . . . scored good and hard to the jaw when Hawkins missed with a terrific left.

The last round was a real hummer and in this session Davies fought in great style while Hawkins appeared to tire a little. Both were given a standing ovation at the end.

Although *Boxing News* reported that it was felt the referee's decision of a drawn match may have 'flattered' Tommy, he was far from happy about it and was convinced he had out-boxed Hawkins. It was, he told Ron Olver in 1989, '. . . much to my disgust, and another of my big disappointments.' Both boxers still had their minds set on the British title and a first notch on the Lonsdale Belt, and Tommy resolved to train for it as hard as he could.

Exactly a month later, on 20th April, Tommy lost for the second time to Ernie Roderick, then British welterweight titleholder, who proved to be a stumbling block for both Tommy and Vince Hawkins.

Sometimes it was very difficult to space fights fairly evenly, what with the war and work commitments, and negotiations between managers and promoters, but it was pretty unfortunate for Tommy that within a week of his disappointment over losing to Ernie Roderick he had two more important fights. He stopped Charlie Knock of Hanley in the seventh round at Wolverhampton on 24th April, and a mere two days later his return bout with Vince Hawkins took place at the Albert Hall. This time the younger man got the decision over eight rounds, but it was close enough for Johnny Vaughan to immediately request that the two men be matched again. Tommy had been understandably tired at their second meeting, but he still had a claim as a contender for the British middleweight crown.

Johnny also had other things on his mind in 1944.

The war had inevitably caused enormous disruption to sporting activities; no less in the Amman Valley than everywhere else. Johnny's boys, and their opponents, had gone to war and it was difficult for them to get leave to box. Those that remained were working flat out in the collieries and, when he could get a bill together at all, most of Johnny's promotions were now for charity. Furthermore, he had had to give up mining himself because by this time, his lungs had been badly affected —he was eventually diagnosed with pneumoconiosis. It had become necessary for him to look at other ways of earning a living.

And so, on 6th June 1944, he and Maud moved to the Mansel Arms in Llanelli, and he became a pub landlord. From here on, his diaries record the difficulties of getting beer deliveries, because it was in short supply, and the number of times he had to close early or open late. But he had chosen the premises with care. Above the bars was a large room entirely suitable for a gym, and it was here that Tommy Davies and the few remaining boxers under Johnny's management came to do at least part of their training.

A little over a month after this move, and having fitted in as much training as he could, Tommy travelled up to Birmingham for his final decisive meeting with Vince Hawkins. Though it hadn't been designated as an eliminator contest, its outcome would affect Tommy's claim as a contender.

The *Birmingham Gazette's* headline announced the disappointing news:

HAWKINS MAINTAINS HIS UNBEATEN RECORD

Vince Hawkins (Eastleigh) outpointed Tommy Davies, the Welsh middleweight champion in a return ten-rounds contest at the Big Top, Birmingham, last night. Hawkins, still undefeated, well deserved his success.

Although Davies displayed his customary skill, Hawkins gathered more points consistently, particularly with his follow-through work and with his crisp punches to the body.

Davies however, gave a courageous display, for he fought under the handicap of an injury to his left eye from the middle of the fourth round, caught by a right clip from Hawkins.

Though the fight seldom reached the standard of the previous bout between the two at the Delicia Stadium, the large crowd were provided with several rousing passages, especially one in the seventh round when Davies came back with such exhilarating style that at one period, Hawkins was rather in trouble.

Subsequently, Hawkins finished stronger and he made the fight safe in his keeping by winning the last round. It was the third contest between the two; Hawkins having won two and the other being a draw.

Tommy was bitterly disappointed. Especially as the following month young Vince Hawkins beat the notoriously difficult Dave McCleave, knocking him to the canvas several times before McCleave retired in round five with a cut eye.

Hawkins had gained stature in the boxing world and was becoming popular among fans.

Going to do some training one morning, he passed two little boys sitting on a wall in his home town. He had to smile at their conversation: one little boy said 'Desperate Dan is the greatest!' and the other replied 'Vince Hawkins could beat him!'

There were no other fights for Tommy until December 1944 when he outpointed Johnny Clements of Coatbridge at Willenhall New Baths. Then on New Year's day he lost to Lefty Satan Flynn at Stoke Newington. Tommy had been so good at getting the measure of the wily Jamaican, having beaten him three times already, that the defeat must have come as a blow. It's true, he may have been distracted by his marriage in January 1945, to Phyllis. It's also true that now he sometimes had to travel by bus or train to Llanelli to meetings and training at Johnny's gym, as well as working punishing shifts in the colliery— but he didn't expect to lose this one and it definitely knocked his confidence.

Early in February he travelled up to Walsall where he beat Hull's Frankie Jackson over eight rounds.

Things were hotting up in the stakes for the British middleweight title in spring 1945.

Jock McAvoy had relinquished the title and the Board of Control apparently sanctioned two eliminators: the first between Vince Hawkins and Ernie Roderick and the second between Tommy and Bert Gilroy.

In the meantime, another contest over ten rounds had been arranged between Tommy Davies and Ernie Roderick for 15th March at the Royal Albert Hall. Tommy lost, but again, it was a close verdict. In April he stopped George Howard of Finsbury Park in an eight-round contest at the Queensberry Club.

It was just before his eliminator contest with Bert Gilroy that Tommy had his biggest disappointment, as he recalled later. 'Gilroy could not make the weight. The Board decided that the other eliminator (between Hawkins and Roderick) would be the contest for the vacant British title. I knew I could have beaten both of them.'

As it was Hawkins lost that championship encounter at the Royal Albert Hall in May, by a long chalk. Barry Hugman's *Boxing Yearbook* summarised the fight:

> Hawkins had age and weight as an advantage. But after receiving damage to his left eye in the fifth, he found the going tough. In the ninth round lefts to the body and chin felled Hawkins for a long count. But although he fought back well, he could not match the skills of Roderick, winning only two rounds on the referee's score card.

It was October 1946 before Vince Hawkins, now more experienced, finally wrested the British middleweight title from Roderick on points.

Boxing News reported: 'Hawkins boxed with confidence and coolness through this battle of wits. Roderick brought all his skill and generalship into play, but had to give way to a strong, forceful youngster who would not yield an inch of ground.'

Vince Hawkins used to tell a story in later years of the bouts with Ernie Roderick:

> Roderick was a very good man. I remember in our first fight I caught him with a right hand. He went back against the ropes and my many supporters yelled, 'Go on Vince, you've got him!' So like a mug I walked in—straight into a right hand which nearly put me down.
>
> In our second fight exactly the same thing happened. But this time, instead of walking forward, I walked to the middle of the ring. Ernie said: 'You remembered from last time, then.'

Tommy was left to reflect on what might have been.

Meanwhile, Ronnie James, who had been on active service since his last fight with Lefty Flynn in July 1943, lost two contests on points to Arthur Danahar of Bethnal Green in March and May 1944.

Danahar was a tough opponent. He had challenged Eric Boon for the British lightweight title in 1939, and though he was stopped in the fourteenth round, his ambition for a British title was in no way dimmed. In the course of his boxing career he beat, among many others, Harry Craster, George Odwell, Jake Kilrain, Lefty Flynn and Ernie Roderick. Danahar may have got a taste for the limelight in his championship contest with Eric Boon because it was the very first televised fight to be publicly screened!

Another Welsh boxer who was around at this time was Gwyn Williams of Pontycymer, who was to win the Welsh welterweight title in 1945. He was in a parachute regiment during the war and took part in the Arnhem invasion. He too fought Arthur Danahar; the first time in the services, and then just at the end of the war. He described Danahar as 'considered by many to be the best welter in the country', and lost to him several times, the first time on a cut eye.

Danahar, who was a hard puncher and usually able to capitalise on any weight advantage, had proved too much of a challenge for Ronnie, but he was considered a suitable opponent at this time. Ronnie was in hard training for an important contest. At long last, the war having intervened, his chance for the British lightweight championship was arranged for 12th August 1944—five years and four months since his unfortunate disqualification in the eliminator bout with Dave Crowley. Now the champion Ronnie had to challenge was Eric Boon, who had taken the title from Crowley in December 1938.

The contest took place at Cardiff Arms Park in front of a crowd of thirty-five thousand fans, and it was 'a cracker', according to Fred Deakin in his book *Welsh Warriors*. He takes up the story:

> James climbed into the ring looking extremely fit and ready for the fight of his life, while the hard punching champion, Eric Boon, had struggled to make the weight. Ronnie James who had always been a slow starter, came out fast for the first round, taking Boon by surprise. He attacked the champion fiercely and Boon fought back with everything he had.
>
> The first two rounds were fairly even as the two hurled heavy shots at each other with both hands . . . The Welsh challenger came out for the third with both guns blazing. He stormed into the champion and drove him round the ring, swamping him with punches from every conceivable angle. Boon staggered and tried desperately to fight back, but he went down for a count of nine.
>
> But now it was all James. He waded into the champion with both hands, hooking, swinging, jabbing, upper cutting, he hit the champion with every punch in the book, and then some of his own.
>
> Before the end of the fight Eric Boon was on the canvas twelve times, but always struggled gamely and bravely back to his feet to take more punishment. No-one ever tried harder to hang on to his crown.
>
> There was a tremendous roar from the crowd in the seventh round when Boon climbed wearily to his feet after yet another visit to the canvas—and dropped the in-coming Welsh fighter with a heavy right hand. However, James was more surprised than hurt and he rose quickly and carried the fight back to the champion.

The end came in the tenth when James floored the badly battered Boon for nine, then finished him off with a right to the head when he climbed exhausted to his feet.

Ronnie James was the Lightweight Champion of Great Britain at last.

He was to hold the title until 1947 when, in effect, he retired undefeated.

1944 ended on a sour note for Ronnie when he was disqualified in the sixth round of a contest against Gwyn Williams who was starting his bid for the Welsh welterweight title.

It was the last time in Ronnie's career that that particular demon struck, and he easily beat Williams on points in July 1945, having lost to Arthur Danahar for the third and final time two months earlier. In one way though, Ronnie got the better of Danahar. For although Danahar went on to knock out Eric Boon in an eliminator for the British welterweight title in February 1946 at the Royal Albert Hall, he never did get a British title. And Ronnie still had his biggest challenge to come.

Tommy was not doing so well in 1945. He was outpointed in three contests through the summer, against George Howard (whom he had stopped inside the distance at their first meeting), Jimmy Ingle of Dublin and Jock McAvoy.

The contest with the undefeated British middleweight champion, Jock McAvoy, who was right at the end of his magnificent career, was part of Tommy's intense preparation for his first, and only, fight outside Britain. It was a close contest, but Tommy had McAvoy down on the canvas and when the decision went to McAvoy, Tommy was not best pleased. He told Ron Olver: 'I got several bad decisions and consider that I should have been given the verdict against McAvoy.'

It was a shame if he felt in any way demoralised because of the enormous challenge he now faced at the Palais des Sports in Paris.

A fortnight before the scheduled fight, Johnny recorded in his diary that he had written requesting a permit for Tommy to box in Paris. He received the contracts for the fight on 6th October. Then he wrote to Jack Solomons reiterating the Board's instructions that Tommy must not box or appear at the venue without a permit. On Sunday, 14th October, Tommy travelled to London for his flight across the channel the following day. He continued his training for the next couple of days before resting prior to his fight at the Palais des Sports.

There, on 19th October 1945, hardly able to believe it, he stared across the ring at Marcel Cerdan, warming up for his contest with our Tommy. At that time Cerdan was French and European welterweight champion, but moving up to middleweight.

Whether Cerdan's team considered that Tommy would be an easy middleweight for their man to beat in order to ease his transition to a heavier division, I cannot say, but the fact is Tommy was utterly out-classed by a man considered by many experts to have been Europe's finest-ever boxer.

Surprisingly, Cerdan's first defeat had been at the hands of Harry Craster at the National Sporting Club back in January 1939 when Cerdan was disqualified in the fifth round for a foul blow. But he had come a long way since then: up until his contest with Tommy, Cerdan had had eighty-three wins, forty-seven of them by knockout, and lost two. Tommy had fifty-nine fights.

There were two minor consolations for Tommy that day. The first was that his agony didn't last long; he was knocked out in less than two minutes of the first round. The second was that he lasted longer than three previous victims of Cerdan's lethal fists; the unwelcome record for the quickest knockout by Marcel Cerdan went to Gustave Humery, who lasted 22 seconds in 1942.

Afterwards, Johnny Vaughan received a brief call from Jack Solomons, who was involved in organising these overseas promotions. He stated that he would not be requiring the services of Tommy Davies again.

I have wondered whether Jack Solomons, still less Johnny Vaughan, were totally aware of Cerdan's record to date. They obviously could not have known that he would go on to become a World champion, but it was pretty clear he was shaping up for it.

"BOXING NEWS" PHOTOS No.38.

Marcel Cerdan (France),
World middleweight champion.

Born in Sidi Bel Abbes, French Algeria, he had a long almost unbroken record of wins in North Africa as well as in Europe. He was known as the Moroccan Bomber and the Casablanca Clouter.

Cerdan's very next contest after Tommy's humiliating defeat was against Assane Diouf for the French middleweight title. Cerdan won by a knockout in the third round.

He later knocked out Leon Foquet in the first round to get the European title. The zenith of his career was September 1948 when he beat champion Tony Zale, to gain the NBA World middleweight title with yet another knockout, in the twelfth. He was the toast of Paris.

In these celebrity obsessed times, Marcel Cerdan is remembered now not so much for his incredible boxing career, but for being the lover of France's favourite singer, Edith Piaf, though this was a final brief period of his life. He was married with three children when he began his affair with 'The Little Sparrow' in 1948.

In June 1949 he lost the World title to Jake LaMotta in his first defence. 'Raging Bull' LaMotta knocked Cerdan down in the first round and he carried on until the tenth with a dislocated shoulder, but had to retire at the end of the round.

A re-match was arranged and Cerdan was due to attend a training camp to make his careful preparations, but he missed Edith and decided to visit her in Paris before beginning his training. He boarded an Air France flight on 27th October 1949. The Lockheed L-749 Constellation crashed into the Monte Redondo on Sao Miguel Island in the

Azores, killing all eleven crew members and thirty-seven passengers, including Cerdan. He was thirty-three years old.

Perhaps, mused Tommy, being Welsh Champion was fame enough for him.

In fact, before Marcel Cerdan's untimely death, Tommy had successfully defended his Welsh middleweight title four times, the first Welsh champion to achieve this record in the middleweight division. He equalled Ginger Jones's record as champion in the Welsh featherweight class and Ivor Pickens had also had four successful defences of his Welsh welterweight title.

Tommy's first defence as Welsh champion took place some eight months after his meeting with Cerdan and was a fairly easy win over Swansea's Taffy Williams. The contest was scheduled for fifteen rounds on 11th June 1946 in Swansea, but Tommy stopped his opponent in the fourth. The following month he won inside the distance again, this time against Alby Hollister of Islington in the eighth round of a ten-round contest. Tommy, who was still keeping his hopes alive of getting an eliminator for the British title, felt encouraged by the victory. At the end of October 1946, after a three month lay-off, he had two fights within four days. After a disappointing points decision went to Johnny Houlston of Cardiff at Trealaw on the 25th, Tommy recovered his equilibrium enough to get a draw with a good middleweight, Alex Buxton of Watford, in Marylebone on the 29th. Buxton was eventually to become British light-heavyweight champion in October 1953.

It was in September 1946 that Ronnie James met the most challenging opponent of his career. As with Tommy's encounter with Cerdan, Jack Solomons was the entrepreneur who brought it about. Solomons had been in America and seen the NBA World lightweight champion, Ike Williams. '. . . he hadn't been impressed,' according to Fred Deakin, who added: 'He was convinced Ronnie James would take him apart.' He knew that the mood in post-war Britain was for big money spectacular fights—what could be more exciting than British champion against World champion? Stage it in Wales and it would be a sellout. The Williams camp said they'd be willing for Ike to meet the British champ at the open-air venue of Ninian Park, Cardiff, over ten rounds in a non-title fight.

Jack Solomons made it plain that he wanted a full fifteen round contest with the NBA World title at stake, or nothing at all. Eventually, Ike Williams' team agreed, and Solomons conceded that Ike would get twenty-five per cent of the takings, while Ronnie got fifteen.

The American party arrived in Britain and Ike Williams continued training under Harry Curley who had travelled over with him. Fred Deakin records that he 'appeared listless and worked half-heartedly, as if it was all too much trouble. But the real experts had seen it all before and the very occasional flashes of brilliance told the truth about the champion's real ability.' However, Peter Brooke-Ball thought: 'He was hardly at his best because the cold climate got to him . . .'

Whether or not he was a hustler, Ike Williams could be awkward and contradictory. The British press didn't know what to make of him. Under the headline 'Prefers a Birdie to a Knockout', Ralph Hadley had this to say: 'At first glance Ike (Isaiah) Williams, part world lightweight champion, now in England on boxing business, is a terrifying person. Not even his best friends would say he has an amiable face. His opponents must find it positively ugly.

'But when Ike talks, and he doesn't talk very much, it's usually about the gentle art of golf—and you forget his expressionless fighter's face.'

Ike Williams,
World lightweight champion.

Jack Solomons, meanwhile, had been put to a great deal of extra trouble by Ike's demand for fresh oranges. 'Oranges!' spluttered Solomons, 'We haven't seen them since before the War!'—rationing and short supplies of many foods continued in Britain until well into the nineteen-fifties. Eventually, he had to arrange for Williams to eat at a cafeteria belonging to the American Embassy, where apparently, they had oranges.

To add to Solomons' troubles it had begun to rain in Cardiff sixteen days before the fight and it just didn't stop. 'On the morning of the fight it was still belting down,' said Fred Deakin, 'and Jack was advised to call it off, but he refused. He assured everyone that the downpour would cease in time for the show to start.

'They said he was mad. The men trying to prepare the stadium complained that the numbers were being washed off the seats faster than they could stick them on.' Solomons must have been wondering why he'd chosen to promote boxing as a means of earning a living when it turned out that Williams was two and a half pounds overweight.

It was Harry Curley's job to get the weight off though, and he did it with no time to spare. At the official weigh-in Ike Williams scaled 9st.8lbs.12ozs and Ronnie James was 9st.8lbs.2ozs.

It suddenly stopped raining. Numbers were stuck back on seats, puddles were mopped up and the lights worked. Although Jack Solomons later said the attendance was about twenty-six thousand instead of the estimated forty thousand, the fans were in great voice on that Wednesday evening of 4th September 1946, for the epic battle—the very first World title fight to be held in Wales.

Ike Williams was six years younger than Ronnie James, and he was acknowledged to be one hell of a puncher. He had actually developed his own unique punch, known as the 'Bolo Punch', which must have been a terrifying sight to face in the ring: he would raise his right hand, throw it back over his right shoulder, bring it round and down low across his body, up from that position and into his opponent's body.

Poor Ronnie soon found out what it was like to be on the receiving end of the 'Bolo' as well as numerous other punches.

Fred Deakin wondered how Ronnie James managed to survive until the ninth round: 'He took an amazing amount of punishment and the champion wasn't even in top gear.

'I honestly don't believe there has been a lightweight since who could have beaten Ike Williams that night, and I include Roberto Duran.'

Ringside, Ronnie's gasps of pain as Williams' body punches tore into him, could be plainly heard. He was down six times in the course of his ordeal and was finally counted out in the ninth, after soaking up more punishment than anybody could reasonably endure.

The following year, Ike Williams beat an opponent who had given him a hiding when he was younger, Bob Montgomery, and became internationally recognised as World champion, adding to his NBA title. He went on to defend this title five times, finally losing it to Jimmy Carter in 1951.

Ronnie had three more recorded fights after that night, in 1947, winning two and then losing to Cliff Curvis in June. Ronnie had trouble making the weight for the fight, coming in thirteen ounces over. Cliff knocked him out in the seventh round. Shortly after this fight, the Board took his undefended British title away from him and Ronnie decided to call it a day. He emigrated to Australia.

For Tommy Davies, who also had three fights throughout 1947, it was the year of the Turpins. Unfortunately, he lost to two of the three famous brothers from Leamington Spa. Randolph Turpin knocked him out in the second round of a contest at Harringay Arena in April, and older brother Dick, who had outpointed Tommy back in 1940, beat him again in Liverpool, when Tommy had to retire in the fifth.

There was no doubt that the Turpins were dominant forces in the middleweight division in Britain during the nineteen-forties and early fifties. Not only were Randy and Dick magnificent champions, but they also had to battle against the disgraceful colour-bar which operated in British championship boxing before this time. In fact Dick had been boxing since 1937, but had to wait until June 1948 to fight Vince Hawkins for the British middleweight title, becoming the first black

British champion ever: 'Hawkins attacked incessantly but the Leamington man brilliantly countered, leaving his opponent battered and bruised.'

The boys' West Indian father had died when they were young—Randy was still at school—but he surely would have been so proud of their achievements in the ring.

In October 1950, Randy took the British middleweight title from Albert Finch who had beaten his brother Dick to gain the crown in April of that year. Four months later he beat Luc Van Dam for the European title.

Frank McGhee, in his book *England's Boxing Heroes*, summed up Randolph Turpin's short life with a quote from poet Thomas Mordaunt:

> *One crowded hour of glorious life*
> *Is worth an age without a name.*

'Randy had his sixty minutes of genuine glory,' he continued, 'on the night of 10th July 1951, and England briefly became a better place to be when, over fifteen rounds, he outpointed Sugar Ray Robinson to become undisputed Middleweight champion of the world.' In the post-war decade of austerity and shortages, McGhee pointed out, it was no exaggeration to say that people 'walked around feeling a foot taller.'

Although he lost the World crown back to Sugar Ray Robinson just 64 days later—Robinson had seriously underestimated Turpin's ability at their first meeting—Randy went on to achieve further glory by winning the British and British Empire titles at light-heavyweight, beating Don Cockell in 1952. He was undefeated as British and British Empire middleweight and British and British Empire light-heavyweight champion, and won sixty-four of his total of seventy-three contests. What made his success all the more remarkable was his unorthodox stance, with his feet planted wide apart. He did though, have an unusually long reach and great physical strength.

When he gave up boxing, his business ventures failed. Randolph Turpin, a truly great boxer, committed suicide in 1966, aged thirty-seven.

In between his fights with the Turpins, Tommy held old opponent Trevor Burt to a draw, at Bristol on 7th July. But realistically, he had reached the end of his bid for a British title. Tommy was perhaps unlucky to have peaked at a time when there were a number of really good middleweights around in Britain, and maybe he didn't always get the breaks, but he was certainly able to tell his five grandchildren that he was one of the most successful Welsh champions.

In January 1948, he turned the tables on Johnny Houlston—and retained the Welsh title—by outpointing him in a title fight at Neath. At the 2 o'clock weigh-in, Tommy was 6 ozs. over weight and given an hour to get it off, succeeding with five minutes to spare which probably affected his stamina for the fight. The *Western Mail* reported:

> The hall was packed to capacity when they faced up, and Houlston made the body his target, making the champion gasp on one occasion; later crossed lightly with the right. Davies retaliated in kind. It was a hard battle, and in the second round Houlston was warned for using his head in the clinches.

HOULSTON DOWN

> Early in the fourth, Houlston was caught with a right to the jaw as they broke, and he took a count of four. The fight was threatening to develop into a maul by the fifth, but they opened out towards the end of the round, Davies having the better of a sharp rally.
>
> The sixth, seventh and eighth were uneventful, with both seeming to take a breather, but they livened up again in the ninth when Houlston was again effective with some two-handed work to the stomach. Houlston shook Davies with a short right hook in the twelfth, but almost immediately ran into a similar punch from Davies and went down for seven.
>
> The thirteenth and fourteenth were by no means exhilarating, with Houlston doing what little clean hitting there was. Davies did more leading in the final round, but with both men looking very tired, it was not a thrilling finish'.

But Tommy had done enough to keep his title. His next defence in July against Ron Cooper of Pyle, again took place in Neath, and was an altogether more satisfying win, Tommy managing to stop his opponent in the fourteenth round.

He was by now having to do an awful lot more work to make middle-weight contests and discussions with Johnny Vaughan convinced Tommy that he might have a go at the Welsh light-heavyweight title.

It seemed like a very good idea in September of 1948 when Tommy was matched with then current Welsh light-heavyweight champion Jack Farr of Abertillery, and knocked him out in the first round. And he finished the year on a high with another win inside the distance, over Ginger Sadd of Norwich at the Gwyn Hall, Neath on 29th November.

But success and titles in boxing largely depend on the quality of the opponent you meet on the day and in a final eliminator for the Welsh light-heavyweight crown, Tommy met a good one.

Dennis Powell of Four Crosses was the little boy in hospital who had been allowed to sit up by the radio at three o'clock in the morning to listen to his hero Tommy Farr fight Joe Louis in America back in August 1937.

Only now of course, he was grown up and had developed into a fighter with ambition who was beginning to be noticed. In fact 1949 was probably Powell's best year; just Tommy's luck to come up against him that May!

Boxing News reported:

> In a final eliminator for the Welsh light-heavyweight title, Dennis Powell, Four Crosses (12st.5lb.), scored the best win of his brief career when he caused Tommy Davies, Cwmgors (12st.1lb.4ozs), Welsh middleweight champion, to retire at the end of the ninth, with a badly cut left eye.
>
> Davies was the boxer and Powell the fighter. As early as the first Davies was in trouble, when a left hook opened a cut over his right eye.
>
> Following a bout of in-fighting in the fifth, Powell seized an opening and caught Davies on the chin with a left swing, dropping him for a count of nine. When he got to his feet, Powell rushed in but was shaken by a left hook to the body. Powell recovered however, and a right to the body again dropped Davies for four.

Keeping the pressure up in the sixth, Powell soon had Davies's face bearing evidence of the force of his punches, and near the end of the round a right jab opened a cut over Tommy's left eye. Davies took another count in the seventh, and now his nose was badly bleeding.

He tried hard but the speed of Powell's punching was too much, and with his left eye in a bad way, it came as no surprise when he retired.

To his credit and in spite of this battering, Tommy went on to successfully defend his middleweight title for the fourth and final time against Des Jones of Tredegar, just three weeks after his encounter with Dennis Powell.

Powell's next move was to win an eliminator in the Welsh heavyweight division in June 1949, before wresting the Welsh light-heavyweight crown from Jack Farr, knocking him out in the first round at Newtown. Finally, in August that year, Dennis Powell met Welsh heavyweight champion, George James of Cwm, taking his title by knockout in the second.

Two years later, an incredulous Dennis lost the Welsh heavyweight title to none other than his hero, Tommy Farr, who was staging his remarkable comeback. Farr went down on one knee in the third, though Powell was warned to keep his punches up. A clash of heads in the fifth round resulted in a nasty cut over Dennis's left eye. Farr played on the wound in the sixth round, worsening the injury considerably. At the bell, the referee, Mr I. K. Powell, went over to Powell's corner and called an immediate halt to the proceedings. Dennis told the *Boxing News* reporter at ringside: 'Naturally I'm disappointed. My training programme was much harder than the actual fight.'

When Randolph Turpin relinquished his British light-heavyweight title in 1953, Dennis Powell was a top contender. He was nominated to fight tough George Walker of West Ham for the title. Gilbert Odd took up the story:

> The pair had met six months earlier at the Empress Hall, Earl's Court, when Powell won the first two rounds by outboxing his vigorous opponent, then was awarded the fight in the third, when the Londoner was ruled out for persistent holding.

Their return battle with the championship at stake, took place at Liverpool Stadium and provided one of the hardest and most gruelling contests between light-heavies that has ever been seen in this country.

Each put full body-weight behind his blows and only tremendous courage enabled Powell to survive a tempestuous fourth round in which he was floored for a long count and saved by the bell, while sustaining a badly damaged left eye.

At the end of round seven, one of the Welshman's seconds was ready to throw in the towel. In fact had he been able to catch the referee's eye, it would have been all over. But the official was too busy entering his score card, so Powell got a reprieve!

There is an old boxing adage that says: no matter how bad you are, the other guy may be worse. And so it transpired. Powell fought back under a handicap; fought so gamely and so confidently, that by the end of the eleventh round, it was the Londoner who had to surrender. For George Walker had also sustained a damaged left eye that had swollen up so badly that he could not see out of it. His chief second told the referee that there was no sense in letting a game fighter carry on under such a handicap.

So Dennis Powell was a British champion at last and how proud he was!

Exactly seven months later, he lost the title to Alex Buxton at Nottingham.

Following Tommy's bruising encounter with Dennis Powell, *Boxing News* ran a report by Bryn Jones under their heading 'Welsh Outlook' which announced that Eddie Thomas would be headlining an open-air venture in Monmouth, 'if all goes well'. It went on to say: 'Randolph Turpin will probably meet Tommy Davies, Welsh middles champion, on this programme and this should make for an interesting return encounter, because when they met at Harringay two years ago, Randy k.o.'d Tommy in a couple of rounds. Davies, strictly a 'home-ground' fighter, is now clamouring for inclusion as a contender for the British middleweight title, and a clean-cut win over Turpin would help his cause considerably.'

The proposed return match between Tommy Davies and Randolph Turpin never did take place and truth to tell, Tommy must have realised his chances of being British champion had all but gone by the summer of 1949.

Actually, Tommy only had two more recorded contests against British boxers; his next three opponents came from much further away. At Haverfordwest Market Hall on 28th November 1949, he outpointed Koffi Kiteman from the Gold Coast (South Africa), but lost the following March to Sammy Wilde from Nigeria, who knocked Tommy out in the third round at Carmarthen. In July 1950, Tommy was at Coney Beach Pavilion, Porthcawl, where he stopped Joe Hyman of British Guiana in the second round.

Without doubt his boxing career was winding down now and his fights were few and far between. In October 1950 he beat Ron Cooper of Pyle for the second time, but lost to Sheffield's Henry Hall on points in December at Carmarthen.

Tommy Davies and Des Jones, Tredegar.

Carmarthen was also the venue for Tommy Davies's last fight. The 'Welsh Joe Louis' as he had been known locally because his fans thought he resembled Louis, bowed out on 19th February 1951, by losing to South Africa's Duggie Miller over ten rounds.

He enjoyed a long and happy retirement, during which time I got to know him well.

Tommy Davies died in December 1998, at the age of seventy-eight.

Ronnie James died in Australia in 1977.

Johnny Vaughan left the Mansel Arms, Llanelli, in 1950, and moved back to Ammanford.

After Tommy hung up his gloves, Johnny did not renew his manager's licence though he continued to take an active role in encouraging both amateur and professional boxing in the valley until ill-health made it difficult.

In September 1959, he and Maud travelled to South Africa, where their son Edgar had become a successful physiotherapist. They stayed for eight months—the warm climate was good for Johnny's chest—returning to Ammanford on 13th May 1960.

During the latter part of 1962, Johnny got in touch with his ex-boxers to ask if they had kept photographs, programmes or dates of any of their fights, so he could compile complete records for them to keep —now his diaries would prove their worth.

Sadly, his health deteriorated before he could complete the task and throughout 1963, the diary made sad reading.

Johnny Vaughan died on 7th March 1964. In our little corner of Wales, and much more widely in the boxing world, he had made his mark.

In a way, this book is about boxers who mostly didn't achieve their coveted goal of British Champion, though they came pretty close. But for me they shone not only as Welsh stars, but because they travelled far and took on the best opponents of their day. It is a remarkable fact that the success of these boxers was largely due to the dedication of one man. Johnny's all-round ability to inspire his Welsh champions as well as the other boxers in his care, cannot be disputed.

Local Boxers Re-union, 1964.
Back row: H. Cooke, Denzil Hopkins, Dai Rees, Dai Morgan.
Middle row: John Jones, Rhys Cae Gurwen, Danny Evans, Dai Farmer Jones,
Benny Price, Geo Davies, Tommy Davies, Jack Walsh (Cross Keys),
Landlord Castle and Raven.
Front row: Ginger Jones, Edgar Vaughan, Archie Rule, Billy Quinlen.

Boxing Presentation to Danny Evans.
Left to right: Tony Lee, Cliff Curvis, Tommy Davies, Big Jim Wilde, Danny Evans.

Edgar was able to complete the boxers' records and he gave them to each one at a presentation evening in 1964.

Maud Vaughan, who lived just up the road from us, grew older and a bit forgetful. We had got to know her as our neighbour over the years. Putting my head round her back door one day to check that all was well, I found her ripping pages out of a small notebook to write 'reminders' for herself. With growing horror I realised the notebook was a diary which had been kept by Johnny.

'Oh yes,' said Maud, 'he kept them for years.' And she produced a shoebox full of small diaries in which Johnny had kept records of the training nights, meetings, correspondence and contests relating to his boxers. Also in the box was the accounts book belonging to Ammanford Athletic Club and Johnny's Boxing Board of Control manager's licence.

That was how Johnny's diaries got saved and, thanks to Mrs Maud Vaughan's generosity in allowing me to use them, how I first got the idea for this book.

Chapter 18

Stories Ginger Told Me

In his later years I used to visit Ginger Jones at his home in the hills above Pontardawe. He was a very interesting man to talk to and the stories of incidents that had happened in his life made fascinating listening.

Once, he told me, he was on his way to catch a train to Paddington because he had a contest lined up in London. It was, he said 'at a time when golden sovereigns were scarce, as they are today, but I had one in the ticket pocket of my wallet, and this in the hip pocket of my trousers.'

He was also wearing 'a heavy overcoat, trilby hat, spats and so forth' for the journey, and 'eating an orange, for I seldom drank fluids to quench my thirst while in training.' Reaching the canal bridge in Pontardawe, a woman ran up from the towpath in an agitated state, shouting that a baby had fallen into the canal. Ginger threw down his orange, scrambled down to the towpath, taking off his overcoat as he went and scanning the water for sight of the child. At last he caught sight of 'the hand of a child protruding out of the water' under the bridge and jumped in. He got engulfed in mud but struggled through towards the child. 'The current is now sweeping the child towards me; I grasp her hand and lift her up, then struggle back to the bank and hand her to a police sergeant who has appeared from somewhere, as there was but one woman there when I jumped in.'

The policeman soon resuscitated the little girl and Ginger, as soon as he knew she was alive, and who still had to catch a London train, rushed back to his digs to change his suit. His landlady immediately hung his wet trousers above the fire in the kitchen so that they would dry out and the mud could be brushed off them. Ginger, now in a clean suit, remembered just in time to retrieve his wallet from the pocket of the soiled trousers, and rushed off to catch the train at Neath.

Once on the train, Ginger soon realised that the gold sovereign was no longer in the ticket pocket of his wallet. Arriving at Cardiff, he sent a telegram back to his landlady warning her to look out for the valued coin, before continuing his journey to London.

The contest went ahead and Ginger 'did what was expected of me' and returned home in a day or two.

'My good landlady told me that she and her husband had searched high and low but failed to find the sovereign, but I knew from her demeanour that she was joking.'

She explained that they had gone through the pockets of the wet trousers on receiving the telegram, finding nothing. However, the following morning her husband, thinking it was worth a try, sieved through the ashes of the previous day's fire and lo and behold! there was the sovereign, blackened but otherwise undamaged.

Years later, at almost the same spot near the bridge in Pontardawe, Ginger helped an old lady across the road. Thanking him, she looked closely at him and exclaimed that he was the young man who had rescued her granddaughter from drowning. The child was now grown up and married with two children of her own.

It was also at Ginger's home, settling for the afternoon in his comfortable living room, that I first heard about his fight, so famous in South Wales at the time, with Panama Al Brown. I have looked many times under Al Brown's record in Nat Fleischer's annual *Ring Record Book* ('the bible of world boxing'), and have never seen this fight mentioned at all. Nor did it get a place in Barry Hugman's 'World Champions who boxed in Britain 1929-1984' section of the *British Boxing Yearbook*. I don't know why. Ginger related this story in an after-dinner speech following the first contest between Cassius Clay—as Ali then was—and Henry Cooper, in 1963. Muhammad Ali himself described the incident that Ginger refers to, in his book *The Greatest*:

305

. . . Cooper came out throwing punches with all his might. I outboxed him and when I started whipping my right to his head, jabbing him with combinations, the blood began gurgling out of a cut above his eye.

It was the third round, and I moved back because my prediction called for the fifth and I wanted to be on time. I dropped my guard and glanced down at ringside at a screaming woman—Elizabeth Taylor and her husband Richard Burton—and suddenly something exploded against my jaw. I was down on the floor. I was dazed and numb. The stadium was roaring. The referee was counting. But before he said four, the bell rang.

Back in my corner, Angelo (Dundee) discovered that the seam of my boxing glove was busted. The cushion was coming out, and the rules and regulations in boxing are strict—the gloves must be in good condition. It took nearly a minute to make the replacement.

Many times I've been asked if I needed that extra minute it took to get the glove, but the truth is I wasn't shaken up that much.

As history records, Ali came out for the fourth with all guns blazing, re-opened Henry's cut and the referee stopped the fight to save Henry from further punishment. Ginger used the much-debated fight as an opening for his speech:

All this ballyhoo and hot air about the Cooper v. Clay contest—the incident was a split glove—brings to my mind memories of a similarly controversial situation which occurred many years ago.

It was 21st September 1931 to be precise, that I opposed the prevailing champion of the world at his weight.

The newspapers, even in those far-off days were prone to 'building up' the boxers far in excess of their true capabilities. This man Al Brown, was reputed to be a killer having beaten all and sundry both in America and in this country.

My unbiased opinion is that he is nothing to some of the men I had met over the years, although one must say he was willowy and moved like elastic thus taking advantage of his physical characteristics; very lean and long. I was undoubtedly the foremost featherweight in Wales at that time and many would say in the country. So I became the obvious choice to meet the world champion who was touring this country at the time, toppling all and sundry—Englishmen, Irishmen, Scotsmen—in which was eventually to be included a Welshman.

My manager Johnny Vaughan of Ammanford, who incidentally trained four Welsh champions at the same time, was approached by the late Mr Teddy Lewis of Pontypridd, who was the advance booking agent in Wales for the majority of the best Welsh boxers, and asked whether he would allow me to box fifteen rounds against Al Brown, the World champion. After a deal of negotiation regarding the purse money I was to be paid, which I may say was not quite as much as our heavyweight champion received last Saturday, matters were decided and I was booked to fight Al Brown.

A privilege granted to Johnny Vaughan, my manager, was that a few days prior to our contest, Al Brown should exhibit himself at a boxing promotion organised by Mr Vaughan at Ammanford in order that the boxing public could see a real live world boxing champion. This day duly arrived; our stadium was packed to the door and during an interval between contests Al Brown, the king of the bantams, stepped into the ring with his entourage.

He was widely acclaimed and cries of surprise were heard all round. He wore a grey check suit of 'plus-fours' and was tall as an oak tree almost, and looking really smart for all that. Eventually I followed into the ring greeted by the usual cheers; they were my own crowd—and on this occasion, by a great deal of laughter. We looked so incongruous, he a tall willowy six feet, and I a dumpy five feet four inches! I was frankly disconcerted but had met, and defeated, tall boxers previously—yet not as tall as Brown.

Not to worry, for as one old wag said: 'The taller they are, the harder they fall,' so I was solaced.

After all the handshaking, compliments paid and received, press photographs taken, etc., we eventually went our several ways. It had been realised weeks before Brown's appearance that night that I had a problem with the difference in our height and reach, which required discussing and planning with my manager and trainer. So from the time a special programme had been worked out, about three weeks prior to the date of the contest, I commenced training with my usual host of sparring partners; all good boys, some of whom were champions in their own class and who gave me every assistance for the biggest fight in my career. After due consultation with my trainer I had to alter completely my modus operandi from the stand-up straight orthodox manner to a crouching aggressive style which in actual fact was foreign to me. Still, one had to adjust oneself to prevailing circumstances and as my opponent was so much taller, my target had to be his stomach as I could hardly reach his face.

Well, after a few weeks of intensive training running around the country lanes, playing tennis and even fishing (as a relaxation), and a couple of days after our introduction to the crowd in Ammanford, the big day arrived.

Off we go to the Mountain Ash Pavilion where the Welsh National Eisteddfod had been held, and which was the only place large enough to cater for the expected crowd. Even so it was far too small and hundreds were turned away. At 2 p.m we weighed in and horror of horrors! I was 1lb over weight, which was the first time in the whole of my career I had not been well under the necessary nine stone. This was undoubtedly due to the scale being faulty at our gymnasium. Well I had to work it off and duly weighed in at nine stone, the featherweight limit.

I then returned to the hotel and had a meal (undercut steak, under-done) and rested in bed until it was time to return to the pavilion. The only time I had butterflies in my stomach was when I realised I was overweight, as it was so unusual. The whole remaining time I was not worried one iota.

The pavilion was packed to suffocation; men hanging on girders, sitting on window sills and a blue haze of smoke over all. It was even suggested by one Cardiff cartoonist that it would have been more just for me to have come straight from the mine into the ring as Al Brown was almost invisible with his colour merging with the smoke haze. I was first in the ring and the crowd started singing the usual hymns—enough to make one cry.

Al Brown followed, to be greeted by the American anthem. Looking across the ring, he was almost indistinguishable.

After the preliminaries we started the contest by me closing in and pummelling him about the stomach but he did not like that and his long arms came across my shoulders and he beat a tattoo on my but-tocks. This method went on for a number of rounds by which time Brown's seconds were 'doping' him with something that looked like whisky in a bottle.

Anyway, we came out for the ninth round at which time press reports say that I was ahead on points and I can picture the incident vividly even now, after thirty-odd years.

Brown swung a low right-hand punch from below his knees intending to catch me in the stomach but at the same moment I was moving in for the opening which he had offered me. His blow connected before time, catching me in a very tender spot and dislodging my protective shield. I collapsed in agony with the crowd yelling 'foul' but the referee W. E. Allen counted the full ten seconds, thus considering me knocked out, for the first time in my professional career. The doctor examined me but found nothing as it was too soon to show any marks. But the following morning my manager and I had to meet Brown and his party at the promoter's office in Pontypridd (taking with me a horse and cart to carry my winnings!) and on arrival I showed Brown and his manager the bruises that had by now appeared on the inside of my thighs.

Ginger looked over at me in mock indignation: 'Do you know what he said to me? He smiled and shrugged his shoulders, and he said: Hey, man, it's all in the game!'

Ginger leaned back and appeared half-asleep. He murmured a rhyme, which I had to strain my ears to catch, and I still don't know whether he made it up on the spot:

> A fighter's life is short at best
> No time to waste, no time to rest
> The spotlight shifts, the clock ticks fast
> All youth becomes old age at last
> All fighters weaken; fighters crack
> All fighters go, and they never come back.
> Well, so it goes –
> Time hits the hardest blows.

The clock ticking was the only sound now. We sat in companionable silence in Ginger's comfy armchairs. Ginger looked at me and I looked back at him: this amiable elderly gentleman with a fading tinge of ginger still in his wiry grey hair. There was a bright twinkle in his eyes. Could he have done enough to beat Panama all those years ago?

I don't know. But that was how he liked to tell the story and who was I to argue?

Bibliography

Ball, Vernon, *For the Love of the Game*. Tempus Publishing.

Bell, Leslie, *Bella of Blackfriars*. Odhams Press.

Bettinson, A. F. and Bennison, B., *The Home of Boxing*. Odhams Press.

Billot, John, *History of Welsh International Rugby*.

Broadribb, Ted, *Fighting is My Life*. Frederick Muller Ltd.

Brooke-Ball, Peter, *Boxing – An Illustrated History of the Fight Game*.

Cordell, Alexander, *Peerless Jim*. Hodder and Stoughton.

Deakin, Fred, *Welsh Warriors*. Crescendo Publications.

Deghy, Guy, *Noble and Manly, a History of the National Sporting Club*. Hutchinson.

Driscoll, Jim, revised, by Jim Kenrick, *Text-book of Boxing*. Athletic Publications.

Farr, Tommy *Thus Farr*. Optomen Press.

Fleischer, Nat, *Ring Record Book and Boxing Encyclopedia*. The Ring Book Shop, 1955, 1965.

Grombach, John V., *The Saga of the Fist*. Barnes.

Harding, John, *Lonsdale's Belt*. Robson Books.

Harding, John with Jack Berg, *Jack Kid Berg – The Whitechapel Windmill*. Robson Books.

Harrison, Paul, *South Wales Murder Casebook*. Countryside Books.

Hugman, Barry, *The Boxing Yearbook*. Newnes, 1985, Mainstream Publications, 2007, 2009.

Jones, Wynford, *Benny's Boys*. Wynford Jones.

Lonkhurst, Bob, *Man of Courage – The Life and Career of Tommy Farr*. The Book Guild.

McGhee, Frank, *England's Boxing Heroes*. Bloomsbury.

Miles, Les, *The Welsh Wizard – Howard Winstone, Concept Associates*.

Muhammad Ali, with Richard Durham, *The Greatest*. Hart, Davis MacGibbon.

Rogers, Peter, *Merthyr's Past Pugilists*. Peter Rogers.

Stead, Peter and Gareth Williams, *Wales and Its Boxers*. University of Wales Press.

Sumner, Andrew, *Be Lucky! The Story of Brian London*. Trafford Publishing.

Toulmin, Vanessa, *A Fair Fight*. World's Fair Ltd.
Welsh Boxing Board of Control Handbook, 1931. Priory Press.
Wilde, Jimmy, *The Art of Boxing*. W. Foulsham and Co.
Willson-Disher, M., *Fairs, Circuses and Music Halls*. William Collins.

NEWSPAPERS

Boxing and Boxing News, in particular articles by Ron Olver and Gilbert Odd, Harry Mullen, Harry Legge and O. F. Snelling, and Richard Barber.

> *Amman Valley Chronicle.*
> *Birmingham Gazette.*
> *Carmarthen Journal.*
> *Daily Express.*
> *Daily Mirror.*
> *Liverpool Evening Post.*
> *Llanelli Guardian.*
> *Rotherham Advertiser.*
> *South Wales Echo and Express.*
> *South Wales Evening Post.*
> *South Wales Guardian.*
> *Sporting Life.*
> *The Belfast Telegraph.*
> *The Times.*
> *Western Mail and Echo.*

WEBSITES

> www.prewarboxing.co.uk
> www.johnnyowen.com
> en.wikipedia.org
> www.boxrec.com

Index

Chocolate, Kid: 12
Churchill, Job: 223, 225, 228
Clancy, Young: 79
Clarke, Fred: 166
Clarke, Jackie: 277
Clarke, Johnny Kid: 138
Clements, Johnny: 284
Cockell, Don: 1, 295
Cocteau, Jean: 93
Conn, Joe: 53
Connolly, Bart: 34
Conquest, Al: 183
Cook, Bernard: 182
Cook, Gordon: 55-57, 58, 96, 97
Cooper, Don: 280
Cooper, Henry: 5, 6, 252, 305
Cooper, Nipper: 42
Cooper, Ron: 297, 300
Corbett, Harry: 78
Cowley, Tom: 135
Craster, Harry: 286, 289
Crawford, Jim: 80, 81
Crawley, Mike: 34
Cresci, Etto: 190
Cripps, Sir Stafford: 151
Criqui, Eugene: 26
Cross, Freddie: 212
Crossley, Harry: 174, 182
Crowley, Dave: 246, 274-275, 278
Cullen, Dixie: 109, 114
Cullen, Maurice: 215
Cullen, Oliver: 75, 134
Cullen, Ted: 135
Curley, Harry: 292-293
Curley, Johnny: 8-9, 73, 78
Curvis, Brian: 147, 197, 198, 211
Curvis, Cliff: 147, 159, 211, 294
Curvis, Ken: 241
Cuthbert, Johnny: 75, 78, 80, 81, 83, 115

Daley, George: 157
Daley, Jerry: 52, 63, 113, 123
Daley, Tommy: 158
Danahar, Albert: 109
Danahar, Arthur: 286-287
Dando, Dan: 58
Daniel, D. J.: 161
Daniels, Gypsy: 39, 64, 161-186
Davies, Arthur: 52, 54, 55-57
Davies, Bertie: 52, 65
Davies, Cncllr. Bertie: 194
Davies, Billy: 277
Davies, Bryn: 157, 210, 275
Davies, Dai: 84, 100, 246
Davies, Dai Chips: 24
Davies, Eddie: 239
Davies, Fred Shoeing Smith: 167
Davies, Gwyn: 190
Davies, Harry: 119

Davies, Hywel Cass: 199
Davies, Idris: 65, 100
Davies, Ivor: 259
Davies, Jackie: 206-207
Davies, John Rhys: 191
Davies, Len Davo: 210
Davies, Ocky: 105, 243, 244
Davies, Rhys: 190
Davies, Selwyn: 63, 84, 136
Davies, Tom (Pontamman): 218
Davies, Tommy (Cwmgors): 160, 210, 259, 270-301
Davies, Tommy (Nantyglo): 246, 275
Davies, Vic: 243
Davis, George: 256-257
Davis, Joe: 163
Dawkins, Ginger: 241, 243, 250, 256
Dawson, Sidney: 99
Day, Glyn: 100
Day, Ivor: 39, 219
Day, Tom: 39
Deerhurst, Rt. Hon. Viscount: 60
Delaney, Fred: 217
Dempsey, Jack: 207, 248
Derrick, Young: 52, 133
Deubbers, Franz: 207
Dexter, Percy: 65, 66
Dexter, Tommy: 82
Di Cea, Dominique: 80
Dicks, Phil: 199
Dickson, Jeff: 9, 179
Diener, Franz: 174
Diouf, Assane: 290
Dobbs, Bobby: 217
Dolby, Eric: 278
Dolling, Dai: 35, 54
Domgoergen, Hein: 173
Donovan, Albert: 228
Dowlais, Tommy: 92
Downes, Terry: 212-213
Downes, Wally: 154
Doyle, Jack Kid: 70
Drew, Ivor: 100
Driscoll, Boyo: 217
Driscoll, Jim: 17, 18, 21, 22, 24, 27, 28, 30, 36-37, 49, 69, 70, 73, 97, 189, 203-204, 217, 270
Duffy, Ben: 157
Duffy, Frank: 278, 281
Dundee, Angelo: 306
Dunstan, Harry: 33
Duran, Roberto: 93, 215, 294

Edgington, Bunny: 228, 239
Edwards, Bryn: 52, 66
Edwards, Cyril: 123
Edwards, Keith: 194
Edwards, Llew: 19, 47, 49-50
Edwards, Martin: 192, 194

Luxton, Alf: 121
Lye, Tommy: 88, 90, 135, 137
Mainwaring, Glyn: 133, 141
Mallin, Bert: 230
Marley, Reg: 130, 204
Manning, Eddie: 239
Marren, Tommy: 109
Marshall, Ben: 58, 99-100
Marshall, Jack: 109, 124
Marshall, Lloyd: 160
Martin, Tommy: 243
Mason, Harry: 9, 66, 108, 111-113, 114, 116, 180
Mason, Johnny: 235
Mason, Mog: 246
Mason, Tuck: 52
Matthews, Billy: 69
Maxim, Joey: 185
May, Tich: 130, 131
McAllister, Dan: 154
McAllister, Jim: 110
McAloran, Frank: 91
McAuliffe, Pat: 119
McAvoy, Jock: 117, 245, 247-250, 285, 288
McCleave, Dave: 256, 258, 278, 284
McCloed, Jacky: 244
McCoy, Kid: 248
McGrath, Paddy: 66, 85
McGuire, Eddie: 240, 241, 260, 261
McKenna, Charlie: 166
McManus, Young: 137, 142
McMillan, Johnny: 141
McMurdie, Harry: 157
McVey, Sam: 110
Meade, Billy: 72
Meade, Neville: 121
Meek, Hilda: 180-181
Meen, Reggie: 175
Mendis, Jim: 174
Mildenburger, Karl: 212
Miller, Freddy: 83, 275
Milligan, Tommy: 109
Mills, Freddie: 153, 184-185, 186, 251, 258
Mills, Roy: 244
Milsom, Ernie: 164
Mizler, Harry: 12, 143, 145-150
Moffat, Cock: 243
Molloy, Jimmy: 278
Montgomery, Field-Marshall: 194
Moody, Frank: 21, 58, 59, 96, 114, 169, 175, 261-263
Moody, Glen: 59, 63, 89, 105, 115, 241, 261-263, 264-265, 277
Moody, Jackie: 59, 103, 114, 134, 220, 263, 278
Moore, Billy: 54
Moore, Jimmy: 278
Moore, Ted: 179
Moran, Owen: 47, 49-50, 217

Morejon, Cheo: 243, 255
Morelle, Louis: 172
Morgan, Bobby: 124, 128
Morgan, Danny: 97
Morgan, Fred: 66
Morgan, George: 89
Morgan, Jack: 239
Morgan, Terence: 128
Moriarty, Con: 52
Morris, Dai: 132
Morris, Elfryn: 259-260
Morris, Evan: 91, 133
Morris, Harry: 234
Morris, Iori: 190-191, 237-246, 269, 277
Morris, Tom: 188
Moss, Moe: 85, 114
Mueller, Hein: 174
Muhammad Ali: 22, 111, 305-306
Mullings, Joe: 175

Nancurvis, Dai: 147, 211
Neale, Wilf: 206
Neusel, Walter: 176, 182, 233
Newton, Andrew: 69
Nicholas, Billy: 52, 96, 97-98, 103
Nicholson, Kid: 171
Norman, Axel: 207

O'Brien, Albert: 256
O'Connor, Dan: 136
O'Connor, Jim: 243
O'Connor, Pat: 265, 279, 281
Odwell, George: 280, 286
O'Flaherty, Jim: 140
O'Keefe, Pat: 33, 69
O'Neill, Jerry: 234
Onufrejczyk, Michael: 267-268
Owens, Johnnie: 270-271

Paillaux, Paul: 169
Papke, Billy: 34
Paris, Arthur: 259
Parker, Chuck: 110
Parker, Douglas: 91, 141, 146
Parkin, Battling Charlie: 254-255, 257-258, 264, 281
Pastrano, Willie: 211-212
Paterson, Jackie: 211
Pattenden, Kid: 171
Patti, Adelina: 166
Pearce, David: 121
Pearce, Edward: 115
Pearson, Will: 69, 72
Peiroe, Eddie: 250
Peregrine, Cliff: 52, 54-55, 57, 65, 84, 130, 132, 194, 195, 234
Peregrine, Gwyn: 52, 55, 57, 130, 132, 133, 194, 234
Peregrine, Keith: 198